Choosing Educational Software

Choosing Educational Software

A Buyer's Guide

Carol Truett
and
Lori Gillespie

Libraries Unlimited, Inc.
Littleton, Colorado
1984

LIBRARIES UNLIMITED, INC.
P. O. Box 263
Littleton, Colorado 80160-0263

The following are registered trademarks of the companies indicated: Apple, Apple II, Apple II Plus, Apple IIe, Applesoft of Apple Computer, Inc.; Astrocade of Astrocade, Inc.; Atari, Atari 400, Atari 800, Atari 1200, Atari 2600 (VCS), Atari 5200 of Atari, Inc.; Betamax of Sony Corp.; ColecoVision of Coleco Industries, Inc.; Commodore, Commodore 64, Commodore 2001, Commodore 4000, Commodore 4000 series, PET 2000, VIC 20 of Commodore Business Machines, Inc.; ComputerTown of People's Computer Co.; CP/M of Digital Research, Inc.; DEC of Digital Equipment Corp.; Heath/Zenith of Heath Co.; HP-80 series of Hewlett-Packard Co.; IBM, IBM-PC of International Business Machines; Intellivision of Mattel, Inc.; M/A-COM OSI of Ohio Scientific; Monroe EC 8800 of Monroe Systems for Business; Odyssey of Magnavox Co.; Osborne 1 of Osborne Computer Corp.; North Star of North Star Computers, Inc.; Pascal of the Regents of the University of California at San Diego; PLATO of Control Data; Sinclair ZX-81 of Timex Corp.; TI 99/4, TI 99/4A of Texas Instruments; TRS-80 Color Computer, TRS-80 Model I, TRS-80 Model II, TRS-80 Model III, TRS-80 Model 16, TRS-80 Pocket Computers of Tandy Corp.; VisiCalc of VisiCorp.

Library of Congress Cataloging in Publication Data

Truett, Carol, 1942-
    Choosing educational software.

    Bibliography: p. 182
    Includes index.
    1. Computer-assisted instruction--United States--
Equipment and supplies--Evaluation. 2. Computer programs
--Evaluation. 3. Computer-assisted instruction--Informa-
tion services--Directories. 4. Computer programs--
Information services--Directories. I. Gillespie, Lori,
1956- . II. Title.
LB1028.5.T69   1984   371.3'3   83-24906
ISBN 0-87287-388-9

To Patrick and Dick
who sacrificed their time with me in order for the
writing of this book to proceed.

CT

To Tim
whose advice and support helped make my
contributions possible.

LG

TABLE OF CONTENTS

PART I

PART II

FOREWORD

Teachers, library media specialists, counselors, and administrators have been inundated with recently developed microcomputer software being marketed for use on their schools' new equipment. But nonstandardization of hardware and software, the high costs involved, and the extreme variability in the quality of available software pose tremendous selection problems for educators. This book is intended as an introduction to software evaluation, sources, and selection aids for the K-12 teacher and the student in the field, as well as those somewhat more experienced in materials selection such as the school library media specialist. Many parents will also find this a useful guide. The unique problems involved in selecting microcomputer software are discussed here in detail and numerous sample evaluation forms and lists of criteria developed by researchers and educational groups are provided. In addition to discussing sources of possible programs, such as publishers' directories and journals, the book describes such aids to selection as microcomputer consortia and user groups.

The chapters of this book are arranged to facilitate its use as a handbook for selection. Chapter 1 reviews the history of microcomputers and the current revolution in the use of computer-assisted instruction (CAI) in education. This survey, while not intended to be a comprehensive history of the topic, should serve as a brief introduction for those with no background at all in the use of microcomputers so they may develop a very basic understanding of the field. Those seeking more in-depth reading may wish to consult some of the numerous works to be found at their local book store or nearby computer dealer.

Many users of educational software feel that their own evaluation of the materials is unnecessary. They may think that software undergoes extensive evaluation in the development process, put a high degree of trust in published reviews of new materials, or feel that they are inadequate judges of a program's worth. After defining evaluation and examining its two stages, chapter 2 will consider and challenge some of these commonly held beliefs. It will provide information gleaned from a survey of software producers and publishers regarding the evaluations undertaken as their software is produced, discuss the value of published reviews, and confront the issues of achievement of objectives and of cost—two factors that should (and must) affect the evaluation and subsequent purchase decision for any educational program.

Finally, the practicalities of who's, when, and where to evaluate software are noted — decisions that must be made before the evaluation procedure is begun.

It is this procedure that is the focus of chapter 3, which looks at the many important steps necessary to a systematic evaluation of instructional software. Included are the wide variety of questions which form the bases of many of the currently available evaluation forms or checklists integral to any good evaluation. These checklists, gathered from individual schools, districts, and other educational groups, are the primary feature of chapter 4, which continues and concludes the exploration into the parts of the evaluation process.

While it might be said that there are no universally accepted standards for selection existing yet in this field, educational groups are rapidly developing their own sets of standards and appear on the verge of producing some mutually agreed upon criteria. But it is important to remember that, as in the evaluation of educational films, the selection decisions for software are often expensive ones for individual schools and districts and, therefore, must not *only* be based upon general criteria and selection standards but must reflect the school's or district's unique curriculum and educational needs.

Before any selection or evaluation of microcomputer software can take place, selectors must secure a listing of programs available. Virtually all of the directories of software which have been compiled and can be used to find educational programs are listed in chapter 5, along with complete bibliographic information including addresses and prices so that works may be obtained for purchase. A description of the contents of each directory is provided. Because some publishers are reluctant to send out preview copies for fear the copyright will not be respected, advice is given concerning how to obtain the necessary software for previewing purposes. The merits and disadvantages of creating one's own programs are discussed, and there are suggestions about other sources for finding programs, including computer journals and user groups. Programs available on either a free or inexpensive basis from nontraditional sources are also considered in this chapter.

In chapter 6, the different types of computer-related journals are discussed and representative titles are given. For example, hardware manufacturers publish such journals as *Apple Education News* designed to promote sales of the company's products but also providing extremely useful information. Other journals such as *Classroom Computer News* cover many subject areas and regularly feature software reviews of recent programs of interest to teachers. Finally, there are journals quite specific in nature aimed at a special audience of microcomputer users. *Access: Microcomputers in Libraries* is an example of one such publication. Focusing on articles geared to the computing needs of library media specialists, it is aimed at serving a small, but important subgroup of users within educational institutions. The selected list of journals in chapter 6 is complete with bibliographic data as well as annotations describing scope, special features, and the nature of included reviews.

In addition to review journals, there are other aids to selection which are described in chapter 7 and include microcomputer consortia, user groups, and regional and state educational organizations. There are many groups actively involved in both the development and evaluation of microcomputer software today. Such groups range from those informal organizations known as user groups (often loosely organized with members from a single school, town, or other organization), to such complex associations as Minnesota Educational Computing Consortium (MECC) which not only evaluates, but actually creates software and sells it not only within the state but also throughout the nation. Also included are such regional development and evaluation laboratories as EPIE and the Northwest Regional Educational Laboratory.

The final chapter, chapter 8, provides a bibliography of sources addressing the selection, evaluation, and design of microcomputer courseware. A few readings on selection of hardware are also included.

Since each chapter has a unique orientation, an organization described fully in chapter 7 may have its publications described in detail in chapter 6 and its evaluation forms represented in chapter 4. To enable easy cross-referencing, an index of hardware, software, organizations, publications, and forms has been provided.

ACKNOWLEDGMENTS

The authors wish to take this opportunity to thank the many people who contributed to the effort which made this book possible. These include the publishers who sent review copies of both the journals and directories described in this book. It also includes the people who furnished information, other materials, and ideas, people, unfortunately, too numerous to mention, but to whom we are nonetheless indebted.

We would also like to thank the office staff of the Department of Educational Administration at the University of Nebraska who so diligently worked producing the many drafts of the manuscript. In particular, our thanks to Marlene Starr who coordinated much of this labor, and to Sherry, Cathy, Karen, and Sue. The outstanding work of Luella Parsons deserves special mention as does the support of the chairman, Dr. Ward Sybouts.

Thanks to one and all.

PART I

1

THE MICROCOMPUTER IN EDUCATION

Everyone today it seems has an interest in microcomputers—parents who are pressuring the schools to buy them lest their children be left behind, teachers who want to use them not only for teaching skills but to manage instruction and handle other clerical details of their jobs, administrators who wish to manage all of their administrative tasks via the microcomputer, and, of course, students themselves (Miller 1980). Many people refer to this new technology as the *microrevolution* and compare its potential impact to that of the industrial revolution (Mathews and Winkle 1981). Instead of producing manufactured goods, people are increasingly involved in the production and rapid manipulation of huge masses of information made possible through the invention of the computer, whose greatest virtue lies in the ease with which it manipulates and maneuvers these data. The recent and extremely rapid development of this new medium has caught many professionals unprepared. Teachers, administrators, and other educators have had to return to school to take courses in this new technology or avail themselves of district-level or other inservice opportunities to keep abreast.

Computers are not a new phenomenon in education; schools, in fact, began using large mainframe systems in the late 1960s. But these early machines did not catch on for several reasons: Cost was often prohibitive for all but the largest school districts; the mainframe's complexity and massive size limited its use; and there was a general resistance to technology as dehumanizing and demeaning. But the advent of the microcomputer has made the first two reasons invalid while the third has been eroded by the forces unleashed by two powerful institutions within society: the home and industry.

> History suggests that a technology will play a central role in the public schools—if and when—it first gains cultural acceptance (i.e., admittance to a large number of homes) and becomes a primary work tool. The first factor reduces opposition to the introduction of a particular technology into the schools; the second factor generates public demand that the schools adopt the technology and provide training in its use (Pogrow 1982, 610).

Educators and even large corporations are having difficulty shielding themselves from the effects of a phenomenon which Pogrow calls

3

"environmental collapse." Environmental collapse occurs when dissatisfied constituents and clients do not try to change an organization but simply abandon it for an economically more compelling alternative made possible by new technology. Pogrow gives numerous historical examples of victims of environmental collapse including scribes, artisans, oceanliners, and the Pony Express, and cites the Chrysler Corporation (before the federal government bailout) and the U.S. Postal Service as possible future victims. "If educators attempt to resist demands for technological relevance," Pogrow maintains, "U.S. education could also become a victim of environmental collapse" (Pogrow 1982, 611).

But one is forced to agree with Klassen (1978) that most educators are unprepared to deal with the new computer technology despite the mandate of parents and businessmen, as well as educational administrators, that they do so. Sylvia Charp feels that in the hands of knowledgeable people, "today's computer becomes a powerful tool that can be used to handle problems of great volume and complexity in attacking educational problems" (Charp quoted in Edwards et al. 1978, 110). Yet most educators feel neither knowledgeable nor comfortable with the microcomputer at this time. A recent survey which queried teachers as to their training in computers found (1) only 17 percent (37,000) were highly trained to instruct in computer concepts; (2) 26 percent (55,000) said they were moderately trained; but (3) *57 percent, or 122,000, were only minimally trained* ("For Your Information" 1982, 8).

Ignorance of computer technology, according to Klassen, "breeds vulnerability and places the destiny of education at the mercy of the technologists. There then enters the risk that the technology will shape education, whereas in fact education should shape the technology to suit its needs" (Klassen 1978, 111). Educators must learn to become involved in the development of new technology and determine what is good for education, not simply fall prey to the latest salesman who drops by with the best pitch. Unless educators become themselves educated, Klassen argues, they will be unable either to evaluate competently or to use appropriately any new technology. We will all be caught in the classic dilemma of the tail wagging the dog.

But even more seriously, we may be left completely behind and fall victim to Pogrow's environmental collapse as this demand for new types of educational training also enhances formerly impractical options or creates totally new ones for education. For example, private schools, according to Pogrow, will be able to offer comprehensive curricula at greatly reduced expense and will become a more viable alternative to traditional public schooling. Equally threatening is the creation of totally new options such as Deken's "electronic cottage" (Deken 1982). The latter would consist of a technologically connected home combining workplace, schooling, and entertainment all in a single location, thereby totally supplanting the school.

This book will provide at least a first step in dispelling technological ignorance in the field of microcomputers. In particular, the major part of this book is devoted to educating the non-programming educator in the areas of selection and evaluation of microcomputer software. This alone should do much to allay ignorance on the part of fellow professionals. Let us begin this process with an introductory look at microcomputers and an examination of the major rationale for their use in education.

INTRODUCTION OF THE MICROCOMPUTER

The microprocessor was first developed in 1971. This tiny electronic computer engraved on a silicon chip is smaller than a postage stamp — some are no larger than the eye of a needle. Chips are used in a broad range of manufactured equipment including watches, calculators, microwave ovens, videotape components, television sets, toys, video games, and even automobile ignition systems. The microprocessor, despite its tiny size, is a tremendously powerful entity responsible for all the microcomputer's fundamental operations of logic and arithmetic; and it is from these latter two that the microcomputer derives its "intelligence."

Despite the development of the microprocessor over ten years ago, it was not actually marketed until 1975; and only since 1978 have microcomputers been extensively used in home, business, and educational settings. This was due to two factors. One was the initially slow rate of development of the hardware, or microcomputer machines themselves. Today, however, "the technical state of the art in computer hardware is subject to particularly rapid change" (Knapper 1980, 29). The greatest deterrent to rapid acceptance, however, has been the even greater lag in the development of computer programs, known as software, particularly in regard to variety and quantity. Indeed, quality of the programs currently being marketed is a continuing problem and is a major motivating force for the writing of this book.

In the fall of 1980, an estimated fifty-two thousand computers were available for instructional purposes in U.S. schools; almost three-fifths of these (59 percent) were microcomputers (National Center for Education Statistics 1982, 2). By April 1982, the number of microcomputers available for instructional use in the public schools had tripled. Students had access to ninety-six thousand microcomputers and twenty-four thousand mainframe terminals in the spring of 1982 ("For Your Information" 1982, 8). In 1980, nearly three-fourths (73 percent) of educational computers were reported to be in secondary schools, one-fourth (24 percent) in elementary, and the remaining 5 percent were found in combination or special level schools. Microcomputers were fairly evenly distributed among the three different sizes of districts classed by student enrollment: small (fewer than 2,500 students), medium (between 2,500 and 9,999 students), and large (10,000 or more students). By contrast, remote terminal computers were concentrated in the medium-sized and large districts (which had 82 percent of these combined) while small districts had only 18 percent (National Center for Education Statistics 1982, 2). The fact that smaller districts can now afford computers (due to the reasonable cost of the microcomputer) has finally truly ushered in the computer era in education which we are witnessing. Today three-fifths of all secondary schools have at least one microcomputer or terminal as do one-fifth of all elementary schools. Of the approximately twenty-nine thousand public schools which have at least one computer, 80 percent have microcomputers only. Only 5 percent have terminals only and 15 percent have both available. In the 1982-83 school year, another seven thousand schools expected to purchase microcomputers and the number of computers was expected to increase by about fifty-two thousand during 1982 (but this had already increased by sixty-five thousand as early as April — see above). ("For Your Information" 1982, 8).

What exactly is it that makes the microcomputer so different and so much more revolutionary than any other technological development which has impacted education? What, in short, do microcomputers have to offer educators? Are they just another fad like the teaching machine which has become so obsolete that the majority of educators today would not recognize one if someone brought it into their classroom? Christine Doerr (1979) cites over half a dozen reasons why the microcomputer is making tremendous inroads in education today, particularly in the public schools which formerly so stubbornly resisted its larger mainframe ancestors.

In the first place, the computers being used today offer opportunities for relevant education—a goal with which educators have been struggling for decades with mixed success. The big push has come from both the home and business to provide computer education to today's youth who will be increasingly exposed to (and in many cases actually using) the computer on a daily basis in the not too distant future. Students must learn the role of computers in modern society to keep the new technology in perspective, to use it to the best advantage, and to protect themselves from possible abuses of their individual privacy.

The vocational or occupational aspect of computer education can certainly not be overlooked. Most jobs of the future will involve computer technology in one form or another whether those jobs are in business, government, medicine, education, or industry. One estimate predicts that by the year 1985 as many as 75 percent of all jobs will involve computers in some way (Williams et al. 1981, 90). To be a "computer illiterate" will be as serious a handicap to tomorrow's jobseeker as being unacquainted with verbal or quantitative skills is today. Also, those entering higher education, including an increasingly larger and older segment of our population every year, will be expected to possess an acceptable level of computer literacy as part of their basic student skills.

Another reason for the microcomputer's appeal lies in its ability to enhance the effectiveness of the individual teacher for achieving what Doerr calls "great teaching" (1979, 12). Indeed, this is one of the micro's greatest strengths. Rather than supplanting the teacher's efforts, the computer can help create a powerful new teaching force surpassing anything yet achieved in education. This is possible because the microcomputer can relieve the teacher of the monotony of drill-and-practice and repetitive rote learning while adding such creative new formats as games, simulations, tutorials, and combinations of these. The microcomputer also can be used by students, as they develop programming skills, to create their own learning activities and lessons for themselves and others, and in the process enhance their own reasoning, logic, and creative abilities. Finally, the computer can do the grade keeping and recording of student progress formerly done manually by the teacher, as well as provide individual student progress profiles and prescriptive learning diagnoses.

Student motivation is another positive force promoting widespread acceptance of the microcomputer. Increased student attendance and unusually high rates of student progress particularly among low-achieving or remedial students are two positive results reported as consequences of this high level of student enthusiasm. Many young people not only have home computers but are avid players of arcade and home video games, and their high interest transfers to the classroom. The more popular educational programs often utilize competition, games, simulations, colorful graphics displays, and other popular features of the commercial amusement-type programs.

One of the highly touted features of the early teaching machines developed by Skinner and other behavioral psychologists was the immediate feedback provided to student responses. Virtually instantaneous feedback continues to be a distinct advantage of this electronic extension of programmed learning: microcomputer-assisted instruction. The better programs provide positive (often entertaining) feedback and also utilize the computer's branching capability to route the student on to new material when correct responses are given. Branching then, relieves the student of boring repetition of material which has already been mastered. Summary scores can be kept and reported and these results can be checked each day to monitor student progress.

For years educators have espoused the virtues and merits of individualized instruction. Now, by using the microcomputer and the creative new programs which are appearing on a daily basis, students can have individualized programs to work with. They can control the pace and progress of these programs and even create their own. The branching capability previously mentioned, which is built into many tutorial and drill-and-practice programs, allows almost unlimited possibilities for individual control and progress over one's own learning.

Last, but not least, the moderate cost and the versatility of the microcomputer have combined to make it the most desirable new technology available to educators. This versatility has caused some educators to predict that management applications of the microcomputer in education may eventually surpass their use as teaching tools. But given the present rapid increase in instructional use of the microcomputer, this is questionable. There is no doubt, however, that the microcomputer is a multi-purpose machine whose full potential appears as yet unrealized.

SELECTING HARDWARE

The ultimate question about the issue of microcomputer use in education today is not *whether* we should use them, but *how* we should use them to best utilize their unique capabilities and get the most for our money. Most of today's classroom teachers, unfortunately, have neither previous formal undergraduate coursework, recent practical experience, nor inservice training in the selection of software and the purchasing and utilization of microcomputers to run this software. The three most popular micros presently in use in education today are the Commodore PET, the Apple II, and Radio Shack's TRS-80. Although in 1978 it was said that from a technical standpoint microcomputers are a long way from perfect, the same thing was certainly true of the first automobiles, and the three models above, plus many other brands, are being used quite successfully in classrooms throughout the country. It is beyond the scope of this book to discuss the merits or faults of individual machines available and due to the rapid developments in the field, today's best buy or model of microcomputer may not be so six months from now. In any case, a number of works both describe and compare the various machines available in terms of capacity, capability, and peripherals (optional equipment) and should be consulted as an aid in selecting a machine. A number of articles addressing hardware selection will be found throughout the bibliography in chapter 8.

Although the selection of computer hardware may be viewed as an enormous task by many educators, due to their lack of familiarity with the equipment and to the relatively large sums of money involved, the decision is actually a limited one. Hardware should be selected with regard to the software capabilities it can offer.

SELECTING SOFTWARE

One authority estimates that computer equipment costs are only about 30 percent of computer expense, with the remaining 70 percent going for software or instructional programs and staff training. It is not difficult, then, to see why choosing the software, the actual instructional programs which will be used in the classroom, should be the first decision made. In fact, choosing the right software will be what makes or breaks the computer revolution according to a recent article in *Education USA*. Quoting a spokesman from the Educational Projects Information Exchange (EPIE) Institute, a laboratory which tests instructional materials and equipment, the article also stated that schools were being presented with "a whole new, and much tougher ball game when it comes to materials selections" ("Software Will Make or Break the Computer Revolution" 1982, 17). Many, if not most, educators will be forced to play in this "ball game" unless they wish to have materials chosen by others and forced upon them whether or not they meet a particular teacher's objectives. Thus, selection will continue to be an ongoing problem faced by today's educators, administrators, library media specialists, counselors, and curriculum specialists; and locating and evaluating microcomputer software will be important considerations. A recent survey of schools found that 60 percent of them bought their microcomputer software from publishers and/or equipment vendors mostly outside the school district ("For Your Information" 1982, 8).

Despite the newness of the field, the variety and quantity of programs already available to educators is truly remarkable, but at the same time overwhelming. Unfortunately, the quality of these programs, as we remarked above, varies from excellent to poor, and many fields or subject areas (e.g., library skills) have been generally overlooked until recently by programmers who tended to focus their efforts on certain areas where educational applications appear most obvious (i.e., mathematics and science). It is to the ordinary teacher and others with little or no experience with computers—who must still choose educational software—that this book is aimed.

The authors, incidentally, contend that anyone can learn how to use a decent commercially produced and marketed program with little or no prior knowledge of microcomputers after about fifteen minutes of teacher- or self-instruction and half an hour of practice. In fact, they accomplish this with undergraduates in a basic audiovisual production and equipment operation course every semester. One does not need to be a computer programmer to utilize computer-assisted instruction effectively in the classroom. Furthermore, with the help of this book, the selection criteria which it provides, and one of the many software evaluation forms to be found in chapter 4, any competent educator can make intelligent decisions in regard to the purchase of instructional computer software.

Some of the problems faced by selectors in making purchase choices on microcomputer software are common to choosing most nonprint media formats. Other problems are unique to computer program selection. For example, finding reviews of a title under consideration has always been more difficult for nonprint items than for books. And, when reviews have been laboriously tracked down, they have often been found to be notoriously lacking in objective criticism and high on description and summary, information one could get from any publisher's catalog or accompanying teacher's guide.

An example of a problem unique to microcomputer software selection, however, is the reluctance of producers to allow preview of programs before purchase, a commonly accepted standard practice in the selection of 16mm films, another costly budget item. But the ease with which an unscrupulous user could copy a microcomputer program, return it to a producer saying it was unsuitable, and then actually use the pirated copy has made software companies understandably reluctant to extend this preview privilege to their customers. There is some evidence, however, that this reluctance is changing and that many producers will now extend their customers limited privileges (see chapter 5).

One solution to the selection difficulties faced by educators is to develop one's own software. Many teachers, in fact, are doing just this. In Lyons Township High School District in LaGrange, Illinois, teachers give their ideas to programmers who translate them into the appropriate software ("Software Will Make or Break the Computer Revolution" 1982). But this is an impractical solution for many school districts due to the high costs involved both in terms of teacher time and computer programming. One skeptic has claimed that schools should not even purchase microcomputers and software if manufacturers don't come up with better products, but the fact remains that schools continue to purchase them. Thus, the majority of educators are likely to continue to become more and more involved in the selection of the commercially prepared and some excellent noncommercial (see chapter 5) software being offered. This book will serve as an invaluable guide and resource for those who must make these decisions and who wish to make them in an intelligent, well-informed manner. An interesting phenomenon which often occurs as teachers are exposed to computers in the classroom is that they end up becoming interested in developing their own student-oriented courseware, but this is by no means a necessity for successful use of CAI in education.

DEVELOPMENT OF COMPUTER TECHNOLOGY

For some people, it is helpful in understanding a field of endeavor if they can place it in historical perspective. Thus a brief history of computers will be presented here. Bitter divides this history into five generations of computer development, claiming we are only at the beginning of the fifth generation which will bring us smaller, faster, and less costly computers (Bitter et al. 1982). The first generation dates from 1946 to 1958, although the first computer or world's largest calculator was actually completed before this — in 1944. That computer was begun by Howard Aiken, a Harvard University professor, in 1937 and finished with the help of International Business Machines (IBM) engineers. The Mark I, as it was called, weighed over five tons, was fifty-one feet long by eight feet high, and contained 760,000 parts plus five hundred miles of wire. Information or data input to the Mark I was accomplished through the use of punched cards. The punch card had been developed much earlier — in response to the need for tabulating the 1880 and 1890 U.S. Census surveys — by Dr. Herman Hollerith who eventually became associated with IBM. James Powers later further refined the punch card tabulating system for the 1910 census; his company, through a series of mergers, eventually became part of Sperry Univac. Results of the Mark I's tabulations were also produced on punched cards with addition and subtraction taking three-tenths of a second and division requiring less than sixteen seconds. All operations were carried out by a system of electrically operated switches and relays. This machine was used extensively during World War II by the U.S. Navy.

The first true electronic digital computer was the Electronic Numerical Integrator and Calculator (ENIAC) finished in 1946. Its thirty ton weight made the Mark I seem small in comparison. ENIAC could calculate in one day what it would take three hundred days to do manually. It also utilized punched card input and output; however, it could only store 20 ten-digit numbers. Some 18,800 vacuum tubes were used in this machine and two and a half years were required just to solder the 500,000 connections required by these tubes. Typical computers of the 1950s which followed their ENIAC ancestor weighed forty tons, took up entire rooms, gobbled large amounts of electrical energy, and required air conditioning. Obviously they were very costly to own and run and only large corporations could afford them. Sperry Univac's UNIVAC I, for example, cost $1.5 million.

Second generation (1959-1963) computers were the result of a new semiconductor material called the transistor which was developed by Bell Laboratories; they received a Nobel Prize for this innovation (Bitter et al. 1982). The major contributions of the transistor lay in its smaller size, lesser power requirements, lesser amount of generated heat, and decreased cost compared to the vacuum tube. Transistors were more reliable thereby cutting maintenance costs; this was due to the fact that they did not generate the same intensity of heat which had formerly resulted in so many burnt out vacuum tubes. Two hundred transistors could fit into the same amount of space required by a single vacuum tube. The cost of 100,000 calculations on this newer computer was $0.25 compared to $1.25 for the same number performed on the older vacuum tube machines. These second generation computers used rings or cores for storage of data.

Third generation (1964-1978) computers were the result of the invention of the chip. A chip is defined as "part of a silicon wafer that is about a quarter-inch square and contains a circuit pattern resembling a miniature wall map" (Bitter et al. 1982, 9-10). Within a single tiny chip there are thousands of transistors, enclosed in a case, all connected to the outside world. Another name for a chip is integrated circuit. Third generation computers are nine hundred times faster than their first generation counterparts and have numerous other distinctive characteristics: They are physically smaller; they are more reliable; they operate with printed circuits; they are capable of talking or communicating with more than one user at a time; and they can be programmed in more one language. A chip has a life expectancy of many years and its manufacture is greatly simplified since it is created as a single entity rather than being laboriously assembled and soldered from separate parts.

Fourth generation (1975-early 1980s) computers are considered by some to be more powerful and versatile refinements of third generation machines. Others consider the development of the large-scale integrated circuit (LSI) to be the technological breakthrough heralding in the fourth generation. An accompanying development was microminiaturization, called the computer on a chip, whereby fifteen thousand transistors were placed within an area one-twentieth of an inch square. This tiny chip or brain can store, process, and retrieve data and is equal in performance to the large computers of only a decade before. Cost is less than one cent per 100,000 calculations and the most significant impact of these micro chips was that almost immediately the cost of electronic products plummeted dramatically. For example, today's digital watch which costs between four and twenty dollars originally sold for two thousand dollars. Desktop computers, which sold for a minimum of twenty thousand dollars initially, now can be purchased for five hundred to twenty-five hundred dollars.

Bitter feels that we are only at the tip of the fifth generation (1980s) of computer development. Hewlett-Packard, for example, announced early in 1981 the development of a new chip that can process one thousand books in a single second and has a 450,000 transistor capacity (Bitter et al. 1982, 11). Truly we are only beginning to develop the potential of this marvelous machine as we explore new frontiers of technology in information storage and processing and push the frontiers of the science of teaching and learning theory further back. To ignore learning about computers or to avoid using them is to be as foolish as those who resisted the early horseless carriage or the Wright brothers' winged invention. Technology is once again providing us with a way to go places and do things we have not done before. Those who choose not to climb aboard will surely be left behind. Now that we have seen where the microcomputer fits in the overall history of computers, let us take a look at the development of the computer's most basic application in education, computer-assisted instruction.

COMPUTER-ASSISTED INSTRUCTION

Computer-assisted instruction (CAI) may be defined as "a process in which the learner interacts directly with lessons displayed on a cathode-ray tube (CRT) or ... printed by a terminal that provides hard copy" (O'Neal, Kauffman, and Smith 1981-82, 160). According to Knapper, CAI as originally conceived was a direct descendent of programmed instruction "and many early uses of computers for teaching purposes constituted adaptations of the teaching machine" (Knapper 1980, 27). Lesson formats in CAI can be tutorial, in which basic information is imparted; standard drill-and-practice; problem solving; simulation; games; or a combination of two or more of these formats. Besides varying in format, CAI can be used in different ways in the classroom.

It can be a tool to supplement classroom instruction; it can be used to actually deliver instruction; or it can be the total instructional system. The latter is also known as computer-managed instruction (CMI). CMI can be used to diagnose, prescribe, present, evaluate, inform, and keep track of student progress just as the individual teacher would. Although many people, even recently, associate the use of computers in education only with CAI, today CAI has generally come to loosely include these CMI applications as well. Many people question whether it is sensible to use the computer solely for tutorial purposes (i.e., as a principal source of information) and this has led to the increased use of CMI applications.

The use of computers in education despite the recent publicity brought about by the introduction of the microcomputer is hardly a new phenomena. The University of Pennsylvania put its first digital computer into use thirty years ago (O'Neal, Kauffman, Smith 1981-82, 159), yet universities and schools were slow to acquire the new electronic devices, and their early use was confined largely to research and management applications called data based management (DBM). It was not until about fifteen years ago that educational institutions began using computers in a classroom setting for instructional purposes, now popularly referred to as CAI.

During the 1960s there was great hope that the computer was the solution to many of the problems facing education including meeting the needs for individualization of instruction, mass instruction to serve the rapidly expanding student population, and instructional accountability. The high costs and the complexity of these early mainframe systems, however, prevented their widespread use although certain systems were fairly successful. One notable example is Control Data's Programmed Logic for Automated Teaching Operations (PLATO) system, developed in the early 1960s by the University of Illinois and now widely marketed in North America and even in Europe (Knapper 1980, 29-30). Although most of the functions generally utilized on PLATO are either tutorial or drill-and-practice in nature, it is capable of many more applications. For example, the display screen used is touch sensitive so students may simply point to the correct answer. Graphics, printing capability, music, and even speeches can be incorporated into lessons. A bulletin board feature allows students to communicate with those in other locations by exchanging notes. Besides choosing from a published catalog containing hundreds of programs, instructors may even produce their own PLATO courses with the company's aid. One user of PLATO, the University of Delaware, had sixty PLATO terminals providing instructional materials at twenty-nine different academic locations (Knapper 1980, 30).

Costs of systems like PLATO have remained fairly high to this day and have prevented this form of CAI from being universally adopted; however, Control Data has begun rewriting many of the mainframe PLATO programs for the microcomputer and these are already being marketed to schools. The use of large mainframe systems with access to remote computers was reported to entail two-fifths of the more than 52,000 computers being used in this nation's public schools in 1980 while the remaining three-fifths of the computers in use were micros (National Center for Education Statistics 1982, 2). However, by fall of 1982, microcomputers comprised 80 percent of the machines in use in the schools while terminals dropped to only 20 percent of the 120,000 reported computers ("For Your Information" 1982, 8). The large cost reductions made possible by the advent of the microcomputer were responsible for this dramatic increase in computer use in U.S. schools.

Almost one-half (48 percent of the nation's school districts provided their students with access to one or more computers for instructional purposes in the fall of 1980; this access is expected to increase to 57 percent at all levels by fall 1983 (National Center for Education Statistics 1982, 10). During the 1981-82 school year, 4.7 million students used computers for an average of nine hours per student spent in computer use ("For Your Information" 1982, 8).

Since the number of microcomputers in the public schools tripled between 1980 and 1982, a mere two year span, predictions as to the percentage of students who will have access to microcomputers in the future seems risky. Much of the money allocated to states through the new federal Block Grant Program, which replaces the former Elementary and Secondary Education Act of 1965 title programs, is anticipated to be spent on microcomputer acquisitions. One study recently reported a mean of five microcomputers in every school in the country, high schools averaging six per school while elementary schools had just over three ("Study Show Schools Take to Computers" 1982, 6). Another source reports less computer availability than this (although the data may not be as current) for an average of 3.2 computers available to students in each of this country's sixteen thousand school districts ("Computer Use" 1982, 143). By level of instruction, according to this same source, computers are primarily available in the secondary schools. Roughly 63 percent of districts with computers are providing them at the secondary level in contrast to 5 percent which have them available solely in elementary schools. Approximately one-fourth of districts provide access at more than one level. The majority of school districts (61 percent) have only microcomputers available.

As early as the academic year 1974-75, Bukoski reported that 58 percent of *all* secondary schools had access to computers and spent an estimated 350 million dollars on computing services (Bukoski 1975). Some had claimed that the number of secondary schools actually using the computer for instructional purposes would double between 1970 and 1975 (jumping from 13 to 27 percent) and predicted that this utilization would double again (to 51 percent) by the year 1984 (Edwards et al. 1978, 32). These predictions are probably low but in any case the fact that by fall of 1982 there were 120,000 computers in use in U.S. schools is indicative of their widespread acceptance.

New CAI Formats

Although early use of CAI was largely confined to tutorial and drill-and-practice formats, today utilization of the computer has expanded to include applications as an educational tool for problem solving, as a director of the learning process, as an interface between student and teacher, and as an instructional management system (O'Neal, Kauffman, and Smith 1981-82, 160). Others have identified twelve common computer applications which may be grouped into the following five broad categories: (1) Computer as Instructor: drill-and-practice, tutorial; (2) Computer as Laboratory: data analysis, problem-solving and simulation; (3) Computer as Calculator:

mathematical calculation; (4) Computer as Object of Instruction: computer literacy, computer science and programming, and data processing; and finally, (5) Computer as Instructor's Aide: computer-managed instruction (CMI), generation of instructional materials, and information and storage retrieval (Edwards et al. 1978, 33).

As we have seen, one of the major deterrents to the use of CAI in public schools in the past has been the cost. Pools of experts on CAI have consistently confirmed that this cost has been considered the major obstacle to its widespread acceptance (Kearsley 1977). However, Hirschbuhl predicts that given the premise that conventional instructional costs will continue to rise as they have over the past ten years, by 1985 the cost of CAI on a per-pupil basis will be less than half the cost of comparable conventional instruction (Hirschbuhl 1977). Research on the cost-effectiveness of CAI (Vinsonhaler and Bass 1972; Mitchell 1973; and Schramm 1974) has shown that both at the elementary school level and in specialized educational settings such as disadvantaged, handicapped, and nursing programs, CAI is as cost-effective as traditional education and can often result in substantial savings of student time. The rapidly developing nature of this technology, in addition, may dramatically reduce costs in the near future as has occurred in the recent past thereby surpassing any cost reduction predictions which we can presently make. Certain educational programs (e.g., special education) where recent federal regulations have necessitated voluminous record keeping on individual students may turn to the microcomputer as the system savior. Control Data, for example, has been working on paperless classroom systems particularly for special education and other situations where extensive monitoring of student progress must be done and recorded (Joiner, Miller, and Silverstein 1980).

An obvious and legitimate concern of educators has been the effectiveness of instruction delivered through CAI. So far, research results have been positive. Numerous studies report significantly greater gains in student achievement among CAI groups over traditionally instructed groups (Ronan 1973; Crandall 1975; and Morgan and Richardson 1976) especially among developmental or basic skills students. Indeed, one experimental group in a remedial reading program in an Akron, Ohio, junior high school averaged three months' growth in reading ability for every month spent in the program. Formerly they had averaged less than one month's growth (Hirschbuhl 1977). Similar findings have been reported in other remedial settings. And although long term retention appeared worse in early research studies, recent reports lean toward equal retention (Joiner, Miller, and Silverstein 1980).

Future studies will undoubtably yield more information regarding the effectiveness of CAI, and as more schools adopt the technology, a wider sample for these studies will be available. As of now, all indications are that, properly developed and used, CAI programs offer much promise for the future of education: a promise that properly educated software choosers and evaluators can help fulfill.

SOME BASIC MICROCOMPUTER TERMS AND PRINCIPLES

Despite the amazingly complex nature of the microcomputer, the terminology and basic principles needed to operate one successfully — using a well-written, commercially prepared program—are few in number and easy to understand. The reason the above statement is qualified by the expression "well-written" is that a poorly written program fraught with programming errors or so-called bugs can cause even a seasoned programmer some moments of hair-pulling frustration. A major premise of this work is that if the average non-programming individual cannot operate a purchased program easily, then it should not be bought. The educator her/himself is the final arbiter of what constitutes a suitable, appropriate software program for oneself or one's students and this should always be kept in mind.

It is hard to find a definition of the term *microcomputer* in any but the most recent dictionaries. A computer is simplistically described as "a programmable electronic device that can store, retrieve, and process data" (*Webster's New Collegiate Dictionary*, 8th ed., s.v. "computer"). Deitel further clarifies this definition by adding that a computer is "a device that is capable of computations and making logical decisions at speeds thousands of times faster than any human" (Deitel 1977, 1). Ankers adds the concept that a computer is a machine that follows a set of instructions, i.e., is programmable (Ankers 1980, 52). This is helpful because many people still think a computer has a mind or brain of its own. But no computer can perform any function for which it does not have specific instructions—a major source of frustration to beginning programmers who want the computer to do what I *want* it to do, *not* what I'm *telling* it to do. In other words, their instructions or commands to the computer, known as a computer program or software, are incorrect.

There are two general types of computer software or programs that tell the computer what to do: (1) the computer's own software system, which consists of programs directing the computer's basic operations and overall general functions, and (2) user's programs, or programs which instruct the computer to perform specific applications (Edwards et al. 1978). Edwards has grouped software and programs into types (table 1.1).

Table 1.1
Types of Software

Computer's Software System	User's Programs
Arithmetic Operations	Problem-solving
Logical Operations	Statistical Analysis
Program Sequencing	Tutorial
Error Checking	Data Processing
Translating	Simulation
Control Procedures	Calculation
Etc.	Drill
	Games
	Etc.

Note: Reprinted by permission from Edwards et al., 3. Copyright © 1978 by Northwest Regional Educational Laboratory. Published by Time Share Corporation, Hanover, New Hampshire 03755.

Some basic principles of computers are helpful to understand before one begins to evaluate and use programs successfully. For example, one principle is that one must communicate with the computer in a language it understands called a user language. This is analogous to speaking to a Frenchman in the French language. The computer in turn translates this program into one that the machine understands, called a machine language. Thus we have two main types of computer languages: user and machine languages. Within the broader category of user languages we also have two subtypes called assembly and high-level languages. An assembly language, itself a program, is "a simple language people can understand" and "gives the user the ability to write a simplified list of instructions (a program) which is subsequently translated into a program made up of machine language" (Frederick 1980, 7). In contrast to assembly language which is more difficult to learn, high-level languages such as BASIC, Pascal, and COBOL are generally easier for the novice or beginning programmer to learn since they are English-like languages specifically designed to make it convenient for the average person to program. BASIC (Beginner's All-purpose Symbolic Instruction Code) is probably the most commonly used high-level language for beginning programmers and for instructional programs. There is even a high-level language, named LOGO, which was developed by MIT professor Seymour Papert especially for children to use in programming.

Machine language, the second type of computer language, is the set of instructions which a computer understands and uses to transform an assembly or high-level language into instructions which it can read and carry out. Machine language is neither read nor learned easily by computer users. All programs are eventually interpreted by the machine into this machine language which is built into the computer itself by professional, highly skilled computer programmers.

While operating instructions or programs written for a computer are called software, the machine and its various attachments, called peripherals, are referred to as hardware. Hardware selection is not discussed in detail in this book. Yet in order to understand and operate software, it is useful to know the various components of the machine. The microcomputer itself is actually the Central Processing Unit (CPU) (see fig. 1.1) and, besides the keyboard which is similar to that of a typewriter, contains the brain of the computer.

> This brain, composed of three interworking parts, receives data from the outside world, processes the data, and sends the processed data back to the outside world. *Chips*, or *electronic circuits*, store the information to be processed and the results of the processing, and are often referred to as the computer's *memory unit*. There is also an *arithmetic/logic unit* that performs all the calculations and makes decisions based on the testing of certain conditions. The *control unit* keeps everything running in a computer and makes sure all the parts work together properly. In most desktop microcomputers all this is enclosed within a box-shaped device containing a keyboard like a typewriter (Bitter et al. 1982, 6-7).

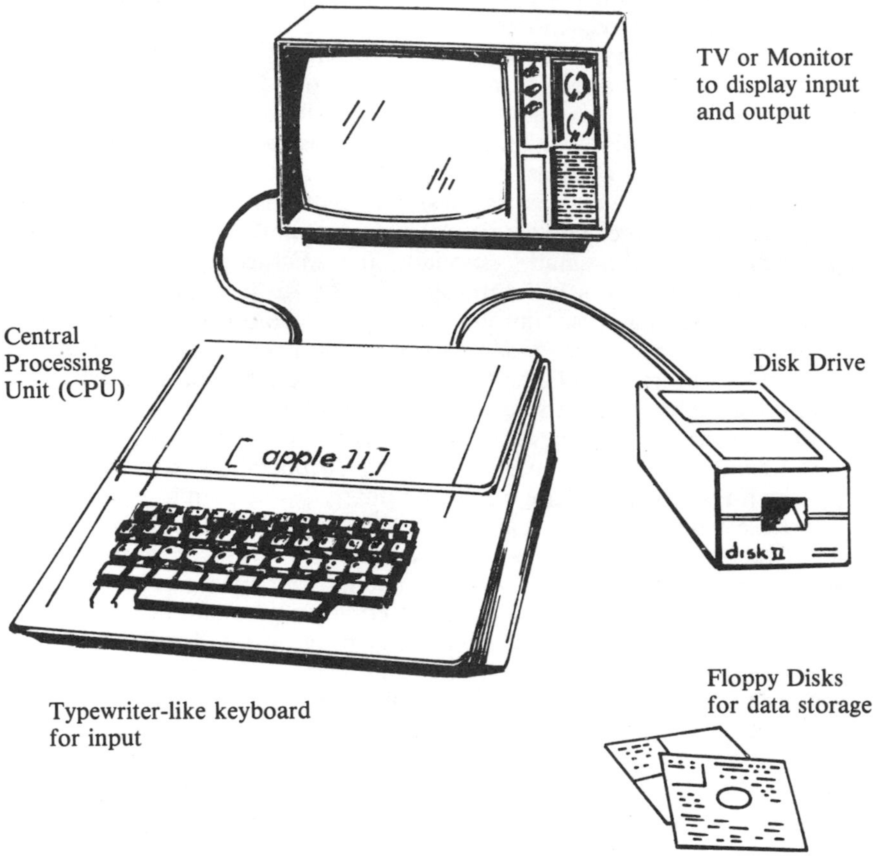

TV or Monitor
to display input
and output

Central
Processing
Unit (CPU)

Disk Drive

[apple]l]

disk ll

Typewriter-like keyboard
for input

Floppy Disks
for data storage

Fig. 1.1. Typical microcomputer system. Artwork by Brandon Whistler.

Other components of the hardware are generally concerned either with input or output of data. For example, the keyboard mentioned as part of the CPU is an input device. Another input device is the floppy disk, so named because of its flexibility. A floppy disk somewhat resembles a record with one or two mylar surfaces and generally measures either 8 inches or 5¼-inches in diameter, the latter size being the most commonly used. It is inserted into a unit called the disk drive which reads and writes the programs and/or data from these disks. An alternative input medium is the less expensive cassette tape although this medium is less desirable than disks which provide more rapid, accurate access capabilities. Certain devices both input and output data; these include monitors made especially for microcomputer use and the ordinary television screen which must utilize an RF modulator to adapt for computer use. A final input/output device to be mentioned is the cathode-ray tube, which is a video screen mounted into a terminal with both a screen and a keyboard (Bitter et al. 1982). The most commonly used display units in education are the television screen and the monitor.

Printers are output devices which permit hard copy of data to be produced and are extremely useful for many purposes although by no means necessary for instructional use of the computer. Two examples should suffice to illustrate where printouts can be helpful. Computer program revision is much easier to do when one sees the whole program at once, often an impossibility on a screen on which only twenty-four lines can be viewed at a time. A second example of where hard copy or printouts are useful is in evaluation of student progress; many CMI programs will print out student grades and scores achieved on exercises and tests.

Printers vary widely both in the quality of their type and in price. For example, a thermal printer, while generally cheaper, must use special thermal paper and does not produce high-quality printouts. A dot-matrix printer will produce fairly good quality type if one with enough dots per square inch is chosen; both upper and lower case letters are available on this type of printer. The best quality print is produced by a daisywheel printer which has type comparable to a better typewriter's (Bitter et al. 1982). A quality printer can easily cost as much as the CPU itself, but no printer at all is really necessary for a majority of the instructional applications of the microcomputer.

Another underlying principle of computers is their use of the binary number system. In this system, there are only two symbols, zero and one, which represent either an "off" or an "on" position, respectively, of an electrical circuit. If the circuit is on, that is represented by the symbol one (1). When the circuit is switched off, this is represented by the symbol zero (0). Bits, corresponding to this on or off switching of the electrical current, are the smallest measure of information that is recognized by the computer.

Eight bits make up what is called a byte. A byte, in turn, "represents an alphanumeric character or a number in the range 0 to 255" (Milner 1980, 19). Or, in other words, a set of consecutive bits (a byte) corresponds to some one character or stroke on the keyboard such as a letter; a number; a space; or a special symbol, e.g., a period (Bitter et al. 1982, 13).

Microcomputers vary as to how many bytes of information or data they can store. This is measured by how many *thousands* of bytes a particular machine's memory can retain at one time. The symbol K stands for kilo or thousand but a K is a little more than 1,000; it represents 1,024 bytes. The more K, the larger a computer's memory capacity or storage space. A unit with 32K or 48K, which is adequate for most instructional purposes, would be capable of storing 32,768 or 49,152 characters, respectively. We say that a computer has 4K, 8K, 16K, 32K, etc., which is another way of expressing its data storage capacity and is always stated in these standard memory size increments.

There are two types of memory utilized in a computer. These are called ROM and RAM storage. Read-only memory (ROM) is data or information permanently stored in the computer; it cannot generally be changed by the user. Certain computers, for example, are designed with a particular language such as BASIC commonly built into them. Random access memory (RAM), on the other hand, consists of temporary storage space and is actually the main memory where user programs and information are written and stored and from which they can be subsequently retrieved, changed, or deleted altogether (Milner 1980, 19). Since there is a limited amount of storage in any microcomputer (expressed in its K), the more storage space taken up by ROM, the less will be available for storing user programs in RAM.

These principles, then, are the most basic of computer information and can help the software user understand how the microcomputer works.

One of the most incidental but significant side effects of using microcomputers in classroom instruction is that both teachers and students pick up terminology and computer expertise quite readily. While the principles and terms just described may appear unfamiliar to the total novice, to someone with any degree of experience in microcomputers this discussion has probably been rather elementary. The remaining chapters are devoted to the evaluation process, sources, and aids for choosing educational software. We hope this chapter has provided the beginner with some basic concepts and background which will prove helpful in reading the rest of the book.

2

GEARING UP FOR THE EVALUATION

One teacher was recently overheard discussing her experiences evaluating instructional software. "We wanted to buy several programs to supplement our language arts curriculum," she said. "We ordered some competing software to compare products from different companies. Thank goodness it all came with a thirty-day return guarantee. We ended up sending more than three-fourths of it back almost right away—some of it wouldn't even work for more than a minute or so without flashing an error message on the screen. Others were so simplistic I knew my junior high students wouldn't stay interested very long." She sighed softly. "It's been really hard finding enough good software to meet our needs."

This Nebraska schoolteacher's experience is, unfortunately, not unique. Many poor programs exist on the market which justify undertaking the evaluation activity described in the following chapters. There are other reasons yet to be discussed, but first it seems appropriate to explore possible causes for this inferior software.

A report released in 1982 by the Office of Technology Assessment (OTA) of the Congressional Board of the ninety-seventh Congress cited four reasons to explain the lack of quality educational software:

> In the first place, many of the technologies are still new. It takes time to learn how to use them and the early attempts suffer from this learning process. Second, production of high quality educational software is expensive. Some large firms that have the necessary capital to produce educational software hesitate to risk development money in a relatively new and uncertain market.
>
> Third, the programmers and curriculum experts qualified to produce educational software are in short supply. Finally, some firms cite the lack of adequate property protection (e.g., copyright, patents) for their information products as a barrier to investment in development (U.S. Congress. Office of Technology Assessment 1982, 19).

It is certainly indisputable that lack of experience with the technology can account for many of the faults in earlier efforts. Any time a new medium of delivery is introduced, time must be allotted for the discovery of its unique advantages and limitations for education. (Consider, for example, the history of instructional television.) Although micros were introduced commercially in the early 1970s, they didn't become a highly regarded educational phenomenon until about 1980. Thus, many of our educational software programs grew out of initial experiments with the medium.

But the microcomputer should not have had to jump so many hurdles. As described in chapter 1, computer-assisted instruction (CAI) was an outgrowth of an educational innovation first developed in the 1950s—programmed instruction. Experience with that learning method should have precluded some of the problems encountered in the development of its grandchild, the microcomputer program, but this has not been the case. Software developers have stumbled over the same rocks that programmed text writers tripped on in the past and the vast research that came out of the programmed instruction movement has been largely ignored by the producers of microcomputer lessons.

Educators are only now beginning to put into practice those ideas about evaluation of programs first proposed in the early sixties by such prominent researchers in programmed instruction as Arthur A. Lumsdaine and Robert Glaser. Contemplate this advice:

A. Prospective users should evaluate each program on its own merits according to its demonstrated effectiveness in producing specified outcomes.

B. In determining the suitability of any program for a particular purpose, the prospective user should first formulate his own objectives in as much detail as possible and then evaluate the program in relation to these objectives in the light of three things:

1. The apparent appropriateness of the program content for his purposes, as based on inspection of the program itself and of the producer's statement of the program's objectives...

2. Consideration of factors affecting practicality, or feasibility of use, such as the cost of the program, initial and maintenance cost of the machine (if required), and factors affecting supervision, scheduling, and other aspects of administration.

3. Evidence on the demonstrable effectiveness of the program in terms of outcomes relevant to the user's objectives. (These may include motivational or attitudinal effects, as well as subject-matter competencies.) (Joint Committee on Programmed Instruction and Teaching Machines 1966, 3-4.)

Note the date of the publication cited above. The quote did not come from any recent literature in our field. It came instead from a report entitled *Recommendations for Reporting the Effectiveness of Programmed Instruction Materials* first written in September 1964 and revised in October 1965. This advice is as pertinent to the educational software of the present as the programs of the past. That these historical admonitions have surfaced once again is a testimony to their solid basis in theory and their practical utility.

Perhaps, as the field of microcomputer e' ation advances, we should look backwards, as well as ahead. We can lear ch from the programmed instruction movement by studying both what worked and what failed. Some of today's microcomputer skeptics, doubting the new medium's continued existence in the schools, often point to the failure of programmed instruction (it declined rapidly in the late sixties) as a fitting parallel to what they say will happen to CAI.

Though the micro does possess some strengths that earlier programmed instruction never enjoyed (massive business and parental support, for one), the parallel might still be drawn—but only if we let it. It is often said that we study history so that we don't repeat it. We should study the programmed instruction movement for the same reason: to learn from it.

The second reason given for lack of quality software in the OTA report is the high cost of development. "The cost to develop just one good—repeat, good—program is roughly $10,000-$12,000 (and that's assuming a 'not-for-profit' producer)" (Braun 1981, 36).

Time, which in business *is* money, accounts for the largest portion of this expense. It takes a very long time to plan, write, and then program a good CAI lesson. Because this "brain time" is the most important ingredient in a quality program, many smaller software developers can produce some excellent work. Their "investment capital" is the intelligence and the experience of their programming team—often consisting of the company's owners who began the collaboration due, at least in part, to their compatible interests. The larger publishing companies, in contrast, often must buy the time of competent programming personnel or purchase programs already developed by independent authors.

But, despite the tremendous investments of both time and money necessary to enter the software business, it is still booming. So much so, in fact, that many enterprising but untalented individuals have contributed their inferior wares to the current market along with the really good products, creating a need for careful evaluation of programming quality as well as suitability.

This is closely linked to the third reason for variable quality computer programs—that qualified curriculum and programming experts are in short supply, and we all know that unqualified individuals seldom produce quality work.

> Part of the problem stems from the fact that much of the software that's currently available was produced by programmers who aren't educators or by educators who aren't programmers. This "cottage industry" of software sprang up a few years ago to meet the needs of educators who were grabbing up the new micros. Many would-be entrepreneurs suddenly found that for a couple of thousand dollars, they could buy a micro, set it up on the kitchen table, stay up late and grind out a program or two, and boom!—they were in business ("Quality Software" 1981, 34).

But apparently things are changing. David Bricklin, coauthor of VisiCalc, a much respected and highly grossing business accounting program, was recently quoted as saying, "You can't just start in the garage as easily any more. The price of entry is going up and up because people are expecting so much from these products" (Taylor 1982, 56). Though speaking for the business software industry, Bricklin's words can be applied to education as well. Most experts in the field of software evaluation now agree that it takes a team approach to produce quality educational programming: a subject matter specialist, an instructional designer, and a highly experienced programmer. Software produced without these important inputs is sure to suffer and as teachers, administrators, media specialists, and parents learn more about what the microcomputer is capable of and what quality programs currently exist, poorly produced programs will no longer be tolerated.

The OTA's fourth and final explanation for lack of quality is the problem of copyright infringement. Certainly, few would argue that a program developer should be compensated for his or her work, but beyond this platitude lies a range of disagreement that will not be explored here. Suffice it to say that the facts should dictate our actions. If good, competent program developers and producers are being discouraged from entering the field (or restricting their previewing privileges) because of violation of their copyrights, that practice is not only illegal, it is counterproductive. Good common sense, as well as our own ethics, must guide us.

Though these four explanations are often given for low quality educational software, the fact remains that good and bad instructional programs exist side by side in the marketplace, signaling the need for developing software evaluation expertise. But before we examine the "hows" of the evaluation process, we need to take a closer look at what evaluation really is, why educators should be involved, who should participate in the task, and when and where it should be undertaken.

TYPES OF EVALUATION

Evaluation has been defined as "the determination of the worth of a thing" (Worthen and Sanders 1973, 19). This implies that in evaluation a judgment must be made about the thing being evaluated, be it a behavioral objective, a curriculum unit, or an educational media product. Many theorists in the field have come to recognize two common types of evaluation generally referred to as "formative" and "summative" evaluation, terms first coined by Michael Scriven, a prominent researcher in the field (Scriven 1967).

Formative evaluation of instructional media products refers to assessments made of the products while they are still under development. During formative evaluation, media producers and development staff act as evaluators and make judgments about the product as it proceeds through its many stages from conception to completion. These assessments produce recommendations that are used in subsequent revisions, contributing to a superior finished product.

Formative evaluation, then, is distinguished by two main characteristics: (1) the product is evaluated repeatedly throughout its stages of development, and (2) information gained through formative evaluations is used for immediate revisions to improve the product before it is marketed.

Summative evaluation, in contrast, is undertaken to assess the worth of the total, completed product and can be conducted before or after the product is marketed. Media producers often perform summative assessments but the frequency and rigor of these total-product evaluations can vary dramatically from producer to producer (and medium to medium) casting some doubt on the usefulness of these assessments. Summative evaluation is perhaps most valuable when undertaken by the consumer, who must determine the worth of the product under examination as well as its usefulness for a particular classroom situation.

Because of the nature of the medium, program revisions of marketed microcomputer software are not the expensive and laborious undertakings they are for a textbook or film. Subsequently, producers will more readily make improvements in an already marketed product to satisfy their customers. This means that a software program offered by a receptive and responsive producer can technically *never* undergo a summative evaluation because it is never finished; it is in a state of "perpetual revision." Magazine and journal reviews become more than recommendations to purchase or pass over—they are tips to a better product. Even the individual consumer evaluations that are the focus of this book can have an impact on future program revisions.

Of course the best information a producer can get about a program's worth will come from the students who work with it. For this reason field testing has strong applications in software development. A well-run, representative field test provides a controlled, yet flexible, setting for student interaction with the program under evaluation and includes the exploration and testing of a wide range of variables associated with the program's use.

Publisher Evaluations

In January of 1983 the authors conducted a survey of educational software producers to discover their methods in field testing currently unmarketed programs. We asked them to identify themselves as either commercial (for profit) or noncommercial (not-for-profit) vendors, but beyond this their responses were anonymous. Fifty-six instructional software producers replied.

Of the respondents, thirty-nine said that they field tested *all* of their software, eight said they field tested *some* (ranging from 10-90 percent), and nine reported no field testing procedures. Questions then addressed the extent of the assessments undertaken as shown by the number of teachers and students used and the locations of the test schools. Tables 2.1, 2.2, and 2.3 (see pages 25 and 26) report this data for the forty-seven publishers who conducted routine or periodic field tests. Results indicated that although a majority of the producers queried did use this important evaluation procedure, factors that could help generalize the results to the full buying public were often not present.

For instance, a comparison of the number of teachers and students utilized show a very low student-to-teacher ratio (less than eight) which is certainly not common in today's classroom environment. Also, schools in varying socioeconomic areas which could provide the most relevant data for programs intended for nationwide distribution were seldom used, further limiting the generalizability of the field test data gathered.

It would seem, then, that simply because a program has been field tested during development does not insure its usefulness as an instructional tool in every classroom. But the field testing process is certainly not a wasted activity. Products that have been field tested by even small numbers of students and

Table 2.1
Number of Teachers Used for Field Testing

Number of Teachers	Number of Respondents	Percent	Percent Adjusted
1-2	12	21.4	26.7
3-6	17	30.4	37.8
7-10	4	7.1	8.9
More than 10	7	12.5	15.6
Uncertain	5	8.9	11.1
No Response	11	19.6	----
TOTALS	56	100.0	100.0

Table 2.2
Number of Students Involved in Software Field Testing

Number of Students	Number of Respondents	Percent	Percent Adjusted
Fewer than 20	7	12.5	14.9
21-50	19	33.9	40.4
51-100	6	10.7	12.8
More than 100	8	14.3	17.0
Uncertain	7	12.5	14.9
No response	9	16.1	----
TOTALS	56	100.0	100.0

Table 2.3
Field Test Locations

Teacher Location for Field Test	Number of Teachers	Percent	Percent Adjusted
Local Schools	25	44.6	53.2
Different Regions	11	19.6	23.4
Other	11	19.6	23.4
No Response	9	16.1	----
TOTALS	56	100.0	100.0

teachers in a local or lab school still have a major advantage over those not tested—they have been *used by students* and influenced by this interaction.

Though only one producer reported relying *solely* on the results from field testing for evaluative data upon which to base revisions (reviews by the authors, in-house staff, or experts in the field were the additional sources most often cited), few publishers doubted the value of direct student/teacher experience with the software. When asked if they felt the procedure improved a product's marketability, thirty-two replied yes, five said no, and eighteen expressed uncertainty. Most comments indicated a feeling that, while the activity contributed to better software, advertising one's participation didn't influence sales. Indicative of this belief were the responses to a question asking if field testing data were included in their programs' documentations—thirty-seven of the forty-seven field testers stated no.

What do these survey results tell educators? Primarily they say that while many software producers are making attempts at learning about their programs' inadequacies to facilitate improvements before marketing, the extensiveness and generalizability of their results are sometimes questionable; thus, consumers must continue to play an active evaluative role. Working together, buyer and seller can establish communication and influence both the development and use of future software. How those communication lines can be strung by individual educators will be discussed in chapter 4, but already many schools (even districts) are offering their services as field testing sites for software producers—one method of directly affecting programs being written while getting a first look at the instructional aids of tomorrow.

Though this idea seems simple, some educators will still balk at the idea of direct participation in evaluation. "No time" is one commonly heard excuse; "No experience" is another. While these will be answered in time, a third excuse requires discussion here: "There are plenty of reviews in computer journals and magazines—I'll just choose my software based on them."

Published Reviews

Though there are indeed many periodicals now available containing software reviews, they, like the programs they are assessing, vary in quality and usefulness. Chapter 6 provides an expository bibliography of most of these publications and should be useful in identifying potentially valuable resources for additional information about a program. They should not, however, be consulted in lieu of a direct evaluation of any software under consideration for purchase. While they *can* relate descriptive data about a selection—its objectives, target audience, equipment requirements, etc.—they *cannot* report how that particular program will work in every learning or operational environment. Along with this limitation is the fact that not all reviewers can be considered knowledgeable "experts." Some, in fact, are not even adequately identified in the publication.

Reviews, then, can be valuable as an additional resource or "second opinion," but must never supplant one's own. Why not? Because that excuse "no experience" mentioned earlier is very wrong. A teacher, media specialist, or other educator has exactly the *right* background to evaluate materials: a knowledge of objectives and ways they might best be achieved, and an understanding of students and their needs.

School Evaluations

A knowledge of objectives and the methods of achieving them inspires personal involvement in the evaluation process. Instructional materials should meet and achieve the objectives established by the teacher, and only the teacher can determine if the objectives design of a certain piece of software meets the classroom needs.

Both content and instructional method are important in this determination. A program designed to teach recognition of the parts of the heart through drill-and-practice might not be the best choice when a teacher desires not only that the terminology but the *functions* of each element be learned. In this case, an animated simulation might be a better alternative.

Sometimes the examination of instructional objectives will lead to a realization that another medium or teaching strategy might better achieve them. Sometimes, two media might be equally effective but one operates at less cost. At that point the educator faces a decision regarding the best use of available resources. When planning a lesson within today's limited public education budget, a teacher should weigh the costs of equally effective materials carefully. It would be foolish to spend hundreds of dollars on a microcomputer program when a free pamphlet, film, or slide series could facilitate the same learning at a reduced price.

Yet more than purely monetary factors can impact cost. Efficiency in achievement of objectives, measured in the amount of time necessary to complete the task, is also pertinent. A microcomputer program designed to run for twenty minutes with each of thirty students must be weighed very carefully against an alternative strategy requiring twenty minutes and accommodating the entire class. Lest one should automatically dismiss the microcomputer as too inefficient a medium for today's schools, one must remember its broad capabilities, both in interactive learning and instructional management. Though perhaps not a suitable replacement for teaching strategies to meet objectives achieved adequately in group activities, the microcomputer's potential for individualized instruction (in special education, gifted programs, and vocational education) cannot be matched in today's public schools where staff reductions have eliminated most teaching aides and other tutors.

An educator, then, must not only look at the factor of cost (in terms of time and money) when evaluating a program's potential for achieving stated objectives, but must also examine alternatives available if the purchase is not made. If no viable alternatives exist (as is the case now in much gifted education), the microcomputer can become a vitally important mechanism, providing instruction and other opportunities that simply would not be available without it. It is in these situations that the computer's full potential and value are realized, in contrast to the wasteful utilization of the medium for such mundane exercises as simple drill-and-practice.

Along with one's focus on learning objectives, knowledge of one's own students—their interests and prior experiences—is important to the useful evaluation of an instructional product. Students from various regions of the country, with dissimilar cultural or socioeconomic backgrounds, and with varied learning styles may react differently to a program. For a teacher in daily contact with specific students, it is fairly easy to identify potential problems with understanding, retention, and a host of other variables that might alter the effects of a published program. Though the best indications of these pitfalls would come from the students themselves (whose input in evaluation will be discussed later), even a lone teacher is a far better judge than some well-intentioned, but far-removed programmer who developed the software initially.

Confronting and dispelling the other barriers to teacher-conducted evaluations is somewhat easier than dealing with the third common excuse "no time." A teacher's day is composed of many activities. These include planning and delivering instruction, record keeping, counseling, disciplining, and a host of other tasks. When then, does such a busy individual have the free time to devote to software evaluation? The answer, perhaps, lies less in the timing of the task itself than in the identities of the evaluators.

Though evaluation can be performed by a single individual, in school settings it should ideally be undertaken by an evaluation committee that can divide the duties among its members or deal with each level of activity as a group. A committee, besides having the obvious timesaving advantage inherent in a division of duties, can be helpful to an evaluation in other ways as well. The most important is a committee's ability to provide a range of experiences and opinions far beyond that of any single evaluator. One committee member may know of a superior program similar to the one being evaluated; another might be an expert in the particular content area under scrutiny; still another, a computer novice, might uncover problems in execution that could slip past a more experienced operator. The list could go on and on.

Though lone evaluators can provide input regarding how a particular program will work in their situations, they are restricted by their own biases. How this can be overcome when one is forced to do an evaluation alone will be discussed later. For now, it is important to note that if a committee can be formed it will result in a far more objective evaluation.

A committee can also add some clout to previewing requests. A publishing company's representative might find it more worthwhile to spend his or her time describing a program to a group of four to six avid listeners than to a single teacher. Written requests for software also will generally get faster and better service when sent by a committee on official school stationery as producers will be less likely to suspect possible copyright infringement when honoring a group's appeal.

There are, however, some problems associated with a committee approach to software selection and evaluation. Because a diversity of personalities and opinions exists, time spent by a committee evaluating a program will be longer than when one evaluator undertakes the entire project. (This is not to say that this extra time will be wasted, though this can happen. If the committee remains task oriented, the additional time spent will provide more detailed information and ultimately lead to a more complete evaluation.) Another concern is the arrangement of group meeting times and locations, as educators seldom get "release time" or extra compensation for their participation. The accessability of both the microcomputers and the programs under review must also be assured so that deadlines for returns to producers can be met. There is also the possibility that there may be disagreement over the final purchasing decision. Some thought should be given ahead of time to how this situation will be resolved. Is it majority rule? Will there be an outside party (perhaps an administrator) to act as the tiebreaker? Or must a "buy" vote be unanimous for a purchase to be made?

Of course, the first step in any committee evaluation project is to form the committee. Care should be taken so that members are chosen who not only have a commitment to the task, but who can each offer a unique outlook or a special talent that will insure their individual usefulness on the team. The committee should include:

1. A teacher from the specific subject area and/or grade level under consideration
2. Students at the specified grade level
3. The media specialist or librarian
4. An "expert" in microcomputers and their capabilities (could be the teacher or media specialist)
5. Administrators
6. Others (parents, central office personnel, etc.)

An examination of the rationale behind the naming of each of these membership categories might be in order here. A teacher from the specific area and/or grade level under consideration is, of course, a necessity for the evaluation of curriculum materials. But it is the inclusion of the second category—the students—that comes as a surprise to many educators. Yet at second glance this seems more than reasonable. Peters and Hepler warn "what students find boring or motivating, effective or ineffective, is often different from what an instructor might conclude" and advise that software evaluation occur with student input (1982, 12). Student representation on an evaluation committee can often not only teach adult members something, but foster student learning as well. Through participation in curriculum decision-making, especially at the junior and senior high levels, students develop an understanding of the educational process and a sense of responsibility toward their own role in it.

The media specialist or librarian, the third category of membership, can provide expert input about general practices of media evaluation which should act as a solid base for software reviews. "An educator wishing to evaluate software should begin with what he or she knows about evaluating any material or media" (Minnesota Association for Supervision and Curriculum Development et al. n.d., 11). Besides this general expertise, the media specialist can also help determine the future organization and physical management of the software being purchased. Several articles have recently been written addressing the cataloging of software, proper storage, and other accessibility concerns.

The fourth member of the team should be someone familiar with micros and their educational applications. Possibly a teacher, this educator can help determine if the software under review will work on the school's existing equipment, and offer expertise in software capabilities and limitations. Other important input can come from administrators versed in budgetary facts and figures essential to the final purchasing decision and from parents who can offer insights into comparisons with home software while operating as active school/community links.

Whatever the final membership, the committee should never exclude any representative from a group that will be directly involved in the implementation and use of the newly purchased software. Overlooking this group will most assuredly lead to, if not the total failure of the program, at least utilization far below the program's potential.

Before proceeding to an examination of the evaluation process, we should take a look at the other two practical concerns associated with software evaluations, namely, when and where to evaluate. The question of *when* actually has two answers.

The first is before purchasing any software. Such evaluation for the purpose of selection is the main focus of this book. This task can consist of short committee meetings to organize, interspersed with individual work with the programs in question, and culminating in a longer conference where evaluation forms are compared and a decision is reached. Certainly, time must be borrowed from other activities if one is sitting on an evaluation committee; but with rotating membership, structured evaluation activities, and comparisons of several programs at one time, demands upon individuals should not be too extensive. Considering the instructional time saved when using a quality program, one's clocked debits and assets might even balance.

Besides this assessment for purchase, a second evaluation should be instituted (and continue periodically) once the new software has been integrated into the curriculum. It should focus on the instructional effectiveness of the new material and might constitute one's very own field test. While the first evaluation judged the program's suitability in terms of stated objectives and an educated guess about its achievement of these objectives, this second evaluation focuses on what is actually occurring as a result of the program's implementation.

> ...many factors extrinsic to the software have a bearing on the effectiveness. Unless the software is meant to be used as stand-alone instruction, the manner in which the teacher introduces it, manages it, intervenes during its use, and follows up the instruction, will impinge upon its effectiveness (Wager 1982, 5).

This second evaluation should take all these factors into account. Perhaps a change in how the program is being used will increase its effectiveness and should be tried. Perhaps, too, the evaluation might reveal that no amount of change in delivery or follow-up can improve a bad purchase, or it might show that the objectives themselves were poorly developed or conceived, relieving the programmer of responsibility but still resulting in an unusable product. Fortunately, because of the ease with which software can be revised, a useless program does not have to be thrown away.

If the program itself is a bad one, one might try to contact the producer and ask to return the purchase even if the thirty days has expired. Some companies may be distressed over the ineffectiveness of their product and value one's continued business over a single sale. Perhaps a revision has already been made and is available free or for a nominal fee. Sometimes, one's copy can be sent and changes made directly on the disk. If the company is not helpful or is no longer in business, a bright student might be able to modify the program, as part of an advanced programming project. A similar solution might be in order if objectives are changed slightly and programming students are *very* talented. If all else fails, one can erase the faulty program and at least salvage a blank disk from the misguided purchase.

The question of *where* to do the evaluation is more easily answered. Every effort should be made to preview the software in the same environment in which it will be used. Most important is the assurance that it will work on the available hardware, but another benefit is the ability to judge how the capacities of the software will relate to the environment. Is the color programmed into the software important for the understanding of the concepts illustrated, thereby requiring a color monitor? Will the music or other sound effects disturb other students sitting nearby? These are questions that can easily be overlooked if the software is previewed in places other than the location where it will be used, and can be of supreme importance to the successful utilization of the newly purchased materials.

These three issues (who should evaluate, and when and where to evaluate) must be considered before the start of the process itself. Once those issues are resolved, the evaluators can move ahead with the activity described in detail in the next chapter.

3

EVALUATING EDUCATIONAL SOFTWARE: THE PROCESS AND THE CRITERIA

A popular proverb which has appeared on greeting cards and T-shirts reads, "You have to kiss a lot of frogs before you find your prince." A parallel can be drawn between this commentary on the dating scene and the evaluation of educational software. "Kissing a lot of frogs" implies a process involving the assessment of a wide range of candidates to identify the "best" choice, not unlike the task of software evaluation. But while kissing can be less than systematic, software evaluation should never be.

Much has already been said about the divergence in quality of current educational software, ranging from excellent to awful. But a systematic process for evaluation (see fig. 3.1, page 34) can help a diligent consumer separate the princes from the frogs and lead to wiser expenditures of the ever-dwindling curriculum material dollar.

There are three common ways that microcomputer software packages currently function in the classroom. They may serve as adjunct materials which supplement regular classroom instruction, currently the most common usage of microcomputer-assisted instruction. They can comprise a complete course in a curriculum unit, delivering and managing all the instruction while maintaining student records. Or, they can be used only as a management system, storing all records on student progress through particular curriculum units though providing no direct instruction (Cohen 1983). Three additional potential applications are cited by Cohen: (1) as a preprogrammed authoring device for creation of student and teacher programs, (2) as a programming course on computer literacy, and (3) as a testing and assessment device which scores and keeps records for the teacher. Given this broad range of possible ways to use software packages, it is important that an evaluator determine ahead of time how a program or courseware package is to be used since this use determines what procedures will be undertaken in evaluating the software as well as the evaluative criteria to be used to judge the program(s). Courseware (CAI programs) to be used with a wide audience, must be scrutinized somewhat differently from information management (CMI or DBM) programs that will be operated by only one person or a small, select group of individuals. Student input, as mentioned in chapter 2, is extremely important in the evaluation of courseware, while assessing management programs can be a more restricted task involving only an instructor or administrator. This chapter will examine the evaluation process with courseware in mind, but evaluators of other educational software should still find this chapter useful as they need only scale down or selectively apply the evaluation procedures appropriate for their purposes.

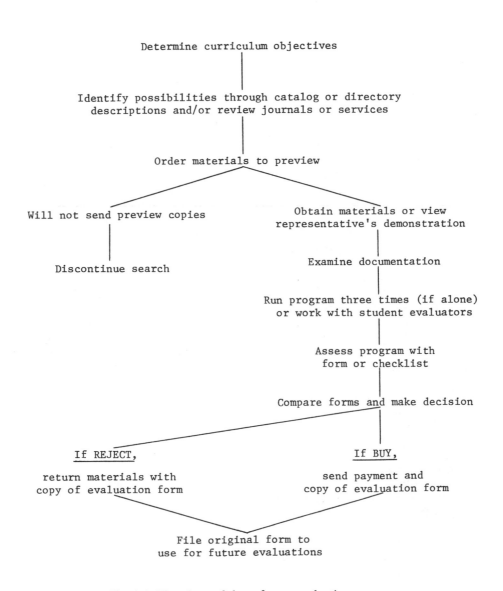

Fig. 3.1. Flowchart of the software evaluation process.

THE PROCESS

Evaluation of courseware normally begins with the determination of instructional objectives that provide the major focus for the entire activity. A program is then sought that can achieve the stated objectives. Occasionally, an evaluation will grow from interest in a particular program heard or read about. In this case, the evaluator looks at the program first and then attempts to fit it (if acceptable) into the existing curriculum plan or develop a new scheme to utilize it. Although this second situation is not the preferred method, it may be more the usual case today due to a somewhat limited selection of quality software. One hopes this will change as the choice of programs expands and a wider range of program options becomes available to suit the many differing objectives.

Assuming that one does begin by formulating instructional objectives, the next step is to identify possible programs that might achieve them. Sources for this information include software directories, company catalogs, consortium newsletters, and journals. School libraries should have at least some of these resources but other places to look include the public library, school district offices or service units, and computer and book stores. Expository listings of program sources can be found in chapters 5, 6, and 7. A collection of several of these selection aids should provide enough information about available programs to begin the task of assembling a list of titles for consideration. As mentioned in chapter 2, this is one of those duties that is made a lot easier through committee effort.

When all possible resources are assembled, one should examine them closely to locate specific programs that, judging by their descriptions, sound potentially useful. These will form the basis for the list of software to be ordered for preview. Not always will sufficient information on which to base this initial selection be given. Though sources vary greatly in the amount of information they provide about a specific educational program, any description is virtually worthless if it does not provide at least enough information to allow the answering of these six initial questions:

1. Will the program suit my objectives?

2. Is it designed for my students' level(s) — i.e., grade and/or reading?

3. Will it work on my equipment?

4. What does it cost?

5. Who provides/publishes the software?

6. How can I order it?

Often omitted in catalog descriptions, for various reasons, are a program's objectives. Sometimes the program's author did not have any well-developed objectives in mind when the program was written, due to a lack of pedagogic or content knowledge. Occasionally, producers feel that the objectives the program can achieve are dependent on the user, and they would rather let consumers discover the potential uses on their own. While there is certainly merit in the notion that different teachers will be able to achieve different things with the same instructional materials, excluding intended objectives from the description removes helpful guideposts in the initial selection process, and, consequently, teachers who have little time to spend on materials selection may pass up potentially useful programs for lack of adequate information about them. Often the omission of a program's objectives results from oversight on the part of an inexperienced software producer and needs to be brought to the company's attention. There is no more important information in a program's description than a list of its objectives. Without it one must try to "guestimate" a product's usefulness from the content area/subject matter information and the approximations given of the appropriate target audience.

Yet sometimes this student-level information will also be omitted, or one is given such a broad range that the data are of little or no value. One program recently encountered was advertised with K-12 as its target audience. While perhaps appropriate for a long and detailed series of programs providing increasing levels of difficulty, this claim is ludicrous for a single program. Using this software across all levels would be akin to offering exercises from the same workbook to students from kindergarten to senior high — far above the level of some, insultingly below the capabilities of others. Though it is true that program levels are sometimes mislabeled, it is better for publishers to have made some attempt to provide this information rather than simply to omit the data entirely.

Information regarding the type of hardware required for a program to operate effectively should also figure prominently in any description used to select software for preview. There are five points for hardware consideration which must be examined: (1) language, disk operating system (DOS), and memory requirements; (2) software medium or format and the number of storage systems necessary for operation; (3) monitor; (4) printer requirements; and (5) other necessary peripherals.

Unfortunately, there is no widely accepted set of manufacturing standards for many types of audiovisual equipment and the microcomputer is no exception. Just as a Betamax videocassette cannot be played on a VHS machine, Apple II software will not run on a TRS-80 computer. Often, even a software program developed to be compatible with one model will not work on another model of the same brand. Owners of the very popular Apple II Plus microcomputer, for example, were extremely concerned about program compatibility when its replacement, the IIe appeared. Fortunately, the Apple company anticipated this reaction and II Plus owners were relieved to learn that approximately 90 percent or more of their programs will reportedly run on the newer model.

Besides assuring machine brand and model compatibilities with a program, one must investigate the language, DOS, and memory requirements of the software under review. An Apple II Plus micro, for example, comes with BASIC as its machine language. Through additions to the expansion slots, other languages may be added including Pascal, FORTRAN, and Apple LOGO. Software is also written in various versions (or dialects) of BASIC such as Applesoft or Integer BASIC. Without an Integer language card, Integer programs cannot be run on an Apple II Plus computer. The language card board which costs around $130, is placed in one of the expansion slots in the back of the Apple. In short, language considerations must be carefully checked during the initial selection for previewing process.

Closely related to language is the computer's DOS. Apples produced after January 1980 operate on a 3.3 DOS system; fortunately the System Master disk which comes with the Apple allows one to upgrade the older 3.2 programs to 3.3. This 3.3 DOS is adequate for games, most educational programs, and some business software. However, CP/M and UGSD Pascal are also available and increase the business application capabilities of the Apple. Again, these entail additional monetary outlay on the part of the user. CP/M, for example, requires the purchase of a Z80 softcard which costs approximately $350.

Since all programs require a certain amount of memory, the stated requirements of a specific program must be checked against the maximum memory of one's machine. Another hardware consideration, that of storage format, becomes important here. Although the most popular microcomputer software formats are 5¼-inch magnetic disk and cassette tapes, some programs with greatly increased storage capability must use a "hard disk" drive and compatible disks. Educational programs do not generally require this greater storage or memory but data based management programs storing large amounts of information do offer potential memory capacity overload problems when one uses the smaller disks.

But even if one does not deal with the larger, hard disks, program format is a consideration due to the incompatibility of cassette and 5¼-inch floppy disk systems. To run a program stored on a floppy disk, a disk drive is needed. Conversely, a cassette tape player is required when working with a program stored on cassette tape. When selecting a program to preview, it is important that the proper format be ordered to match the existing hardware, or the software will be unusable.

Not only are a program's requirements for the *type* of storage and playback equipment important, but also crucial is the number of *systems* needed. Some programs, for example, require two disk drives for their effective operation, and this will limit the possible software purchases for use with a microcomputer that is equipped with only a single-drive unit.

Closely associated are a program's monitor requirements. Some programs rely heavily on color for their maximum effectiveness, and a black and white monitor will often render them essentially useless. In contrast, a color monitor can create visual distortion when doing data entry or word processing, eventually leading to eye strain and fatigue.

Certain programs also require the use of a printer for maximum effectiveness. Two examples are word processing and student-record keeping software. Without a printer capable of producing hard copy of the results of these programs, their full potential cannot be realized.

Other peripherals may also be necessary to run certain pieces of software. If they are not available and must be purchased, user costs will, of course, increase. Prices vary greatly, and a printer alone can run from three hundred dollars to several thousand dollars. Graphics tablets, voice synthesizers, and other peripherals can increase expenditures extensively as well.

Along with the possible cost of additional hardware, the direct cost of the software itself should be carefully scrutinized. Price information can very quickly eliminate some programs which have, up to this point, satisfied the conditions of objectives/level suitability and equipment compatibility. It would be useful if, accompanying the cost information, all software directories would include information regarding the producers' policies toward second, "backup," and multiple copies. Some companies make an additional copy available free of charge; others sell one for as much as one-half the original purchase price. (For additional information about this issue, and suggestions for negotiations, see chapter 5.)

Having the name and address for a program's producer/publisher is important because it can frequently give an indication of the software's quality. Because a good product seldom comes from a company with a history of inferior work, those with a minimum of time to devote to software evaluation will find themselves returning again and again to those producers whose programs they have come to trust. This practice will undoubtedly help spell the ultimate demise of many of the poor quality software publishers.

Occasionally a source for program information will provide all the necessary data to facilitate ordering for preview with the exception of the address or telephone number of the company to contact. Periodicals and similar publications are probably the worse offenders in this area and should be informed of the omission whenever it is noted. Sometimes, a program is not available through its production house, but instead must be obtained through a "jobber" or distributor of materials, and this information should also be included.

Upon choosing the programs to preview, ordering the materials can be achieved through a simple phone call to the producer or distributor or through a more formal, written request. Official school stationery should always be used in these matters, as should an administrative co-signature. Due to a fear of copyright infringement, some companies do not offer free previewing privileges. They may instead distribute a sample copy, called a demo disk, which contains excerpts from a variety of programs, or they may operate on a thirty-day money-back guarantee policy. Although buying a program based on a small excerpt displayed on a demo disk is not recommended (the program's *one* highlight could be shown), one should take advantage of the thirty-day return offer if free previewing is not available. Though bookkeeping can get frustrating and keeping a "fair" program because it's already paid for might be tempting (obviously one of the producer's reasons for instituting the policy), this option is certainly the next best thing to free previewing. Chapter 5 lists thirteen jobbers who extend this thirty-day return privilege.

Educational software publishers in the author's 1983 survey (see chapter 2) indicated that previewing was still being offered to schools by many (61.8 percent did offer preview versus 38.2 percent who did not), which is good news for educators. Previewing provides the opportunity to undertake an evaluation before making a monetary commitment to the material—a definite plus for the budget-conscious.

Another free previewing option deserves mention here. Some of the larger publishing companies have sales representatives who are available for demonstrations of software and other instructional materials. This procedure allows for question and answer exchanges concerning program design and suggested uses. Sales representatives are a direct link to the company and are able to solve problems and transmit requests and recommendations. One should involve them whenever possible in selection activities.

If it is difficult to get sales representatives to visit a school due to its size or location, one might go to computer stores and ask for demonstrations of educational software from qualified sales people. Many microcomputer manufacturers publish their own instructional software (Radio Shack is a good example) and much can be learned by watching, or preferably sitting at the keyboard, while a program is demonstrated. While violating the ideal previewing situation of working with the software on one's own equipment, this method is certainly preferred over buying solely from a program's written description in a publisher's catalog.

As for companies that offer no type of previewing policy and expect their customers to buy on faith, the best advice is to forget them. There is still too much variation in the quality of software to take such a risk. Many companies have already loosened their preview policies and others are sure to follow as they realize that responsible educators refuse to buy blind.

THE CRITERIA

We have seen that evaluation is an activity that requires, ultimately, a judgement about the materials under review. To make an intelligent and informed decision, criteria must be developed to give the evaluator a framework for the task.

Educators for decades have been obsessed with the development of criteria for the selection and/or evaluation of the entire range of instructional materials, from textbooks to 16mm films. It is not surprising, therefore, that during the past few years a great deal of time, money, and effort has been expended to develop evaluative criteria for microcomputer software programs as well. A lack of quality control or industry standards on the part of producers themselves has accelerated efforts of users and consumers to come up with their own criteria suitable for this new media format. A whole new vocabulary, in fact, has been developed to aid in this evaluation process (Kansky, Heck, and Johnson 1981) with terms like "user friendly" and "crash-proof" joining our linguistic repertoire as we undertake this novel activity.

The criteria for software evaluation, while somewhat different from that used for other media, have certain universal aspects. This is most obvious when one examines the questions to be asked in evaluating a program's documentation, i.e., the written material accompanying the software. This investigation of a program's printed instructions and other adjunct materials is the first important step in the actual evaluative process.

Examining the Documentation

Besides repeating the program objectives, grade or ability level, equipment required, cost, and publisher's data listed in the original description, the documentation should provide at a minimum (1) directions for the user, (2) a validation statement of the program's effectiveness (see chapter 2), and (3) a teacher's manual containing a vocabulary list, suggested preparation and follow-up activities, and an evaluation tool or description of the assessment instrument contained in the program. In short, the same information that should come with any well-conceived and designed instructional material, whatever the medium, should accompany courseware.

Unfortunately, this is one area in which many software publishers could greatly improve their products. Some provide no documentation at all. Documentation when it is provided ranges from a single xeroxed sheet to a thick, slick packet. And though many professional publishers could certainly enhance the appearance of their materials, it's what is inside all that brightly colored plastic that really matters. Missing or unclear directions can prove fatal to an educationally sound and beautifully developed program. A piece of software devoid of any supplemental activities stands a poor chance of being effective with a wide range of students. Proper documentation is essential—which explains why its evaluation should be undertaken before that of the actual program. Kelly (1982) even recommends one purchase the documentation of prospective software before previewing the program. Product manuals generally cost between twenty-five and thirty-five dollars (a fraction of the cost of many programs) and can give an excellent indication of the software's capacities, with the documentation's fee often being deductible from the program's purchase price.

Whether the documentation is obtained separately or as part of the preview package, the following questions must be asked about its quality and condition:

1. Is the documentation complete?

2. Does it include a validation statement?

3. Are the instructional objectives clearly stated? Are they:
    - Relevant?
    - Important?
    - Compatible with the curriculum?
    - Based on sound educational theory?

4. What student materials are provided?
    - Instructions?
    - Worksheets?
    - Follow-up activities?

5. What teachers' materials are provided?
    - Instructions?
    - An evaluation tool or description of the program's assessment tool to gauge student progress?
    - A bibliography of resources?
    - An estimate of time required to complete the program and activities?
    - A summary of the content and activities of the program?
    - Suggestions for how to use the program in a variety of classroom situations?
    - Skills needed before students can effectively use the program plus pre- and post-instructional activities?
    - Ways to modify the program?

6. Is there technical documentation provided, including the explanation of any special software/hardware interface which must be understood for successful program operation and program code listings?

7. Is there a flow chart or diagram showing the general logic of the program(s)?

8. Is written documentation free of errors (grammar, spelling, punctuation) and clear and concise in style?

9. Does written documentation provide enough instruction so that a user with no previous computer experience can run the program?

10. Are error messages appearing in the programs defined?

A final consideration related to documentation is:

11. What type of packaging is provided for the courseware and supporting materials?
    - Does it hold both the software components plus all the afore-mentioned documentation materials?
    - Is packaging in a box, notebook or other binder, plastic pockets, etc.?
    - Is this packaging sturdy enough to hold up under classroom use?
    - Does packaging allow components to be divided and used by different teachers in varying locations particularly where packages contain programs which cut across grade levels?

Examining the Program

Evaluating the documentation lets the previewer note the inclusion or omission of all of the above information, but the only way to see how accurate and useful it is, is to run the program. Though the use of several student evaluators can provide the most valuable input during this phase, when one is forced to do an evaluation alone, most literature recommends making a series of runs.

First, one should go through the program as a "model" student would, trying to follow the directions, answering questions, and performing the required skills. After completing the first run (often impossible due to poor documentation), work through the program again, this time making typographical errors, answering improperly or not at all, and hitting command keys at will. This unruly behavior at the keyboard is called "trying to crash the program." Students, especially bright ones, love to engage in this activity. A very good program will withstand such abuse and continue to run; a weaker program will "go down" (simply stop, often leaving the screen blank and/or the disk drive whirring) or begin responding strangely. Even if your students are closely supervised when using the micro, the program's ability to withstand crashing should still be tested. Some very poor programs will stop running if a simple yes or no question is answered any other way, or will go down if a single key is pressed accidentally. A program this touchy will be a constant source of frustration to most students and many teachers and should be avoided.

If a program successfully weathers both runs, one should go through it one more time, this time applying a range of criteria to determine the strengths and weaknesses of the software. A valuable aid in this task is an evaluation form or checklist that can serve as a reminder of the desirable characteristics sought. Examples of these forms are reproduced in chapter 4, but what follows here is an extensive list of the questions that form the basis for these checklists and should serve as a useful stimulus to the exploration of the program. When we venture into the realm of courseware with special instructional objectives and purposes in mind, it often becomes difficult to judge both educational value and achievement of objectives as we sit before the keyboard.

Often, special features that exploit the unique capabilities of the microcomputer are offered in a program (synthesized voice, high-resolution graphics, etc.) that can awe a novice operator and cloud the real value of a program. "If these features actually lead to greater student acceptance and/or increased program effectiveness, then they deserve promotion. Otherwise," Wager warns evaluators, "they should be regarded merely as sale gimmicks" (Wager 1982, 6).

Remember to take special care to consider student input if possible and observe carefully all student output and feedback as your young evaluators work through the program.

Educational Value and Instructional Objectives

The following questions can help guide an evaluation of software concerning educational value and instructional objectives:

1. Does the software appear to achieve its stated educational objectives?

2. Does the program produce positive affective outcomes on the part of the student?

3. Is learning generalizable to a range of situations which the student is likely to encounter in real life?

4. Are graphics, color, or sound used?
   - Is such use appropriate for enhancing the educational objectives or is it merely window dressing, possibly even distracting student attention?
   - Do the graphics utilize principles of good message design and focus attention on important learning concepts or content?

5. Is the mode of instruction used tutorial, drill-and-practice, simulation, gaming, problem-solving, testing, or a combination of these modes?[1] Is this mode:
   - Appropriate for the type of material presented?
   - Appropriate for the student level?

6. Does the instruction presented take advantage of the microcomputer's instructional strengths or simply provide information which could be learned as well through some other means (e.g., a written text)?

Content

A program's content must be evaluated closely to determine both the accuracy of information and the appropriateness of structure. Ask these questions when evaluating this component of a program:

1. Is the content appropriate and appealing to the intended level of its users?

2. Does the content appear factual and accurate?

3. Will the content become dated quickly?

4. Is the content free from racial, ethnic, and sexual stereotypes?
   - Is one group overrepresented?
   - Is one group generalized about falsely?

5. Is the content free from spelling, grammatical, or other errors?

6. Is the software well-organized? Does it:
   - Proceed logically if sequential?
   - Move from the concrete to the abstract, simple to complex, familiar to unfamiliar?
   - Present small enough units of information so that students can learn easily rather than giving it all in hard to digest lumps?

7. Can modification in content (e.g., changing number or word lists) be made by the teacher?

8. Does the program content or design refrain from focusing on undesirable practices (violence, etc.)?

9. Does the structure allow for a variety of outcomes (different endings, etc.) so students will not become bored with the program?

User Interaction

The ability to actively involve the student in his or her own learning is the microcomputer's chief advantage over any other instructional delivery device. Because of this, it is extremely important that educational programs designed to be used with the micro take full advantage of this interactive potential. A program that only requires a student to "Press Return to Continue" will probably suffer a long and lonely existence on the shelf while students discover and learn with more stimulating fare. When examining a program's user interaction capabilities, ask these questions:

1. Does the program effectively involve the student in active learning experiences providing a maximum amount of hands-on time for the learner?

2. Does the program provide varying levels of difficulty according to the skill level of the learner?

3. Does the program have instructions at the beginning in nontechnical, easy-to-understand language?

4. Are the instructions:
   - Able to be bypassed by knowledgeable users?
   - Presented in an interactive mode within the program itself?
   - Inserted as prompts throughout the program if difficulty is encountered?
   - Programmed to appear, thus providing help, following an incorrect response?

5. How much control is granted to the user or learner?
   - Can the student alter the rate of the presentation of the text and/or problems presented on the screen?
   - Can the student decide where to enter the program?
   - Does the program permit the student a choice of sequence of concepts to be studied?
   - Can the student exit the program at will?
   - Can the instructions be reviewed at any time?
   - Can the students redesign any program parameters such as the number of examples provided, number of programs to be completed, etc.?

6. What type of reinforcement or feedback is used?
   - Is it immediate?
   - Is it too frequent?
   - Too infrequent?
   - Is every correct response rewarded or does the program simply progress as a means of reward?
   - Does feedback over-elaborate with phrases like "tremendous," "terrific," and "wow" that can become tiresome and seem unwarranted for the type of success achieved?
   - Is the feedback relevant for the user's age and grade level?
   - Is it of good quality?
   - Non-threatening?
   - Does the program correct errors before continuing? How?
   - Does the feedback reinforce wrong answers by providing more rewarding graphics or situations for the wrong response?
   - Is feedback quantitative so that students know the number or percentage of correct answers given?

7. Is there provision for review?
   - Is it optional?
   - May the students review without repeating the entire lesson?

8. Is the program motivational?
   - Does it capture and hold student interest?
   - Is it fun to use?

9. How much creativity does the program allow for?
   - Does it allow the student to make a maximum number of decisions?
   - Does it allow for open-ended questions?

10. Can the program be used effectively with more than one student at a time?

11. Does the program foster positive cooperation or competition?

12. If the program is likely to be used by non-readers, does it:
    - Have a minimum of typing?
    - Provide voice-synthesized instruction and coaching?
    - Depend heavily on graphic representation of concepts?

Technical Considerations

Technical considerations relate to programming and ease of use. They are important for both students and teachers since it is a major contention of the authors that one should not have to be a programmer to use microcomputer software any more than one should have to be an auto mechanic in order to drive an automobile. The evaluation of a piece of courseware's programming components can be guided by these inquiries:

1. Does the program run?

2. Is it well done?
    - Is the program quick and easy to load?
    - Is the response time quick enough to allow for rapid student input and response or does the student spend an undue amount of time waiting for the computer?
    - Does the program have polish?
    - Does it always respond to or call for appropriate user response?
    - Does it lack obvious programming flaws?

3. Is the software user-proof so that accidental or incorrect student responses neither wipe out nor lock the program?

4. Are error messages clear and unambiguous?

5. Is the program "user friendly"? Does it:
    - Accommodate a variety of anticipated student responses (e.g., accepting "one" for "1")?
    - Allow someone with absolutely no programming skills or prior computer knowledge to run it?

6. Is the use of sound optional so that it may be turned off when its use would be distracting in the classroom?

7. Is the screen format uncluttered and easy to read?

8. Are the graphics understandable?

9. Would lack of a color monitor render the graphics ineffective?

Record Keeping

Beyond the above considerations, one of the most unique and useful capacities of the microcomputer is its ability to keep track automatically of student progress through courseware materials. Though most currently marketed programs are not equipped with this capability, those that are provide a big bonus to educators and should be strongly considered for purchase, providing they are otherwise evaluated as quality programs. Good record keeping abilities should allow for the tracking of an entire class of students, not merely the accounting of one student's work. As programming sophistication improves, one can look for this feature to accompany the majority of quality courseware, providing dual utility and increasing cost-effectivenss.

The final step in the software evaluation process involves using a checklist. The procedure for using and organizing checklists is discussed in chapter 4, which also includes sample forms.

Done systematically and frequently, the task of software evaluation can become easier and more rewarding, resulting in wiser expenditures of a school's instructional materials budget in these times of inflationary prices and decreasing public allocations.

In many cases a number of comparable programs all achieve the same ends or objectives, but one is cheaper and, therefore, should be purchased as the most cost-effective. Lest we place too much emphasis on what selection criteria to use or which checklist to follow, one should consider thoughtfully this final bit of advice:

> The classification of an item of software as good or poor (useful or useless) is, in the final analysis, a professional judgment. It is our privilege to make such judgments and our fate to live with the results. All the world's questions, checklists, consultants, and research are means, not ends, in this decision-making process (Kansky, Heck, and Johnson 1981, 603).

NOTE

1. For those not familiar with instructional modes, the following definitions are provided:

A *tutorial* presents material and actually teaches it to students.

Drill-and-practice drills the student on previously learned material.

A *simulation* models a situation in the real world impossible to duplicate in the classroom or dangerous to perform (perhaps a laboratory experiment) because it may have harmful consequences if errors occur.

Gaming involves introducing an element of competition or the concept of winning into the program.

Problem-solving involves applying learned skills and/or information to the solution of some problem.

Testing in computer programs is similar to testing in any other instructional format but when implemented via computer-managed instruction it may be controlled by the program itself as to timing, frequency, remediation, and the reporting of results.

4

EVALUATION FORMS

Evaluation forms, or checklists, as we have seen in the last chapter can contribute both guidelines and structure to the evaluative process. Uniformity can also be obtained by being consistent in the use of a form or checklist. If at all possible, the same form should be used throughout the school and preferably throughout the district. This allows the evaluators to become very familiar with the tool which in turn leads to shorter evaluation time and makes for easier comparisons between two or more competing pieces of software. If evaluations of several programs dealing with essentially the same subject matter and objectives have been undertaken, an evaluation form allows for a comparative study of each program's capabilities and facilitates a choice. In the case of a single program evaluation, the checklist documents the software's ratings and provides solid evidence upon which to base a final purchasing decision.

Questions often arise at this point asking for clarification of what constitutes an "acceptable" rating for buying purposes. Certainly what will be regarded as "acceptable" should be determined before the evaluation takes place. The selection committee should examine the form prior to using it and decide the minimum acceptable levels for each criteria and the overall rating, if provided. This bit of valuable foresight will shorten decision time after completion of the form for the program under review because there will be a set of firm standards upon which to base a judgment. This minimum rating, however, should not be regarded as carved in stone. If a particular program comes close to, but does not quite reach, the minimum levels, it might still merit consideration and further discussion. This is especially true if the program deals with a subject area for which few current software offerings are available, or if some extra time spent in student introduction or follow-up could substantially increase its effectiveness.

This bit of flexibility in judgment should never, of course, be carried to the extreme. Just because there are few, say, CAI programs on health doesn't mean one should purchase any mediocre one that comes on the market. Yet it is important to realize that the minimum "acceptable" levels for one kind of software might not be the same for another. Requirements should be very stringent for commonly produced programs (i.e., drill-and-practice), because they must be very exceptional to justify their use on the microcomputer when a simple worksheet might achieve the same ends far more efficiently in terms of time and money spent. Simulations, by contrast, often cannot be as successfully performed with many of the more traditional media devices, thus minimum acceptance levels for simulations might be somewhat lower, at least until greater expertise is reached in their development.

Even after the "buy" or "reject" decision has been made for a single program or set of software, the committee's work is not complete. Copies of the evaluation form should be made and returned to the publisher accompanying either the rejected software or the check for purchase. Software publishers are eager to hear from both prospective and former customers and find their comments and suggestions a valuable source for future program development and refinement. Enclosing a copy of the evaluation form is the easiest way to accomplish this communication and influence the quality of future microcomputer projects.

The original of the form should be kept as a committee record and filed, probably by broad subject categories subarranged alphabetically by program title for future reference. This file will become a valuable source of program information especially useful for the prevention of duplicate evaluations. It is a tremendous waste of time and effort to repeat evaluations of programs deemed worthless in the past in a long-forgotten review. A systematically arranged record of previous evaluations will keep this from happening. The forms can be kept in three-ring binders at first and eventually transferred to a more manageable system (perhaps microcomputer disk), as the collection grows. A school might also consider expanding a file's usefulness by offering it to parents seeking instructional program information to help them in selecting software for home computer systems.

Below are listed the sample evaluation forms to be found on the following pages:

Chapter 5 starts on page 87.

CALIFORNIA LIBRARY MEDIA CONSORTIUM FOR CLASSROOM EVALUATION OF MICROCOMPUTER COURSEWARE 1983
(Revised)

FOLD HERE AND STAPLE TO RETURN (ADDRESS ON REVERSE)

....

Program title _____

Title on package/diskette _____

Microcomputer(s) brand/model _____ Memory needed _____ K

Language _____ BASIC (or _____) Version/copyright date _____ Cost _____

Publisher _____

Peripherals needed: _____ Disk drive(s) _____ Cassette ____ Printer (Other _____)

Other materials/equipment needed _____

Backup copy available? Yes _____ No _____ Network/Hard Disk Possible? Yes _____ No ____

★ ★

Reviewed by _____

Grade level/subject/position _____

School/District _____

Address/Phone _____

May we use your name in the published review? _____
THANK YOU FOR YOUR CONTRIBUTION! PLEASE RETURN IMMEDIATELY TO THE ADDRESS ON THE
BACK.

(Evaluation form continues on page 50.)

_____

Reprinted by permission of California Library Media Consortium/San Mateo County Office of Education.

PROGRAM TITLE: _____ SUBJECT AREAS: _____

SUGGESTED GRADE LEVELS (Circle) K 1 2 3 4 5 6 7 8 9 10 11 12 College Teacher-use
TYPE OF PROGRAM (Check all that apply):

___ authoring system	___ demonstration	___ logic, problem-solving	___ tutorial
___ business applications	___ drill/practice	___ simulation	___ utility
___ classroom management	___ educational game	___ teachers' utility	___ word processing
___ database management	___ game	___ testing	___ Other:_____

SCOPE: (Check one):
_____ one or more programs on single topic   _____ one program in an instructional series
_____ group of unrelated programs   _____ multi-disk curriculum package

EVALUATION CRITERIA

YES NO N/A   GENERAL DESIGN: ___EXCELLENT ___GOOD ___WEAK ___NOT ACCEPTABLE

— — —   1. Creative, innovative use of computer?
— — —   2. Effective, appropriate use of computer?
— — —   3. Follows sound instructional organization?
— — —   4. Fits well into the curriculum?
— — —   5. Free of programming errors, problems?

   CONTENT: ___EXCELLENT ___GOOD ___WEAK ___NOT ACCEPTABLE

— — —   6. Branches to easier or harder material in response to student performance?
— — —   7. Factually correct?
— — —   8. Free of excessive violence or competition?
— — —   9. Free of stereotypes - race, ethnic, gender, age, handicapped?
— — —   10. Interest, difficulty, typing, and vocabulary levels are appropriate?
— — —   11. Modifications of data, speed, word lists., etc., by instructor are possible?
— — —   12. Punctuation, spelling, grammar correct?
— — —   13. Responses to errors are helpful, avoiding sarcasm or scolding?
— — —   14. Responses to student success are positive, enjoyable and appropriate?

   EASE OF USE: ___EXCELLENT ___GOOD ___WEAK ___NOT ACCEPTABLE

— — —   15. Answers may be corrected by user before continuing with program?
— — —   16. Instructions within program are clear, complete, concise?
— — —   17. Instructions can be skipped or recalled to screen?
— — —   18. Instructions on how to end program, start over, are given?
— — —   19. Menu allows user to access specific parts of program?
— — —   20. Paging speed and sequence can be controlled by user?
— — —   21. Screens are neat, attractive, well-spaced?
— — —   22. Sound, if present, is appropriate and may be turned off?

MOTIVATIONAL DEVICES USED: ___EXCELLENT ___GOOD ___WEAK ___NOT ACCEPTABLE
(Check all which apply):

_____ graphics for instruction	_____ color	_____ game format	_____ sound _____ timing
_____ graphics for reward	_____ scoring	_____ random order	_____ personalization

DOCUMENTATION: ___ EXCELLENT ___GOOD ___WEAK ___NOT ACCEPTABLE
(Check all available):

___none	___instructions appear on screen	___tests
___instruction manual	___suggested classroom activities	___workbook
___teacher's guide	___instructional objectives	___student worksheets

OVERALL OPINION

___Great program. I recommend it highly!
___Pretty good, useful.
___OK, but you might wait for a better one.
___Would select only if modifications were made.
___Not useful.

INSTRUCTIONAL CONTENT AND OBJECTIVES
(PLEASE USE ADDITIONAL SHEETS IF NEEDED)

● Describe content and main objectives of this program:

  In your opinion, were the objectives met?
● What classroom management, testing, or performance reporting is provided?

  How many students/classes can be managed by this program?
  Is the management system easy to use?

● Describe any special strengths of program:

● Comments/concerns/questions:

● Comments comparing with other programs which are similar:

● Suggestions to author/publisher:

BRIEFLY DESCRIBE STUDENTS & THEIR RESPONSE TO PROGRAM

Grade level(s) where used: _____ Subject: _____
Behavior observed that indicates learning took place:

Other reactions:

Any problems experienced?

Any quotes you want to share?

COMPUTER SOFTWARE SELECTION CHECKLIST

Response

A. **CONTENT** — The same considerations apply as for other instructional media. Overall:

1. Is the content appropriate to your needs? — Yes — No

2. Does it support your curriculum objectives? — Yes — No

B. **INSTRUCTIONAL DESIGN** — Numerous types of programs are available. The following are common examples and some of the concerns of each:

1. **Drill and Practice** — provides practice for a skill taught previously.

   a. Is there a variety of levels of difficulty? — Yes — No

   b. Is additional practice provided as needed? — Yes — No

   c. Does the program provide management feedback—record student performance? — Yes — No

   d. Are positive and negative feedback given, as well as any necessary hints? — Yes — No

2. **Tutorial** — conducts actual instruction, generally in the form of a dialogue between the student and the computer.

   a. Is there an appropriate amount of interaction? — Yes — No

   b. Is evaluation included? — Yes — No

   c. Can appropriate segments be accessed by the student without going through the entire sequence? — Yes — No

3. **Simulation** — generates models of environments, experiments, etc.

   a. Is there a reason for using a simulation rather than actual experience, for example, danger or expense? — Yes — No

   b. Are opportunities to generalize provided? — Yes — No

   c. Is graphic representation utilized? — Yes — No

   d. Are any assumptions identified? — Yes — No

   e. Is the simulation based on a valid model? — Yes — No

4. **Game** — generally includes randomized events, provides an opportunity to "win," and presents some obstacles to "winning."

   a. Is the game appropriate to your needs or objectives? — Yes — No

   b. Is it instructional as well as diverting? — Yes — No

   c. Is the student motivated toward learning rather than just winning? — Yes — No

---

Reprinted by permission of Minnesota Dept. of Education.

Response

5. **Information Retrieval** — Information (data) is generated in the form of lists, graphs, tables, etc.

    a. Is documentation easy to understand?   Yes   No

    b. Is storage capacity adequate?   Yes   No

    c. Is speed of operation or access adequate?   Yes   No

6. **Utility** — a support program for the teacher to generate student activities, e.g., crossword puzzles, word games, individualized spelling or math drills, etc.

    a. Is the utility program flexible?   Yes   No

    b. Is it easy to use?   Yes   No

    c. Is it well documented?   Yes   No

7. **Management** — record keeping of student performance, which may be an integral part of another program or used alone as a source of diagnosis and prescription.

    a. Is it easy to use?   Yes   No

    b. Is format suitable for reporting?   Yes   No

    c. Does it insure student privacy?   Yes   No

(N.b. Combinations of the types of programs listed above are common, so it may be difficult to label some programs as to specific type.)

8. Is the program free of racial/sexual, social **stereo-types,** inappropriate language, etc?   Yes   No

C. PRESENTATION

1. **Purpose** — Is the intended use—initial instruction, remediation, guided practice, independent practice or enrichment/extension—evident?   Yes   No

2. **Directions** — Are they clear to the students?   Yes   No

3. **Objectives** — Does the student know what is to be gained by using the program?   Yes   No

4. **Feedback** — Is it effective from the students' perspective?   Yes   No

    a. Does the feedback vary with the performance?   Yes   No

    b. Does the learner get a correct answer after three or less wrong attempts?   Yes   No

    c. Does the feedback lead to additional learning or merely state "right" or "wrong"?   Yes   No

5. **Display** — Is the program visually appealing, attractive, readable?   Yes   No

6. **Ease of use** — Can the program be used independently with a minimum of teacher preparation or intervention?   Yes   No

(Evaluation form continues on page 54.)

Response

7. **User Control** — Does the student have control over rate of presentation?　　Yes　　No

   a. Can the student begin the instruction at a level appropriate to his or her ability?　　Yes　　No

   b. Can the student seek help from the program?　　Yes　　No

8. **Theoretical Basis** — Does the instructional design reflect sound learning theory?　　Yes　　No

9. Is the **order of presentation** logical and sequential?　　Yes　　No

10. Have any **critical prerequisite skills** been identified?　　Yes　　No

   a. Is it clear what the student must know or be able to do before using the program?　　Yes　　No

11. **Intended or Appropriate Audience**

   a. It is clear for whom the program was designed?　　Yes　　No

   b. Is it clear for whom it is appropriate?　　Yes　　No

D. TECHNICAL DESIGN

1. Is the program "error free"?　　Yes　　No

2. Does the program make effective, purposeful use of color, graphics and sound, or are they used just for "show"?　　Yes　　No

3. Does the program adequately provide for misspelled words, or variations of responses.　　Yes　　No

E. SUPPORT MATERIALS

1. Are the **objectives** of the support materials clearly defined?　　Yes　　No

   a. Do they match/complement those of the program?　　Yes　　No

2. Is it evident whether support materials are **optional or required** for proper use of the program?　　Yes　　No

3. Do the support materials provide the teacher with **additional background,** i.e., a bibliography or other resources, sample run of the program, etc.?　　Yes　　No

4. Are the **student materials** effective, attractive, appealing, useful, etc.?　　Yes　　No

F. EQUIPMENT — Have the following factors been taken into account and found acceptable or available:

1. Appropriate computer?　　Yes　　No

2. Language?　　Yes　　No

3. Memory?　　Yes　　No

4. Disk or Tape?　　Yes　　No

5. Special equipment such as a printer, light pen, paddles, joy stick, etc.?　　Yes　　No

microSIFT COURSEWARE EVALUATION

NORTHWEST REGIONAL EDUCATIONAL LABORATORY

Package title _____ Producer _____

Evaluator name _____ Organization _____

Date _____ ☐ Check this box if this evaluation is based partly on your observation of student use of this package

SA - Strongly Agree   A - Agree   D - Disagree   SD - Strongly Disagree   NA - Not applicable
Please include comments on individual items on the reverse page.

CONTENT CHARACTERISTICS

(1) SA A D SD | NA | The content is accurate.

(2) SA A D SD | NA | The content has educational value.

(3) SA A D SD | NA | The content is free of race, ethnic, sex and other stereotypes.

INSTRUCTIONAL CHARACTERISTICS

(4) SA A D SD | NA | The purpose of the package is well defined.

(5) SA A D SD | NA | The package achieves its defined purpose.

(6) SA A D SD | NA | Presentation of content is clear and logical.

(7) SA A D SD | NA | The level of difficulty is appropriate for the target audience.

(8) SA A D SD | NA | Graphics/color/sound are used for appropriate instructional reasons.

(9) SA A D SD | NA | Use of the package is motivational.

(10) SA A D SD | NA | The package effectively stimulates student creativity.

(11) SA A D SD | NA | Feedback on student responses is effectively employed.

(12) SA A D SD | NA | The learner controls the rate and sequence of presentation and review.

(13) SA A D SD | NA | Instruction is integrated with previous student experience.

(14) SA A D SD | NA | Learning can be generalized to an appropriate range of situations.

QUALITY

Write a number from 1 (low) to 5 (high) which represents your judgement of the quality of the package in each division:

____ Content

____ Instructional Characteristics

____ Technical Characteristics

(Evaluation form continues on page 56.)

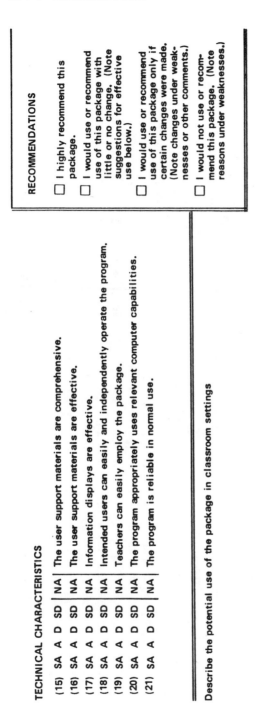

TECHNICAL CHARACTERISTICS

(15) SA A D SD | NA | The user support materials are comprehensive.

(16) SA A D SD | NA | The user support materials are effective.

(17) SA A D SD | NA | Information displays are effective.

(18) SA A D SD | NA | Intended users can easily and independently operate the program.

(19) SA A D SD | NA | Teachers can easily employ the package.

(20) SA A D SD | NA | The program appropriately uses relevant computer capabilities.

(21) SA A D SD | NA | The program is reliable in normal use.

Describe the potential use of the package in classroom settings

Estimate the amount of time a student would need to work
with the package in order to achieve the objectives:
(Can be total time, time per day, time range or other indicator.)

RECOMMENDATIONS

☐ I highly recommend this package.

☐ I would use or recommend use of this package with little or no change. (Note suggestions for effective use below.)

☐ I would use or recommend use of this package only if certain changes were made. (Note changes under weaknesses or other comments.)

☐ I would not use or recommend this package. (Note reasons under weaknesses.)

Strengths:

Weaknesses:

Other comments:

Reprinted by permission. Developed by Northwest Regional Educational Laboratory under contract No. 400-83-0005 with National Institute of Education.

microSIFT COURSEWARE DESCRIPTION

NORTHWEST REGIONAL EDUCATIONAL LABORATORY

Title _____ Version Evaluated _____

Producer _____ Cost _____

Subject/Topics _____

Grade Level(s) (circle) pre-1 1 2 3 4 5 6 7 8 9 10 11 12 post-secondary

Required Hardware _____

Required Software _____

Software protected? ☐ yes ☐ no   Medium of Transfer: ☐ Tape Cassette ☐ ROM Cartridge ☐ 5″ Flexible Disk ☐ 8″ Flexible Disk

Back Up Policy _____

Producer's field test data is available ☐ on request ☐ with package ☐ not available

INSTRUCTIONAL PURPOSES & TECHNIQUES
please check all applicable

☐ Remediation ☐ Tutorial
☐ Standard instruction ☐ Information retrieval
☐ Enrichment ☐ Game
☐ Assessment ☐ Simulation
☐ Instructional ☐ Problem Solving
   management ☐ Other
☐ Authoring
☐ Drill and practice

DOCUMENTATION AVAILABLE
circle P (program) S (supplementary material)

P S Suggested grade/ability level(s)   P S Teacher's information
P S Instructional objectives   P S Resource/reference information
P S Prerequisite skills or activities   P S Student's instructions
P S Sample program output   P S Student worksheets
P S Program operating instructions   P S Textbook correlation
P S Pre-test   P S Follow-up activities
P S Post-test   P S Other _____

OBJECTIVES ☐ Stated ☐ Inferred

PREREQUISITES ☐ Stated ☐ Inferred

Describe package CONTENT AND STRUCTURE, including record keeping and reporting functions

use back for more space

Reprinted by permission. Developed by Northwest Regional Educational Laboratory under contract No. 400-83-0005 with National Institute of Education.

Texas
Education
Computer
Cooperative

ID # _____

COURSEWARE EVALUATION FORM

PART I. IDENTIFICATION

    A. Package Name: _____

          Single Program _____   Series _____

    B. Distributor: _____

          Address: _____

                    _____

          Telephone: _____

    C. Microcomputer

        Type: __APPLE __3.2 __PET __TRS-80 __MODEL I

                __3.3   __MODEL III

        Memory Required: __16K __32K __48K __64K

        Special Language Required: __Integer BASIC
                                      (APPLE)
                                __Pascal

        Storage Medium: __Tape Cassette __5" Diskette

        Equipment Requirements: __One Disk Drive

        __ Two Disk Drive __Color __Printer

        __Voice/Sound Instrument __Game Paddles

        __Other: _____

ID # _____

COURSEWARE EVALUATION FORM

NAME OF PACKAGE _____

PART II. Instruction

A. Grade Level: K 1 2 3 4 5 6 7 8 9 10 11 12

B. Instructional Technique:

____Drill and Practice

____Tutorial

____Simulation

____Problem Solving

____Educational Game

C. Instructional Activities:

____Classroom Text Dependent

____Direct Teacher Supervision Required

____Student Workbook Required

D. Special Characteristics

Timed Environment	___Yes	___No
Student Branching Allowed	___Yes	___No
Material Modification Allowed	___Yes	___No
Student Statistics Provided	___Yes	___No
Distracting Sound	___Yes	___No

E. Approximate Student Instruction Time

Lesson _____

Total Package _____

(Evaluation form continues on page 62.)

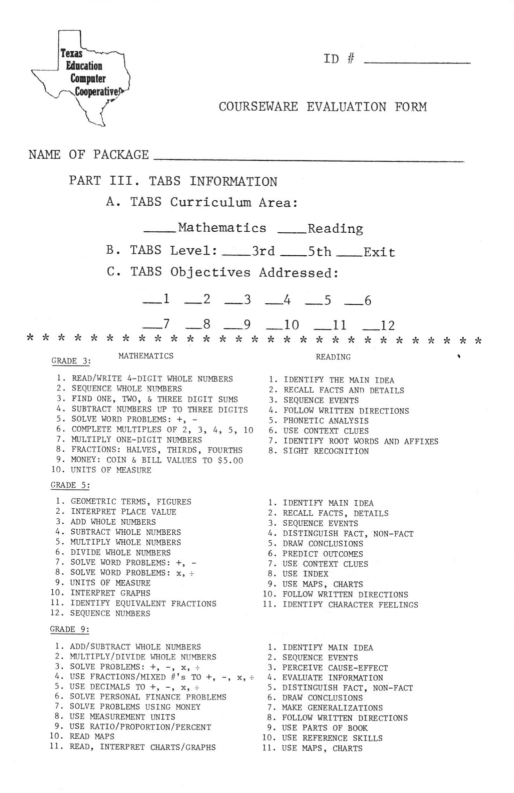

Texas Education Computer Cooperative

ID # _____

COURSEWARE EVALUATION FORM

NAME OF PACKAGE _____

PART III. TABS INFORMATION

A. TABS Curriculum Area:

____Mathematics ____Reading

B. TABS Level: ____3rd ____5th ____Exit

C. TABS Objectives Addressed:

__1 __2 __3 __4 __5 __6

__7 __8 __9 __10 __11 __12

* *

GRADE 3:

MATHEMATICS

1. READ/WRITE 4-DIGIT WHOLE NUMBERS
2. SEQUENCE WHOLE NUMBERS
3. FIND ONE, TWO, & THREE DIGIT SUMS
4. SUBTRACT NUMBERS UP TO THREE DIGITS
5. SOLVE WORD PROBLEMS: +, -
6. COMPLETE MULTIPLES OF 2, 3, 4, 5, 10
7. MULTIPLY ONE-DIGIT NUMBERS
8. FRACTIONS: HALVES, THIRDS, FOURTHS
9. MONEY: COIN & BILL VALUES TO $5.00
10. UNITS OF MEASURE

READING

1. IDENTIFY THE MAIN IDEA
2. RECALL FACTS AND DETAILS
3. SEQUENCE EVENTS
4. FOLLOW WRITTEN DIRECTIONS
5. PHONETIC ANALYSIS
6. USE CONTEXT CLUES
7. IDENTIFY ROOT WORDS AND AFFIXES
8. SIGHT RECOGNITION

GRADE 5:

1. GEOMETRIC TERMS, FIGURES
2. INTERPRET PLACE VALUE
3. ADD WHOLE NUMBERS
4. SUBTRACT WHOLE NUMBERS
5. MULTIPLY WHOLE NUMBERS
6. DIVIDE WHOLE NUMBERS
7. SOLVE WORD PROBLEMS: +, -
8. SOLVE WORD PROBLEMS: x, ÷
9. UNITS OF MEASURE
10. INTERPRET GRAPHS
11. IDENTIFY EQUIVALENT FRACTIONS
12. SEQUENCE NUMBERS

1. IDENTIFY MAIN IDEA
2. RECALL FACTS, DETAILS
3. SEQUENCE EVENTS
4. DISTINGUISH FACT, NON-FACT
5. DRAW CONCLUSIONS
6. PREDICT OUTCOMES
7. USE CONTEXT CLUES
8. USE INDEX
9. USE MAPS, CHARTS
10. FOLLOW WRITTEN DIRECTIONS
11. IDENTIFY CHARACTER FEELINGS

GRADE 9:

1. ADD/SUBTRACT WHOLE NUMBERS
2. MULTIPLY/DIVIDE WHOLE NUMBERS
3. SOLVE PROBLEMS: +, -, x, ÷
4. USE FRACTIONS/MIXED #'s TO +, -, x, ÷
5. USE DECIMALS TO +, -, x, ÷
6. SOLVE PERSONAL FINANCE PROBLEMS
7. SOLVE PROBLEMS USING MONEY
8. USE MEASUREMENT UNITS
9. USE RATIO/PROPORTION/PERCENT
10. READ MAPS
11. READ, INTERPRET CHARTS/GRAPHS

1. IDENTIFY MAIN IDEA
2. SEQUENCE EVENTS
3. PERCEIVE CAUSE-EFFECT
4. EVALUATE INFORMATION
5. DISTINGUISH FACT, NON-FACT
6. DRAW CONCLUSIONS
7. MAKE GENERALIZATIONS
8. FOLLOW WRITTEN DIRECTIONS
9. USE PARTS OF BOOK
10. USE REFERENCE SKILLS
11. USE MAPS, CHARTS

ID # _____

COURSEWARE EVALUATION FORM

NAME OF PACKAGE _____

PART IV. EVALUATION

A. Presentation

	Poor	Fair	Good	Very Good	Excellent
Ease of Use	1	2	3	4	5
Reliability	1	2	3	4	5
Motivation	1	2	3	4	5
Frame Display	1	2	3	4	5
Documentation	1	2	3	4	5

B. Content

	Poor	Fair	Good	Very Good	Excellent
Accuracy of Content	1	2	3	4	5
Appropriate Feedback	1	2	3	4	5
Appropriate Level of Difficulty	1	2	3	4	5
Appropriate for Computer Use	1	2	3	4	5
High Educational Standards	1	2	3	4	5

C. Comments to Distributor: _____

_____

_____

_____

_____

_____

Please Use One Form Per Program

EQUIPMENT:

COURSEWARE EVALUATION FORM

Microcomputer Evaluation and Resource Center
Indiana Department of Public Instruction
Division of Instructional Media

TITLE OF MATERIAL: _____ SERIES: _____

FORMAT: _____ LANGUAGE: _____ COPYRIGHT DATE: _____

MANUFACTURER: _____ VENDOR: _____ PRICE: _____

SUBJECT AREA: _____ GRADE LEVEL: _____

PURPOSE/OBJECTIVE(S): _____

Please evaluate this courseware item on each of the following criteria. For each criterion circle a rating of (1), (2), (3), (4), or (5) — (1) represents a very low level of compliance, (5) represents a very high level of compliance.

*Achieves stated objective?	1	2	3	4	5 N/A
*Is suitably structured for purpose?	1	2	3	4	5 N/A
*Provides information displays which are concise and easily understood?	1	2	3	4	5 N/A

*Allows user to review incorrect responses?	1	2	3	4	5	N/A
*Provides positive reinforcement to user?	1	2	3	4	5	N/A
*Effectively uses computer capabilities, including sound and graphics?	1	2	3	4	5	N/A
*Holds interest?	1	2	3	4	5	N/A
*Provides worthwhile learning experience?	1	2	3	4	5	N/A
*Accompanies effective support material?	1	2	3	4	5	N/A
*Is compatible with existing course and/or unit curriculum?	1	2	3	4	5	N/A

COMMENTS: _____

_____

_____

_____

_____

DPI 3/82

Reprinted by permission of Indiana Department of Public Instruction, Division of Federal Resources and School Improvement.

CURRICULUM REVIEW
COURSEWARE EVALUATION FORM

Program Title _____

Publisher/Supplier _____

Supplier's Address _____

Copyright Date _____ Approx. Running Time _____

Hardware Required _____ Language _____

Packaging/Price _____

Grade Level _____ Subject Area _____

Content Focus

• What is the program's major function in the classroom: initial instruction, drill and practice, gaming, simulation, problem solving, exploration, informational, record keeping, testing, or other?

• How is the basic content presented to the user?

• What is the target audience: average, remedial, gifted, or special needs?

• Does the content's difficulty suit the intended users?

Educational Purpose

• Does the program accomplish its stated objectives?

• Is each objective appropriate for the level of instruction?

• Can the user recover from an error without rerunning the entire program?

• Does the program provide immediate feedback for the student?

• Are the feedback signals suitable for right and wrong responses? Are there appropriate branching instructions?

• Does the program evaluate final student mastery or provide total scores?

• Does the program require much teacher direction or intervention?

• Is there an adequate sense of user control for pacing and review?

• Does the student gain any new skills or concepts from using the program?

• Is the basic instructional approach sound? a good method for teaching this content?

• Is the instructional approach consistent with the teacher's overall teaching method?

• What kind of teacher preparation is necessary?

• How does the teacher obtain results of student progress?

• Is the program best suited for individual or group use? flexible?

• Is the content factually accurate? free of political, racial, or sexual bias?

• What is the value of having this content in a software format? Would print (a textbook or worksheet) accomplish the same educational purpose?

Method of Operation

• Is the program difficult to operate?

• Does it load properly and run without system errors?

• Are the instructions on the screen clear?

• Does the length of the program affect student attention span or subject coverage?

• Can the user interact with the computer (i.e., query and respond at will)?

• Can the user skip over familiar instructions?

• Can the user get help for problems by returning to the instructions?

Technical Features

• Does the program include suitable documentation? (printed versions of goals, objectives, operating instructions, prerequisites, teaching suggestions, correlations with standard texts—i.e., teacher's guide material)

• Is the screen formatting clearly presented: adequately spaced, uncluttered, clearly labelled, easy to read?

• Is the grammar, spelling, and punctuation correct?

• Do the graphics and sound motivate the student?

• Do the graphics and sound contribute to learning, or are they superfluous or even distracting?

• What about the use of animation, color, voice input/output, light pen, or other technical enhancements?

• Is the packaging durable and are the components easy to store?

Recommendations

• What degree of success did this program have in your classroom? (Identify general type of community, school, and students involved in the test.)

• Did the students like it? learn from it? want to use it again?

• What are its major strengths and weaknesses?

• Are there ways the teacher can modify it to compensate for serious drawbacks?

• Are there ways the publisher should modify it in future editions?

• Does it stand on its own, or should it be supplemented with other types of material?

• Is it worth the purchase price?

Lincoln Public Schools

INSTRUCTIONAL SOFTWARE EVALUATION SHEET

PROGRAM NAME: _____

_____ COST _____

SUBJECT AREA: _____

PROGRAM SOURCE   HARDWARE REQUIREMENTS

  Name: _____   COMPUTER: _____

  Address: _____   MEMORY: _____

  _____   PERIPHERALS: _____

                                            LANGUAGE: _____

PROGRAM CLASS   PROGRAM USES

  ☐ Isolated program   ☐ Drill or practice

  ☐ Part of a ____program cluster   ☐ Tutorial

INTENDED AUDIENCE(S)   ☐ Simulation

  ☐ Teachers   ☐ Instructional gaming

  ☐ Students in grade(s)____   ☐ Problem solving

  ☐ Remedial students   ☐ Informational

  ☐ Gifted students   ☐ Other (Specify:_____

  ☐ Special needs students   _____).

INSTRUCTIONAL SETTING   CRITICAL PREREQUISITE SKILLS

  ☐ Groups   _____

  ☐ Individuals   _____

GENERAL DESCRIPTION OF WHAT THE PROGRAM DOES _____

_____

_____

_____

APPROXIMATE EXECUTION TIME: _____

REVIEWER _____ DATE _____

Draft copy 9/30/82

Reprinted by permission of Lincoln Public Schools. Designed by Charles D. Friesan and Ronald O. Massie. Modeled after NCTM evaluation sheets.

Instructional Software Evaluation Sheet   Page 2

DESIGN   Yes   No

1. Is the program about the right length, neither too long to
   maintain interest nor too short to cover the subject well?   ☐   ☐

2. Do the graphics and sound contribute to the program's effectiveness?   ☐   ☐

3. Is the screen formatting well done?   ☐   ☐

4. Does the program allow for student interaction with the computer?   ☐   ☐

5. Is the difficulty of instruction adjusted according to student
   responses?   ☐   ☐

6. Does the program maintain a record of student performance that
   is available to the learner and the teacher at the end of the
   lesson?   ☐   ☐

7. Will the management components really make the teacher's job
   easier?   ☐   ☐

8. Is the program easy to use?   ☐   ☐

9. Are the instructions (documentation) clear?   ☐   ☐

10. Can the user get help by returning to the instructions or
    content material?   ☐   ☐

11. Can the user skip over familiar instructions?   ☐   ☐

CONTENT

1. Is the program instructionally sound?   ☐   ☐

2. Is the content and spelling correct?   ☐   ☐

3. If supplementary materials are included, does the quality meet
   your instructional standards?   ☐   ☐

4. Are safeguards built into the program so that the user cannot
   foul it up by giving inappropriate responses?   ☐   ☐

5. Does this program do things that a good workbook cannot do?   ☐   ☐

6. Is the computer's reaction to right answers more appealing than
   its reaction to wrong answers?   ☐   ☐

7. Will kids like the program?   ☐   ☐

8. Do you like the program?   ☐   ☐

9. Does the quality and instructional need for the program justify
   the price?   ☐   ☐

10. Does the program accomplish the purpose for which it's intended?   ☐   ☐

Microcomputer Software Evaluation

Evaluator _____ Date _____

Title of Program _____

Title of Package _____

Publisher _____

Author(s) _____ Target Audience _____

Copyright Date _____ Estimated Used Time _____

Subject Area _____ Specific Topic _____

Instructional Objective(s) _____

_____

Instructional Prerequisite(s) _____

_____

Hardware Requirements _____

_____

User Worksheets Required?   ___Yes ___No   User Worksheets Provided?   ___Yes ___No

Can the Menu Be Displayed?   ___Yes ___No   Can the Program Be Listed?   ___Yes ___No

Can the Program Be Modified? ___Yes ___No   Is the Program Copy Protected? ___Yes ___No

Backup Copy Provided?   ___Yes ___No   Teacher's Guide Provided?   ___Yes ___No

Medium Of Transfer   ___Tape Cassette ___5" Disk ___8" Disk ___ROM Cartridge

Memory Required   ___8K ___16K ___32K ___48K ___64K ___More Than 64K

Instructional Purpose (check all that apply) ___Remediation ___Regular ___Enrichment

Type of Program   ___Single   ___Component of Series

Instructional Technique (check all that apply)

____Drill and Practice ____Problem Solving ____Tutorial ____Exploration

____Game ____Simulation ____Informational ____Management/Administration

Suitable For: ___Individual Instruction ___Small Groups ___Large Groups

Other Comments _____

_____

Reprinted by permission of Patricia Kennedy and Nancy Haas.

Check the rating that reflects your evaluation of the computer software.
Comment if the appropriate rating is <u>NO</u>.

	Yes	No	NA
1. Is the content accurate? Comment:	____	____	____
2. Does the content have educational value? Comment:	____	____	____
3. Is the content complete? Comment:	____	____	____
4. Is the content free of bias and stereotype? Comment:	____	____	____
5. Is the content sequenced properly? Comment:	____	____	____
6. Is the feedback appropriate? Comment:	____	____	____
7. Is the level of difficulty appropriate for the target audience? Comment:	____	____	____
8. Does the program accomplish the stated or implied objectives? Comment:	____	____	____
9. Does the program accept a wide range of possible responses? Comment:	____	____	____
10. Does the teacher's guide provide relevant information? Comment:	____	____	____
11. Is the program easy to load into the computer? Comment:	____	____	____

(Evaluation form continues on page 72.)

	Yes	No	NA

12. Is the text free from spelling and punctuation errors? ____ ____ ____
   Comment:

13. Are the text and directions easy to read? ____ ____ ____
   Comment:

14. Is the user given adequate time to read and respond? ____ ____ ____
   Comment:

15. Do the color/graphics/sound enhance the program? ____ ____ ____
   Comment:

16. Can the user control the rate and sequence of presentation? ___ ____ ____
   Comment:

17. Does the program branch to the correct level of difficulty
   contingent upon the user's responses? ____ ____ ____
   Comment:

18. Are the supplementary worksheets adequate? ____ ____ ____
   Comment:

19. Is the program packaged in a secure container? ____ ____ ____
   Comment:

20. Are the user's correct and incorrect responses recorded? ____ ____ ____
   Comment:

21. Can the teacher retrieve the user's final score? ____ ____ ____
   Comment:

22. Is a pretest and a posttest included? ____ ____ ____
   Comment:

23. Is a classroom management system included? ____ ____ ____
   Comment:

Major strengths of the program:

Major weaknesses of the program:

Recommendations:

PROGRAM EVALUATION FORM

PROGRAM NAME:

COLOR OR BLACK/WHITE

GRAPHIC OR NO-GRAPHIC

MUSIC OR NO-MUSIC

PROGRAM TYPE:

CAI-DRILL & PRACTICE
CAI-TUTORIAL
CAI-PROBLEM SOLVING
CAI-GAME
CAI-SIMULATION
CMI
ADMINISTRATIVE

AUTHOR:

ADDRESS:

LEVEL:

K-12
ELEMENTARY
JUNIOR HIGH
SECONDARY
POST-SECONDARY

SCHOOL / POSITION:

SUBJECT:

DESCRIPTION:

TYPE OF COMPUTER: APPLE II
                  TRS-80
                  OTHER

REMARKS:

TIME REQUIRED: MINUTES

RATING: 1   2   3   4   5   6   7   8   9   10
        ----------------   ---------------------   ---------
        NOT ACCEPT-   ACCEPTABLE WITH   ACCEPT-
            ABLE   MODIFICATION   ABLE

DISK#(OFFICE USE ONLY):

EVALUATOR'S SIGNATURE:

Reprinted by permission of Nebraska Clearinghouse for Microcomputer Software.

SCHOOL MICROWARE EVALUATION FORM   (COPY AS NEEDED)

Your Name _____

Address _____

Organization _____   Position _____

Supplier _____   Tel: _____

Product Name _____   Price $ _____   No. of Progs.
Subjects and Grades   Est. Student   Under This Name
to Which Applicable   Time Required

FUNCTIONAL DESCRIPTION - Describe the program in terms of its goals and what it does to achieve them. Give as much detail as possible (use extra sheets as necessary).

PRELIMINARY CONSIDERATION - Does this program contribute to the teaching of topic(s) which should be taught in today's schools? Yes ____ No ____ If No, give your reasons for this answer in the Comments section at the end of the form and omit the balance of the questionnaire.

INSTRUCTIONS - Enter a number in the blank to indicate the extent to which the product fulfills the description in the item, as follows: 2 - Completely, 1 - Partially, 0 - Not at All. If the item is not applicable to the product, enter N/A. If the item is unclear, enter U. Elaborate on answers as necessary in Comments at end or on extra sheets, giving item numbers.

DOCUMENTATION - List materials accompanying the program, e.g., teachers guide, student workbook.
    1. Indicate types of information included.
_____ a. Suggested course/subject, grade levels.

_____ b. Goals.

_____ c. Performance objectives.

_____ d. Suggested teaching strateg(ies).

_____ e. Correlation with standard texts.

_____ f. Prerequisites for use of program.

_____ g. Student exercises, teacher answers.

_____ h. Operating instructions.

_____ i. Listing and sample runs of program(s).

_____ j. If a simulation, description of the model used.

_____ k. Suggested topics for follow-up discussions.

_____ l. Suggested references/activities for follow-up.

_____ 2. The documentation is written clearly.

_____ 3. If a workbook is included, the format and content are appropriate.

INSTRUCTIONS GIVEN TO USER BY PROGRAM
    1. The instructions are adequate regarding:
_____ a. The instructional task to be performed.

_____ b. Details of how to interact with the program.

_____ 2. User has the option of skipping instructions if already known.

STUDENT-COMPUTER DIALOG

---- 1. Output is displayed screen by screen (paged) rather than scrolled.
---- 2. If output is paged:
---- a. User has control over continuing to the next page.
---- b. Amount of information in each page is appropriate.
---- c. The perceptual impact (amount of type and lines) is suitable.
---- 3. Output is spaced and formatted so as to be easily readable.
---- 4. Language is well suited to most students' reading ability.
---- 5. Uses correct grammar,spelling, hyphenation and punctuation.
---- 6. Any grid or coordinate system used is consistent with common conventions.
---- 7. Students can respond with common symbols & ways of using them, e.g., right to left entry of sums.
---- 8. Accepts abbreviations for common responses.
---- 9. Provides for individual needs, e.g., opportunity to work with harder or easier material.
---- 10. Dialog is personalized, i.e., makes appropriate use of student names.
---- 11. Uses devices to get & maintain interest, e.g., variation of computer responses, humor, pace change, surprise.

COMMENTS – Please use this space and additional sheets as necessary to provide any information which you believe would help someone who is thinking about buying of the product being reviewed. In particular, indicate what you like best and least about the program. Also, list any changes which should be made.

12. Makes good use of any special features computer:

a. Graphics _____   b. Color _____   c. Sound _____

---- 13. Reinforcing responses (indications of right, wrong, etc.) are appropriate.
---- 14. The number of wrong answers allowed is reasonable.
---- 15. Responds appropriately if allowed number of wrong answers is exceeded.
---- 16. Provides opportunity to get help if difficulty is encountered.
---- 17. Minimizes bad entries via devices such as objective formats (multiple choice,etc).
---- 18. Deals well with inappropriate entries, i.e., response to typing errors, etc., is intelligible and useful.
---- 19. Required entries are within students' capabilities (esp. typing, vocabulary).
---- 20. Reports student performance periodically and at end of session.

MISCELLANEOUS CONCERNS

---- 1. If a simulation, the program gives a sufficiently accurate representation of the situation simulated.
---- 2. The concepts and vocabulary required to use the program are reasonable.
---- 3. Operates properly and is free of bugs.
---- 4. Is well structured and documented internally to facilitate any necessary debugging/modification.

Revised 8/82

Reprinted by permission from *School Microware Reviews*, Winter 1983. Publication restraints have necessitated the redesigning of this form. Content has not been altered.

SOFTWARE EVALUATION CHECKLIST

PROGRAM NAME: _____ SOURCE: _____ COST: _____
SUBJECT AREA: _____ REVIEWER'S NAME: _____ DATE: _____

1. INSTRUCTIONAL RANGE
- _____ grade level(s)
- _____ ability level(s)

2. INSTRUCTIONAL GROUPING FOR PROGRAM USE
- _____ individual
- _____ small group (size: _____)
- _____ large group (size: _____)

3. EXECUTION TIME
- _____ minutes (estimated) for average use

4. PROGRAM USE(S)
- _____ drill or practice
- _____ tutorial
- _____ simulation
- _____ instructional gaming
- _____ problem solving
- _____ informational
- _____ other (_____)

5. USER ORIENTATION: INSTRUCTOR'S POINT OF VIEW

	low · · · · high	
flexibility	· · · ·	
freedom from need to intervene or assist	· · · ·	

6. USER ORIENTATION: STUDENT'S POINT OF VIEW

	low · · · · high	
quality of directions (clarity)	· · · ·	
quality of output (content and tone)	· · · ·	
quality of screen formatting	· · · ·	
freedom from need for external information	· · · ·	
freedom from disruption by system errors	· · · ·	
simplicity of user input	· · · ·	

7. CONTENT

	low · · · · high	
instructional focus	· · · ·	
instructional significance	· · · ·	
soundness or validity	· · · ·	
compatibility with other materials used	· · · ·	

8. MOTIVATION AND INSTRUCTIONAL STYLE

	passive · · · · active	
type of student involvement	· · · ·	

	low · · · · high	
degree of student control	· · · ·	

	none poor · · · good	
use of game format	· · · ·	
use of still graphics	· · · ·	
use of animation	· · · ·	
use of color	· · · ·	
use of voice input and output	· · · ·	
use of nonvoice audio	· · · ·	
use of light pen	· · · ·	
use of ancillary materials	· · · ·	
use of _____	· · · ·	

9. SOCIAL CHARACTERISTICS

	present and negative	not present	present and positive
competition	_____	_____	_____
cooperation	_____	_____	_____
humanizing of computer	_____	_____	_____
moral issues or value judgments	_____	_____	_____
summary of student performance	_____	_____	_____

Reprinted by permission of William P. Heck, Jerry Johnson, and Robert J. Kansky, *Guidelines for Evaluating Computerized Instructional Materials*, NCTM.

1. The grade levels and ability levels for a particular program are primarily determined by the concepts involved. Other important factors are reading level, prerequisite skills, degree of student control, and intended instructional use. It is possible for a program to be flexible enough to be used across a wide range of grade levels and ability levels.

2. Some programs are designed for use by individuals. Others have been or can be modified for participation by two or three persons at a time. Simulations or demonstrations often pose opportunities for large-group interaction. A given program may be used in more than one grouping, depending on the instructor.

3. The time required for the use of a program will vary considerably. Include loading time for cassettes. A time range is the appropriate response here.

4. Instructional programs can be categorized according to their uses. Some programs may have more than one use, thus falling into more than one of the following categories:

Drill or practice: Assumes that the concept or skill has been taught previously.

Tutorial: Directs the full cycle of the instructional process; a dialogue between the student and the computer.

Simulation: Models selected, alterable aspects of an environment.

Instructional gaming: Involves random events and the pursuit of a winning strategy.

Problem solving: Uses general algorithms common to one or more problems.

Informational: Generates information (data).

5. These are factors relevant to the actual use of the program from the point of view of an instructor.

Flexibility: A program may allow the user or the instructor to adjust the program to different ability levels, degrees of difficulty, or concepts.

Intervention or assistance: A rating of "low" means considerable teacher intervention or assistance is required.

6. These are factors relevant to the actual use of the program from the point of view of a student.

Directions: The directions should be complete, readable, understandable, and complete. If in response to student input, the output understood), and use appropriate examples.

Output: Program responses should be readable, understandable, and complete. If in response to student input, the output should be of an acceptable tone and consistent with the input request.

Screen formatting: The formats during a program run should not be distracting or cluttered. Labels and symbols should be meaningful within the given context.

External information: A program may require the user to have access to information other than that provided within it. This may include prerequisite content knowledge or knowledge of conventions used by the program designer as well as maps, books, models, and so on.

System errors: System errors result in the involuntary termination of the program.

Input: A program should ensure that a user knows when and in what form input is needed. It should avoid using characters with special meanings, restrict input locations to particular screen areas, and require minimal typing.

7. These are matters relevant to the subject-matter content of the program.

Focus: The program topic should be clearly defined and of a scope that permits thorough treatment.

Significance: The instructional objectives of the program must be viewed as important by the instructor. Also, the program should represent a valid use of the computer's capabilities while improving the instructional process.

Soundness or validity: The concepts and terms employed should be correct, clear, and precise. Other important factors are the rate of presentation, degree of difficulty, and internal consistency.

Compatibility: The content, terminology, teaching style, and educational philosophy of the program should be consistent with those generally encountered by the student.

9. Competition, cooperation, and values are concerns that may be a function of the way a program expresses them. (War gaming and the "hangman" format are sample issues.) Also, the "humanizing" of the computer may serve for motivation or to reduce anxiety, but it also may become tedious, misleading, and counterproductive.

The summary of student performance can be dichotomous (win or lose), statistical (time expended or percent of items correct), or subjective (as in the evaluation of a simulation). It may be for student, teacher, or both.

▦ SAMPLE SOFTWARE DOCUMENTATION SHEET

PROGRAM NAME: _____

SUBJECT AREA: _____

PROGRAM CLASS

____ isolated program

____ part of a ____ program cluster

INTENDED AUDIENCE(S)

____ teachers

____ students in grade(s) _____

____ other _____

_____

PROGRAM USES: (1 = primary, 2 = secondary)

____ drill or practice

____ tutorial

____ simulation

____ instructional gaming

____ problem solving

____ informational

____ other _____

_____

CRITICAL PREREQUISITE SKILLS

_____

_____

NAME(S) OF PREREQUISITE PROGRAM(S)

_____

_____

_____

NAME(S) OF FOLLOW-UP PROGRAM(S)

_____

_____

_____

DATE OF THIS DOCUMENTATION

_____

PROGRAM SOURCE

name: _____

address: _____

_____

_____

phone: _____

program cost: _____

SYSTEM REQUIREMENTS

computer: _____

language: _____

memory needed: _____ bytes

input mode: cassette

_____-inch diskette

cartridge

other _____

_____

output mode: color monitor

B/W monitor

printer

plotter

other _____

_____

CLASSROOM VALIDATION (describe)

_____

_____

_____

TIME FOR AVERAGE
EXECUTION ____ minutes

OVER ➡

GENERAL DESCRIPTION OF THE PROGRAM (i.e., purpose of the program)

SPECIAL PROGRAM CHARACTERISTICS (e.g., use of graphics or sound, designed for use by groups of two or more persons at a time, level of difficulty can be modified by teacher (only) or student, exit from program is controlled by the teacher (only) or student, etc.)

DIRECTIONS FOR USE OF THE PROGRAM (e.g., directions not presented in the program itself but needed for program execution, directions regarding the use of the program within the total instructional process, notes regarding program options, etc.)

ANCILLARY MATERIALS REQUIRED (e.g., books, worksheets, charts, data lists, dice, geometric shapes, lab equipment, etc.)

ADDITIONAL DOCUMENTATION AVAILABLE (check box for each type)

☐ sample run (location _____)

☐ program listing (location _____)

SOFTWARE EVALUATION REVIEW AND RATING FORM

Name of Series or Diskette:_____ Date: _____

Name of Program: _____

Name of Distributor or Manufacturer: _____

Reviewer's Name: _____

Description and Instructional Objectives: _____

_____

Equipment Required:

_____ DOS Version	_____ Cassette Recorder
_____ Printer	_____ Game Paddles
_____ Dual Disk Drive	_____ Other_____
_____ Color Monitor	

Subject Area:

( ) Art	( ) Grammar	( ) Math
( ) Business	( ) History	( ) Music
( ) Computer Science	( ) Home Economics	( ) Physical Education
( ) Distributive Education	( ) Industrial Arts	( ) Reading
( ) Foreign Language	( ) Literature	( ) Science

Grade Level:

( ) Elementary	( ) Senior High
( ) Lower Elementary	( ) Games
( ) Upper Elementary	( ) Teaching (Administrative)
( ) Elementary-Junior High (Middle)	( ) Non-Teaching (Administrative)
( ) Junior High	( ) Demo
( ) Junior-Senior High	

Indicate prerequisite skills required for student use:_____

_____

Instructional Strategy:

( ) Drill and Practice	( ) Problem Solving	( ) Remediation
( ) Tutorial	( ) Materials Generation	( ) Enrichment
( ) Simulation	( ) Game	( ) Other: _____

The computer is the most appropriate medium to teach this material.
Agree 1 2 3 4 5 Disagree

The program includes sufficient documentation (written materials telling when and how to use the program) to aid teachers and students in using the program.
Agree 1 2 3 4 5 Disagree

The program allows the user to skip over directions or beginning material if he/she wants to.
Agree 1 2 3 4 5 Disagree

_____

Reprinted by permission of Columbus, Nebraska, City Schools.

The program allows adequate student interaction;

Agree 1 2 3 4 5 Disagree

The package makes good use of the motivational devices of:

Timed Responses, etc,   Agree 1 2 3 4 5 Disagree

Scoring: Agree 1 2 3 4 5 Disagree

Graphics: (graphs, moving picture etc.) Agree 1 2 3 4 5 Disagree

Personalization: (informal, conversational, addressing student by name, etc)

Agree 1 2 3 4 5 Disagree

COURSEWARE REVIEW AND RATING FORM
SUMMARY EVALUATION

1. Student interest:

   very interesting   A B C D F   uninteresting

2. Ease of use: easy to use   A B C D F   awkward

3. Educational content and/or value:

   much A B C D F little

4. Program polish: well done A B C D F amateurish, sloppy, incomplete

5. Instructions: very clear A B C D F none

6. Use of Graphics: excellent use A B C D F no use

7. Program responds a great deal differently for good students and poor students:

   a great deal A B C D F no difference is seen

8. Use of computer delivery:

   very effective, can't be done A B C D F There are better ways to achieve
       as well by any other means   this objective

OVERALL VALUE:

every school should have this program A B C D F not worth the effort to load it

Please provide a paragraph summarizing your reactions to the program. Include
strengths and weakness of the program.

PART II

5

SOURCES OF MICROCOMPUTER SOFTWARE

The question of software availability should never follow the purchase of computer equipment. If it did the result might well be the new computer owner's discovering with dismay that the programs which are most relevant to his or her needs are only available for another brand of computer. The initial questions to be raised by anyone purchasing a microcomputer must be what software is available for the brands under consideration and where can this software can be found.

Five major sources of computer software have been identified: in-house programming, commercial vendors, computer magazines or journals, user groups, and research efforts (Miller 1980). The latter are often the products of consortia or national or regional clearinghouses whose work is supported by outside funding from state or federal agencies. These groups are discussed, along with the availability of the software which they produce, in chapter 7. They are often an important source for high quality educational software and should be an initial source consulted by educators purchasing instructional programs.

However, most selectors of software will at some time or other buy commercial software. Buying commercial programs, unfortunately, brings no guaranties of quality software. Inaccurate content, misspelled words, poor programming, and incompatibility are all possibilities which can render purchased software unfit for use.

Before an intelligent purchasing decision can be made in regard to any consumer product, including commercial software, a necessary first step should always be a survey of the market to see what is available. Getting a firm grasp on what was available in the area of microcomputer software may have been quite difficult a year ago, but the amount of bibliographic control which has been achieved most recently has been rather remarkable. This control has been achieved primarily through the development of two major selection aids which have long been used as a matter of standard practice in the selection of both print and other nonprint formats. These two aids are the directory, or bibliography, which lists titles available generally without providing any evaluative criticism, and the journal, which provides reviews of the titles chosen for purchase consideration. The journal review is often used as a finding device by the selector who, after learning of the existence of a particular title and ascertaining that it has been favorably reviewed, may purchase it without further evaluation, may order a preview copy and then do his or her own evaluation before actual purchase, or may seek other reviews in additional sources to verify a positive recommendation before acting. Since chapter 6 discusses microcomputer reviewing journals at length, as well as other journals which provide useful computer information, the reader is referred there for this information.

This chapter focuses instead on sources of programs. In addition, there are brief discussions in this chapter on how to obtain software for preview and on programming one's own software.

SOURCES OF COMMERCIAL SOFTWARE

Comprehensive Overview

Those wishing to obtain an excellent overview of educational computing resources could profitably consult the annual *Classroom Computer News Directory of Educational Computing Resources.*

Another excellent computer resource which, although it also does not list software, is a valuable tool for finding names of software producers for specific applications is the *Microcomputer Market Place.*

1983 Classroom Computer News Directory of Educational Computing Resources, edited by Peter Kelman. Watertown, Mass.: Intentional Educations, 1982. 199p. $14.95 paper; $29.95 hardcover ($10.50 if ordered with a year's subscription to *Classroom Computer News* for $16.00). ISSN 0733-3129, ISBN 09607970-0-9.

Order from: Intentional Educations, Inc.
341 Mount Auburn St.
Watertown, MA 02172

The *Classroom Computer News Directory* contains no actual software listings but is instead a comprehensive guide to microcomputer resources including people, places, other directories, journals, and organizations involved in computing, to name just a few. It is divided into six major parts. "Part I—Sources: People, Places, and Things" includes the following chapters: "Ideas, Information, and Materials," embracing anthologies, bibliographies, indexes, online sources and databases, other databases, resource centers, and research and development; "Software," including directories of software, software review sources, and clearinghouses; "Associations" in educational technology and computing science, and other educational associations with an interest in microcomputing; "Periodicals" on educational computing and computing in general, and educational journals which include computing articles, and microcomputing newsletters; "Funding" information sources and organizations which have specific funds for educational computing applications; and "Miscellaneous" resources, which includes materials and organizations of a national scope which do not fit into other categories such as a journal of want ads for hardware purchasers, a directory of projects using microcomputers for instructional and administrative purposes nationwide, and an association for those interested in the children's computer language called LOGO.

"Part II—Computer-Specific Resources" contains listings of periodicals, software directories, and user groups on a national and regional basis for the following major microcomputer brands: Apple, Atari, Commodore, Radio Shack, Sinclair, Texas Instruments, and others not yet as widely used in education but nonetheless popular including Heath/Zenith, Hewlett-Packard, IBM, M/A-COM OSI, and North Star. This section also contains an article entitled "Ten Rules for Evaluating Computer Systems."

"Part III—Local and Regional Resources" is a unique listing of persons, places, and organizations which may be contacted throughout the United States and Canada in an effort "to facilitate the sharing of information and ideas among computer-using educators in the same region." Resources in the United States are grouped under Central Region, Eastern Region, Southern Region, Southwestern Region, and Western Region. The United Kingdom is also included as are all the provinces of Canada. Under each U.S. and Canadian section are listed government contact persons who have been designated to deal with educational computing and *Classroom Computer News (CCN)* contact persons who have agreed to refer educators to computing resources and answer questions when possible. Under each state may be found the Department of Education and *CCN* contact, and a list of ongoing projects, user groups, resource centers, organizations, computer learning places, and software clearinghouses.

"Part IV—Continuing Education," another unique section, is an alphabetically arranged, state-by-state listing of accredited colleges (including community colleges) and universities which offer courses in the two broad areas of computer science and educational computing. Each broad area is broken down into eight specific courses in a table which indicates which ones are offered at each institution. Programs are also identified as to level: associate, undergraduate, master's, or doctoral degree.

"Part V—Calendar" contains a two-page month-by-month listing of national conferences followed by a regional compendium of conferences, fairs, and workshops. Each listing includes the location, dates, contact persons or associations, and telephone number where available.

"Part VI—Yellow Pages" is a classified section of commercial resources arranged under the following categories: books and periodicals; book publishers; computer courses and camps; computer stores; computer supplies and catalogs; consultants and programmers; databases; furniture and supplies; hardware: accessories and supplies; hardware: components; hardware: network systems; hardware: peripherals; hardware: systems, service and repair; software: catalogs; software: individual programs; software: magazines; and software: publishers and distributors. An index of advertisers and subjects preceeds the "Yellow Pages."

This is an extremely useful directory for those who need an overview of educational computing resources. If it is updated annually as planned, it should provide an excellent state-of-the-art survey of microcomputer activities.

Microcomputer Market Place. New York: Dekotek, 1982. 207p. $75.00 paper.
ISSN 0735-1925, ISBN 0-911255-00-1.

Order from: Dekotek, Inc.
Box 1863
Grand Central Station
New York, NY 10163
(212) 360-2251

Subtitled *A Comprehensive Directory of the Microcomputer Industry*,
this work is distributed to libraries in the United States and Canada by Gale
Research and is available in quantity at a discount. The directory, similar to
Literary Market Place for books, is divided into twenty-two chapters
beginning with a listing of one thousand software publishers. While the
amount of data for each publisher entry varies, in general the following is
provided: name of company; address; telephone; key company personnel;
number of employees, products published and distributed; applications (e.g.,
education, games, home use); hardware brands; whether outside authors are
published; key contact person; desired submission format; and availability and
price of catalog. This is followed by a hardware compatibility index which
groups software companies under the computer brand for which they furnish
software and covers 90 percent of the approximately seventy hardware systems
currently available.

The next eleven chapters list available software under these broad
categories or applications: business; home; games; preschool education;
elementary education; high school education; college and adult education; and
scientific, utility, and special applications. Particular applications are
identified within each broader category and names of companies publishing
each type of software are listed alphabetically under the appropriate topics.
The special applications section groups software producers under special
industries, professions, or businesses such as agriculture and medical.
Software distributors (i.e., jobbers) and suppliers of microcomputer products
as well as complete systems each have separate index sections.

Other features of the directory include a listing of computer publications,
associations, and software producers/developers/consultants, as well as other
services; and a calendar of meetings and events. This is a useful publication,
not only for schools and universities, libraries, retail stores, and home
computer owners searching for program publishers but also for computer
programming authors seeking potential markets for their software. While it
does not contain actual software listings, it is an invaluable resource for the
information outlined above.

Software Directories

Directories provide an initial listing of commercial and sometimes other
types of programs for purchase consideration. Most of these directories are
arranged by subject and generally also type of program since the majority of
users will be seeking a program in a particular subject area (e.g., an eighth
grade mathematics program) or a certain type (e.g., word processing). This
arrangement facilitates finding programs since titles are often unknown or

nonstandardized, and authors are extremely unlikely to be known by a potential software purchaser.

A few directories like *Swift's Educational Software Directory* are arranged by some means other than subject. *Swift's* groups its programs under type of software producer; hence, one must use the subject index in the quite likely event that one is unaware of what publisher has produced a program in the subject area desired.

Selectors can narrow their search by determining ahead of time the selection criteria used in compiling a directory. For example, certain directories such as *Swift's*, the *School Microware Directory*, or the *TRS-80 Educational Software Sourcebook* are limited to educational programs and, therefore, are unlikely sources for finding video game listings. Other directories are limited to programs which will run only on one brand of computer (e.g., *Swift's* and the *Sourcebook* above) while still others list only programs which they have available for purchase (e.g., *Queue*).

The majority of directories are non-evaluative in their listings. That is, they list any software which meets the general criteria for inclusion in that directory and for which they can obtain the necessary listing information such as title, publisher's name and address, price, etc. Most, in fact, print a disclaimer disavowing any responsibility for the quality of the software listed. There are two directories which are notable exceptions to this pattern. They are *The Book of Apple Software 1983* and *The Book of Atari Software 1983*, both of which follow a similar format. Each contains hundreds of the most popular software programs for its computer brand and gives a thorough evaluation and a rating (using a scale of A to F) for every program listed. Ratings are provided for such criteria as ease of use, reliability, value for the money, and educational merit. Another exception is the *Electronic Games Software Encyclopedia* which also rates programs.

Excluded from the following directory list are mere catalog listings from individual publishers and other items considered to be mainly promotional in nature. Every attempt has been made to ensure the accuracy of the information included although it is possible that some information may have changed between the writing and the publication of this chapter. (The authors are particularly grateful to the publishers of the directories which follow, almost all of whom provided free copies for preview purposes to facilitate the writing of this chapter.)

The Blue Book for the Apple Computer: The Complete "Where To Find It" Book of Software, Hardware, and Accessories for the Apple II. 2d ed. Chicago: WIDL Video, 1982. Unpaged. $24.95 paper. ISBN 0-684-17793-5.

Order from: WIDL Video, Chicago
5245 W. Diversey Ave.
Chicago, Illinois 60639
(312) 622-9606

This directory attempts to list all software, hardware, and accessories currently available for the Apple computer. There are over 2,300 software and hardware listings and 450 sources for these products including complete names and addresses.

The main part of the directory is composed of software programs alphabetically arranged under fifty-seven broad subject categories. Included under education are advanced mathematics, basic learning skills, biology, business management, chemistry, computer science, demonstration programs, electronics, elementary mathematics, energy, engineering, foreign language, general science, graphics, health, language arts, music, physics, school administration, social studies, statistics, utilities, and word processing.

The resource section, or second major part, lists boards, peripherals, accessories, systems to increase data storage, devices to control power supplies, regulation and static control, special Apples (e.g., an Apple for the Arabic language), networking systems, and time-sharing and communications hardware.

Final sections contain books, magazines, other Apple publications and a miscellaneous section with such items as Apple sketch pads for writing programs and graphic aid sheets.

Each listing has a unique identification number, gives the program/ product's title or name, a source number which refers the user to the directory of producers and suppliers, and a comprehensive description of the product. System requirements such as the program format (cassette or disk), storage size (K) of the computer needed to run the program, number of disk drives, language, and peripherals needed (e.g., printer) are stated. Documentation or users' guides are noted and the prices are given for most items. Illustrations are provided for many of the programs and products described. Users of this directory may keep current by subscribing to the publisher's Apple Software Update Service which comes in a three-ring binder supplemented by four quarterly updates of new material throughout the year.

This directory, while featuring exclusively Apple compatible products, is in no way connected with the Apple Computer Company. Products included are not endorsed by the publisher.

The Book of Apple Software 1983, edited by Jeffrey Stanton, Robert P. Wells, and Sandra Rochowansky. Los Angeles: The Book Company, 1983. 491p. $19.95.

> Order from: The Book Company
> 11223 S. Hindry Ave.
> Los Angeles, CA 90045
> (800) 421-3930
> in California call collect
> (213) 417-3003

A unique publication which not only lists and describes over five hundred of the most popular programs currently being sold, this directory also evaluates and rates each software title included. While this volume is limited to Apple programs, there is a companion volume for Atari computers — *The Book of Atari Software 1983* — similar in format and content. There are four major software sections grouping programs by type: (1) "Business," which includes modeling, general business, accounting, word processing, database management, stock market programs, mailing lists, and personal finance; (2) "Education," including reading and language skills, mathematics, science, health and body, and geography and social studies; (3) "Utility Programs," which contains general utilities, assemblers, compilers, languages, communications, and graphics; and (4) "Games and Entertainment," including a wide variety of games grouped by type (e.g., fantasy and role playing, puzzle and strategy, etc.). The final two sections are "Apple Hardware" and "Software Houses," alphabetically listing software producers' mailing addresses and telephone numbers. An alphabetical index by product name is included in the directory.

Within each software section, programs are listed by title and the following are given for each: company, language, hardware requirements, department (e.g., education), suggested retail price, availability (whether or not a program is available from many or only a few dealers using a scale of 1 to 10, 10 meaning it is available from most dealers), whether disk or tape, separate ratings for eight to twelve individual items which vary with the type of software being reviewed, and an evaluative description of the program. Educational software is rated on nine items which include: overall rating, educational value, vendor support, ease of use, documentation, visual appeal, error handling, reliability, and value for money. The scale used is A to F: A = Superior, B = Good, C = Average, D = Poor, F = Unacceptable.

There are twenty-six reviewers listed in the introduction to the directory although individual program reviews are not signed. Special features include charts which compare different programs of the same type (e.g., word processor programs) and articles describing the types of programs. The section on word processing is particularly good. Typical educational listings are about half a page in length, but some, like the one on LOGO, run to three pages. Increasing the number of pages devoted to educational programs (currently approximately 45 pages compared to over 190 on games and entertainment) would greatly enhance the usefulness of this directory for educators. Format is excellent and extremely readable and many listings contain a sample screen from the program. A few errors were found upon perusal (e.g., while Milliken's Math Sequences were listed in the directory, Milliken's name and address could not be found in the listing of software houses), but the directory remains extremely useful despite its limitations.

The Book of Atari Software 1983, edited by Jeffrey Stanton, Robert P. Wells, and Sandra Rochowansky. Los Angeles: The Book Company, 1983. 350p. $19.95.

> Order from: The Book Company
> 11223 S. Hindry Ave.
> Los Angeles, CA 90045
> (800) 421-3930
> in California call collect
> (213) 417-3003

Similar in format and arrangement to *The Book of Apple Software 1983*, this directory lists and evaluates hundreds of programs for the Atari 400 and 800 or 2600 (Video Computer System or VCS). Besides the well-known Atari games, programs are included for a broad range of other areas including business, education, and word processing. Listings provide basic ordering information, a concise description, and an evaluation and rating for each program. A rating system using the letters A through F allows the user to tell at a glance if the program is worthy of purchase consideration. This directory, which will be updated frequently, considers itself the only consumer guide to Atari software.

Commodore Software Encyclopedia. 3d ed. West Chester, Pa.: Commodore Electronics, 1983. 890p. $19.95 paper. ISBN 0-672-21944-1.

Order from: Howard W. Sams and Company, Inc.
4300 W. Sixty-second St.
Indianapolis, IN 46268

A truly comprehensive encyclopedia of Commodore software available for the PET/CBM computers, this directory is divided into fifteen· major sections. Before these sections, however, the following information is provided: (1) a seven-page hardware overview list describing Commodore computer models and peripherals such as disk drives, printers, communications modems, and other hardware; (2) directions for using the encyclopedia; (3) a description of the fifteen categories of software, and (4) information on Commodore computer customer support service with address and telephone number.

The fifteen categories or sections are (1) business; (2) word processors; (3) utilities; (4) engineering aids; (5) personal aids; (6) games; (7) VIC 20; (8) Commodore 64; (9) publications (which lists books, not software); (10) firmware; (11) hardware; (12) selected products of Canada; (13) selected products of Europe; (14) communications; (15) and education subdivided into administrative aids, math and science, and verbal skills and social studies. A standard format is used for all software listings. Following the product name is a description of the program provided by the manufacturer or vendor. Hardware requirements are given as to Commodore model required, memory, and any special equipment. Vendor's name, retail price and a product code complete each listing. All products marketed and supported by Commodore also have the company logo and certain listings also state that they are officially approved by Commodore. This means the product was favorably reviewed and Commodore believes it to be a highly meritorious one. While other listings may not carry this approval seal, a sample has been provided to Commodore and been found to have worked at least reasonably well. The education section contains 280 pages of software listings; however, there are additional listings in other sections which are educational (e.g., an attendance report program in the Canadian software section).

A final section contains new releases for Commodore including both commercial and public domain software. The appendixes list vendors alphabetically giving addresses and telephone numbers and provide user group information arranged by state (with some foreign countries). The final appendix provides a comprehensive directory of Commodore dealers throughout the United States.

The program index arranges software titles alphabetically under, first, Commodore model, and, second, subject category providing an excellent overview of the directory's contents. Black section tabs, large type, and wide margin layout, combined with the extremely comprehensive scope of this work make it a required purchase for Commodore computer users seeking software in all subject areas.

Educational Software Directory: A Subject Guide to Microcomputer Software, compiled by Marilyn J. Chartrand and Constance D. Williams. Littleton, Colo.: Libraries Unlimited, 1982. 292p. $27.50 paper. ISBN 0-87287-352-8.

Order from: Libraries Unlimited, Inc.
               Box 263
               Littleton, CO 80160
               (303) 770-1220

This is a subject listing of software packages (i.e., sets) and individual programs for use in the classroom, K-12, chosen on the basis of educational value. Some programs can be used in high school and college. Criteria for selection included the following: (1) subject matter had to be appropriate to the learning environment and to the computer medium itself (which excluded strictly adventure games or programs which simply reproduced a book); and (2) program had to be usable for the intended grade level; furthermore, (3) any program which was listed in its catalog with a cursory or unclear description and whose producer did not provide better information was excluded unless favorably reviewed in the journal literature. All information contained in the catalog was obtained from publishers' and/or distributors' literature, published reviews, hardware manufacturers' data, or telephone interviews with vendors; no software was actually examined by the compilers. Approximately one hundred organizations provided information.

Software listings are arranged under twelve broad subject categories: general, basic living skills, business education, computer literacy, courseware development (including programs which aid teachers in writing their own software), fine arts, foreign languages, language arts, library skills, mathematics, science, and social sciences. Entries appear within each subject category in alphabetical order by either package or individual program title. Entries for packages contain individual program names and descriptions of each; programs sold individually have separate entries. Each software entry provides the following: an ID number, either the package or the program name, publisher's name (address or phone numbers can be found in the back of the directory), availability from other distributors or supply houses, original release date, grade level, media format in which the package is available, hardware requirements (including model name and number, memory, and necessary peripherals), language (generally BASIC), price, source code, description of the package or program, and a listing of each program title if the item is a total package. Description is taken from catalogs or printed reviews and includes such information as intent, type of feedback, method of presentation, sequencing, reports to the instructor, and documentation. Programs listed appear to be compatible with some of the most commonly used microcomputer systems in education (e.g., Apple II, Commodore PET, Atari 800, TRS-80 models I and III), although programs for others such as North Star are also included.

The four additional sections include an alphabetical listing of software publishers and distributors, a bibliography of software and computer-assisted instruction citations, a subject index and a title index. The publishers' directory, besides providing complete mailing address and telephone number (including toll free 800 numbers when available), also gives such useful information about each company as the availability of demonstration disks, preview arrangements, backup copy and warranty policies, how to order the software, and discounts offered. The annotated bibliography has three sections: "Getting Started," "Selecting and Designing Software," and "Case Studies." The margin index system, keyed to black edge markers, facilitates using the directory.

This directory's page layout and format are excellent for finding programs easily and obtaining basic information quickly. The binding is extremely sturdy (exceeding textbook standards), facilitating extensive and prolonged use.

Electronic Games Software Encyclopedia. New York: Reese Communications, 1983. 114p. $3.95 paper. ISSN 0736-8488.

Order from: Reese Communications, Inc.
460 W. Thirty-fourth St.
New York, NY 10001

This directory describes and rates over five hundred computer games including those for the home arcade systems, the best known and most widely distributed of which is the Atari 2600 (the VCS); and those for the more versatile, multipurpose home computers (e.g., Apple II). The encyclopedia is divided into two major sections according to which type of system the software is compatible with. Game listings in both sections follow the same format and provide name of game; computer brand and model; producer (but not address); retail price; number of players; and ratings for graphics/sound, play-action, solitaire, head-to-head, and overall. In addition, home computer games identify medium and memory requirements plus game category (i.e., adventure, scrolling shoot-out, etc.).

The first major section includes video games for the following machines: Astrocade, Atari 5200, Atari 2600, ColecoVision, Intellivision, and Odyssey. The introduction to this section provides an overview of the six most popular machines in this category while a section at the end provides a more in-depth look at each of these machines and a brief discussion of some of their better known cartridges.

The second major section, which focuses on home computers, commences with an overview of the four most popular brands in this category—the Apple II, the Atari 400, 800, 1200 series, the IBM, and the Commodore VIC 20. Games are then listed and rated by brand under each of these. An article providing a player's guide to computer games and the video game Hall of Fame (most popular games) conclude the directory. Parents seeking purchasing advice and an overview of video games will find this guide useful as will educational programmers who wish to study arcade game techniques in order to incorporate some of the latter's highly motivating features into their software.

Hewlett-Packard Series 80 Software Catalog. 2d ed. Reston, Va.: Reston, 1982. 601p. $12.95. Updated semiannually. ISBN 0-8359-6983-5.

Order from: Hewlett-Packard
Personal Computer Division
Series 80 Users' Library
1010 N.E. Circle Blvd.
Corvallis, OR 97330
(503) 757-2000
(800) 367-4772

Subtitled *Catalog of Application Packages and Contributed Programs*, this directory is a "definitive source for programs available to use with the HP-85, HP-86, and HP-87 personal computers from Hewlett-Packard" including engineering and scientific problem-solving, business applications, and educational/training software. Listings have been compiled and evaluated by the Hewlett-Packard staff and include programs available from both Hewlett-Packard and outside sources. Also included are CP/M programs for use with the HP CP/M System module.

The catalog is divided into two main sections: "Application Packages" and "Contributed Programs." The first section contains commercial programs developed either by Hewlett-Packard or HP PLUS Software Suppliers.

The second section contains programs contributed by Series 80 users and owners as well as by Hewlett-Packard. The latter programs are available for purchase through the Hewlett-Packard Users' Library at nominal cost. Software entries generally include product name; model number of required Series 80 Personal Computer; peripherals or enhancements, needed or optional; a product description including special feastures; retail price (if an application package) or Users' Library price if it is a contributed program; company name and address of contributor or supplier (if not Hewlett-Packard); telephone number; contact person(s); and often additional information such as customer support provided, customer training and documentation, and additional ordering information. Application packages are arranged under the following categories: business/finance, engineering, medical arts/sciences, and other. Contributed programs are grouped under the following areas: business/finance, engineering, math/numerical analysis, probability/statistics, life sciences, physical sciences, social/behavioral sciences, medical arts/sciences, home computing/games, and other. Separate alphabetical indexes of programs by product name or title for each section appear at the end of the book, and there is a numerical listing of all program titles. There are also two cross reference listings of programs which refer the user to Series 80 solution book programs which includes learning programs in math, science, and electrical engineering.

Though of limited usefulness for the K-12 teacher because the majority of programs are for business or industry, some of these may be useful in upper high school grades, particulary in accelerated or business/vocational programs. The Users' Library provides a valuable source of inexpensive software for System 80 users.

Instructor Computer Directory for Schools, edited by Katharine G. Cipolla. New York: Instructor Publications, 1982. 140p. $19.95 paper. Published annually in September. ISBN 0-15-0004357-0.

Order from: Instructor Books
Box 6177
Duluth, MN 55806
(800) 346-0085

The 1982-83 first edition describes itself as a buyer's guide to the selection of microcomputers and peripherals, courseware, computer-assisted and computer-managed instruction systems, books and resources, magazines and journals, and free materials. A slick cover publication, this directory contains nearly two thousand products and four hundred company listings, complete with descriptions, equipment requirements, grade and subject codings, prices, addresses, and telephone numbers. The editors attempted to be encyclopedic rather than selective in their inclusion policy and state that a listing in the directory does not imply endorsement.

The directory is organized into four sections:

1. "Hardware," including peripherals, arranged according to the name of the computer system or peripheral.

2. "Software," with over one thousand listings arranged alphabetically under the following subject categories: art and music, computer literacy, early education, language arts (subdivided into grammar, reading, spelling, vocabulary, writing, and other language arts), languages, lesson writing systems, life skills and guidance, management (subdivided into administration, classroom, library, and special education), mathematics (subdivided into algebra, arithmetic, geometry and trigonometry, graphing, problem solving, and other mathematics), science (subdivided into chemistry, general science, geology and astronomy, life sciences, and physics), word processors, and other software. Each listing gives a brief description of the program, machine compatability, grade level, price, and producer.

3. "Publications," including separate annotated listings of books, magazines, and other resources, which give publisher, author/editor, and prices but do not give addresses for ordering the publications.

4. "Companies," the final section, lists producers/publishers and distributors alphabetically by company name giving address, telephone number, and a phrase describing the nature of the company's products.

The directory is useful for educators as a buying guide in locating program names since it limits software to those with educational value and includes programs for half a dozen brands and over a dozen models of the most popular computers.

International Software Directory: Microcomputers. Fort Collins, Colo.: Imprint Software, 1982. 595p. $59.95 paper. ISSN 0732-3611, ISBN 0-908352-17-0.

Order from: Imprint Software
1520 S. College Ave.
Fort Collins, CO 80524
(800)525-4955
in Colorado call
(303) 482-5000

A companion volume to *The International Software Directory, Volume Two: Minicomputers*, this is volume one of the set. *ISD* is based on the International Software Database, which contains details of over ten thousand programs covering every conceivable application from sophisticated industrial systems to simple domestic packages. While it is not clear how many listings are included in each of the two volumes, the database from which they are generated is accessible on-demand and online, the latter through Lockheed Dialog Information Services. This database is updated on a daily basis.

Like a *Publishers' Trade List Annual* for the software industry, the main section of the directory is arranged alphabetically by name of publisher or producer. Under each company's name are given complete address, telephone number, and terms or information on discounts and credit cards accepted, followed by a listing of programs in International Standard Program Number (ISPN) order, an alphabetical listing by title or name of program. Under each program listed are a description of the software, date of release, warranty availability, whether sole vendor, whether part of a package, whether source code is available, whether updates are available, special equipment needed, system needed, subject code, size of memory needed, distribution medium, and price. If users order software of $250 or more through a special shopping service provided by the publisher, called One Stop Soft Shop, they can receive a complete year's worth of quarterly updates to the directory. Telephone numbers are provided for this service, including toll free access.

There are six indexes in the directory. Four system indexes provide a valuable reference tool by listing programs according to computer system, operating system, language, and microprocessor. Within each system classification programs are listed by subject, then by price. Two additional indexes are a subject index and an alphabetical index, the last listing all programs by title. A page tabbing system for each directory section and each of the six indexes facilitates use of the directory and is keyed to the table of contents. Subheadings under the main heading "Educational" include: Administration, Admissions, Computer Assisted Instruction, Computer Managed Instruction, Counseling, Lab Experiments, Languages, Libraries, General, and Testing.

Listings appear incomplete or missing altogether for some of the major educational software publishers (e.g., McGraw-Hill, Milliken) and a lack of grade level information is a distinct disadvantage for educators in choosing appropriate programs. *ISD* does include programs for many of the less common systems and models of computers, although it is probably more useful for vocational or accelerated student program courseware selection.

JEM Reference Manual, compiled by Denyse Forman, Stuart Crawford, Ross Tennant, Vicky Ogloff, and Donna Iverson. Victoria, B.C.: Software Research, 1980. 850p. $75.00.

Order from: Software Research Corporation
Discovery Park
University of Victoria
Box 1700
Victoria, B.C. V8W 2Y2 Canada
(604) 477-7246

This is a revised, expanded edition of an earlier work called the *Reference Manual for the Instructional Use of Microcomputers* and contains information "to assist the educator in locating, selecting, and integrating commercially available courseware into the elementary, secondary or university curriculum." The manual includes (1) an annotated index of over one thousand educational programs cross-referenced by subject and grade level, (2) catalog reproductions from over fifty publishers and distributors of educational software, (3) descriptors and evaluations of over two hundred programs from well-known publishers and distributors of software, (4) an alphabetical listing of publishers and distributors of computer-related products, (5) a listing and description of peripherals and expansion options for the Apple II microcomputer, (6) an annotated index of books, magazines, and journals related to microcomputer technology and computer literacy; and (7) an update supplement of fifty additional software evaluations.

LAMA Software Directory: The Reference of Apple Computer Software. Bloomingdale, Ill.: LAMA Publications, 1982. 92p. $7.95; $4.95 for a single copy, paper. Published three times a year: January, May, and September.

Order from: LAMA Publications
Box 201
Bloomington, IL 60103

The *LAMA Software Directory* contains over five hundred program listings for Apple compatible software arranged under fifty headings with major and minor subject categories. Listings are grouped under the following: business, educational/classroom, games, home use, music, scientific/engineering, specific profession, statistics/mathematics, system, and word processing.

The educational/classroom section is subdivided into computers, grammar, mathematics, reading, religion, science, spelling, teacher aides, and writing. There is also a section of educational games. Most listings provide title, description, Apple configuration required, price, and order information including complete name, address, and telephone number. Most programs are available from local Apple dealers.

The publishers plan to produce new issues every four months incorporating such additional features as software reviews, Apple users' club news, an Apple calendar of conferences and conventions, and hardware listings. Currently the directory is published three times a year—in January, May, and September—with a year's subscription costing $7.95. Forms are included in the back so that vendors may submit program listings with a $15 minimum charge for this service.

There are fifteen pages of educational programs listed (compared to twenty for games); thus the directory has limitations for educators, and, of course, the listing fee may deter many educational software houses from submitting their programs. A good beginning directory because of its reasonable price, this is particularly so if one subscribes and receives the many new listings scheduled for publication every four months.

Marck Catalogue #3. Branford, Conn.: Marck, 1982. 116p. $4.95.

Order from: Marck
280 Linden Ave.
Branford, CT 06405
(203) 481-3271

A catalog of business and education software for Apple II, Atari, PET, and TRS-80 computers, this edition combines the 1981 *Catalogue #2* and *#3* in what is considered the third edition. Software programs from over fifty publishers are included arranged in two separate sections since catalogs #2 and #3 are not interfiled. Each catalog lists programs first by computer, then by subject embracing language and reading (including foreign languages), skills for aptitude/competency tests, history and geography, mathematics, statistics, economics/political science, biology, chemistry (including pharmacology), physics, astronomy, solar energy, geology, music, sociology and psychology, agriculture, data processing, business (including accounting systems, forecasting, budgeting, investing), electronics/electricity, basic living skills, utility programs for education and business (including grading, testing, enrollment, rosters, data presentation, computer language and programming aids, and office management), computer-assisted instruction, and general usage programs.

In addition to a listing of publishers, there are bibliographies of books about computers and computing, listings of simulations and strategy games, and information about the SPIN/SPIF electronic database which may be used to search the catalog's holdings. Besides selling software, Marck offers consulting and training in the microcomputer area. Educators should check to see if this useful catalog is available to them through a local telephone modem via their computer.

MECC Instructional Computing Catalog. St. Paul: Minnesota Educational Computing Consortium, 1982. 28p. No charge.

Order from: MECC Distribution Center
2520 Broadway Dr.
St. Paul, MN 55113-5199
(612) 638-0627

The *MECC Catalog* contains educational courseware for the Apple II and Atari computers available for purchase from the Minnesota Educational Computing Consortium. Subject areas/applications included are assembly language, training materials, computer literacy, health maintenance, nutrition, mathematics, general science, music, earth science, graphing, language arts, reading, social studies, geography, home economics, art, business education, industrial arts and safety education, special education, and teacher utilities. Program listings are grouped by computer brand and subject area and provide grade level, a description of the program, catalog number, model and computer memory required, format, documentation, and price.

Documentation provided with MECC programs contains learning objectives, lesson plans, student exercises, and worksheets. Although MECC does not provide preview copies of its software, there is a demonstration disk available for purchase containing eight programs and a support manual. The catalog also includes a section of classroom programming texts and in-service training products. In general, programs are compatible with either the Apple II with 48K of memory and DOS 3.3, or the Atari 400 or 800 computer with 16K of memory. Within the state, educators should request the Minnesota version of the catalog.

MECC offers a licensing arrangement to nonprofit educational institutions whereby they may obtain courseware at reduced rates and duplicate or distribute manuals and diskettes to their clientele, also at a reduction. Those seeking institutional license information should call MECC for further details.

MECC has been a nationally recognized leader in the field of educational computing consortia (see description in chapter 7) and its software programs have become some of the best known examples of educational courseware (e.g., Lemonade, Oregon Trail). Their catalog is an invaluable source for locating quality educational software at reasonable prices thus making it an excellent initial reference source for educators as well as parents seeking programs for home computer use.

Queue. 2 vols. plus supplement. Fairfield, Conn.: Queue, n.d. 155p. $8.95.

Order from: Queue, Inc.
5 Chapel Hill Dr.
Fairfield, CT 06432
(800) 232-2224
in Connecticut, Alaska, Hawaii, and Canada call
(203) 335-0908

The two volumes of *Queue*, including *Catalogue #8* containing software for the elementary grades and *Catalogue #9* for high school and college, plus the supplement (*Catalogue #14*), contains educational software for Apple II, Atari, Commodore PET, and TRS-80 computers. Queue claims to be the oldest distributor of educational software in the world, publishing its first catalog in March 1980. The major difference between Queue's and other distributors' catalogs is that its catalogs are updated monthly by *Microcomputers in Education*.

Both catalogs are arranged by broad subject categories. *Catalogue #8* for the elementary grades contains listings under computer education; language arts; reading; elementary education; microcomputers in education; reading — extra special; developmental learning; mathematics — elementary (K-5); mathematics — intermediate (Grades 6-9); science; and social studies. *Catalogue #9*, for high school and college, groups programs under mathematics, reading, English, biology, chemistry, speed reading, physics, foreign language, SAT and GRE preparation, computer programming, typing, word processing, and games and simulations. Besides title, each entry provides name of the software producer; a brief description; occasionally a reference to a review of the program; grade or reading level; compatible computer; and format such as disk, cassette, etc. Use of the catalogs would be facilitated by an index of titles. Addresses for the producers/publishers are not given since Queue is a distributor of their materials (jobber).

School Microware Directory, edited by Bob Haven. Dresden, Maine: Dresden Associates, 1982. 120p. $16.00 per issue. Published semiannually in fall and spring.

Order from: Dresden Associates
             Box 246
             Dresden, ME 04342

Subtitled: *A Directory of Educational Software for Apple, Atari, CBM, PET, VIC-20, TRS-80 Models I-III and Color Computer, and CP/M.* This directory forms a companion volume to *School Microware Reviews* (see discussion under software review journals in chapter 6) and contains a listing of precollege educational software for eight popular brands of microcomputers. A recent issue contained two thousand products from 216 suppliers.

The main part of the directory, Section II, contains instructional software programs listed alphabetically under the following broad subject categories: business, career/occupational, comprehensive programs (useful in most subjects), computer science/literacy, driver education, English (including literature), library skills, fine arts, foreign language, guidance, health, home economics, industrial arts, mathematics, miscellaneous (including basic skills), physical education, science, social science, and special education. Broad categories are subdivided by subject and then topic and sequenced from lowest applicable grade level. A second part of the main section contains summary listings of programs available by hardware system or brand. A final subsection lists all packages and tells what programs are included in each of them. Three additional sections comprise the remainder of the directory: a listing of software for administrative applications, an alphabetical listing of software suppliers' addresses and telephone numbers, and a description of the User Software Review Program. A glossary and two indexes (one to administrative software, the other to instructional courseware) by titles or name of program conclude the directory.

Instructional software descriptions include for each program the following information: department or broad subject category, specific subject, name of the program, type of program designation (e.g., tutorial, skills practice, simulation), graded level(s), product description, hardware systems for which the product is supplied, programming language in which the program is written and the minimum hardware required (i.e., size of computer memory required), format available (disk, tape, etc.), supplier, price, whether program is part of a package and if so where the complete package contents are listed elsewhere in the directory, and total number of programs if it is a package. A special feature is the inclusion for several hundred entries of references to reviews in professional and commercial journals whose titles are listed in the introduction.

The administrative software listing begins with a useful chart summarizing administrative programs available which support school departments such as the library, the principal's office, and the business office. Very small print makes the directory a little hard to read, but otherwise it is an excellent, comprehensive source of educational software.

Skarbek Software Directory. 3d ed. St. Louis: Skarbek, 1982. 435p. $14.95 paper.

> Order from: Skarbek Corporation, Inc.
> 1531 Sugargrove Ct.
> St. Louis, MO 63141
> (314) 567-7180

The *Skarbek Software Directory* contains over one thousand programs for the Apple computer, alphabetized by title within the following broad subject categories: business, database, education, entertainment, graphics, home and personal, programming aids and utilities, special interest, vertical market (including programs for such diverse areas as agriculture, law office management, medical, and property management), and word processing. Each entry includes title of program, publisher, a brief description of the program content, and the price. Some listings in education also give the grade level. Memory needed, or storage capacity of the computer, is mentioned only if more than one disk drive or additional accessories are required to run the program and one assumes program compatibility with the Apple II Plus model unless the listing specifically states that the program is written for the Apple III computer. Prices are for diskette format unless otherwise indicated.

At the end of the directory, there is an eight-page dictionary defining some common computer terms and an alphabetical vendor list complete with addresses and telephone numbers. There is also a subject index which, despite the name, is actually an alphabetical title listing of all programs described in the directory.

A total of sixty-three pages is devoted to educational software. Since there is no specific subject index to the programs listed (e.g., multiplication facts drill, addition facts), it is a little difficult to find an appropriate program unless one already knows the title. The lack of grade or reading levels for most programs also somewhat limits the usefulness of the directory.

Swift's Educational Software Directory: Apple II Edition. Austin, Tex.: Sterling Swift, 1982. 358p. $14.95 paper. ISBN 0-88408-150-8.

> Order from: Sterling Swift Publishing Co.
> 1600 Fortview Rd.
> Austin, TX 78704

Swift's claims to be the most comprehensive list available anywhere of educational software for the Apple II computer with an Applesoft card (i.e., language card) or the Apple II Plus. Programs included fall within the following broad categories: computer literacy or awareness, computer-assisted instruction, courseware development languages and lessons, administrative applications, statistical packages, utility programs (e.g., word processors, plotting programs). All traditional school subjects are included: math, language arts, social studies, science, social science, medical courseware, library courseware, and "self help" lessons. Games included are only those which have a clearly defined educational objective; adventure games are excluded.

Basic arrangement of the directory is by type of software publisher or producer, subarranged alphabetically by name of the company, grouped within the following six major chapters: "Software from Apple Computer, Inc.," "Traditional Education Publishers," "Other Educational Publishers," "Education Software Houses," "Non-Commercial Software," "Other Education Software." Chapter 7 of *Swift's* is a brief listing of education software distributors or jobbers who sell software produced by others. Chapter 8 is a list of publications, both professional and commercial, which have served as sources for the reviews cited in some but not all of the directory listings. Since users generally wish to locate a program on a specific subject, there is an index of software by discipline (subject) and grade level following the master index, which lists all software programs alphabetically by title or program name.

Included under the publisher's name are mailing address, telephone number, often a brief statement of the publisher's software development activity, policy on providing backup disks, and the sort of guarantee which the company offers. There is also information about a company's discount policy on multiple copies or institutional purchases, when these are available. Programs listed under each publisher generally give a description of the program, price, grade level, memory and language requirements, and references to reviews. Programs marked with a special symbol are considered exemplary by the publisher of the directory. Program descriptions are based either on actual examination of the programs or on material supplied from the program's publisher, including ads or other announcements.

TRS-80 Applications Software Sourcebook. Fort Worth, Tex.: Radio Shack, n.d. 263p. plus indexes. $2.95.

Order from: Radio Shack
                Box 17400
                Fort Worth, TX 76102

The *Sourcebook* is a comprehensive, nonselective listing of over twenty-three hundred software programs for use on models I, II, and III, the Color Computer, and the Pocket TRS-80 microcomputers by both professional and amateur programmers who have requested that their programs be listed. Software must be ordered directly from the author (person or company) at the address given, although Radio Shack programs are available at Radio Shack outlet stores. Radio Shack has neither examined nor tested the programs offered by other persons, firms, or companies and does not guarantee any programs except for their own which are offered under Radio Shack's standard terms and conditions.

Programs are listed alphabetically by title under the following broad subject categories: business/accounting, business/inventory control, education—classroom, education—home, game, home/personal use, specific industry/profession, and statistics/math. Computer printout format entries include for each title listed: name of program, minimum equipment required, brief description, source (including name of company and address), telephone number, media format available, and price. The index by application (subarranged alphabetically by title of program) in front of volume three, the most recent edition of the directory, provides a table of contents, and there is a combined index by author (person or company) and by program title at the end of the book.

There are over thirty pages devoted exclusively to listings of educational software but users should consult the *TRS-80 Educational Software Sourcebook* if they wish to see a more comprehensive listing of solely educational programs (see discussion below). Many of the business and/or professional programs listed are of potential use for high school vocational or business education curriculums.

TRS-80 Educational Software Sourcebook. Forth Worth, Tex.: Radio Shack
   Education Division, n.d. 228p. plus indexes. $4.95 paper.

   Order from: Local Radio Shack dealer
                or:
                Radio Shack Education Division
                400 Atrium, One Tandy Center
                Fort Worth, TX 76102
                (817) 390-3832

The *TRS-80 Educational Software Sourcebook* lists programs of an instructional nature for all five models of the TRS-80 currently in use including the Model I, Model II, Model III, Color, and Pocket computers. The major section of software listings is arranged by subject, subarranged by title or name of the software program. Subject categories include business/ finance, computer science, foreign language, language arts, mathematics, reading, science, social studies, teacher/administrator tools, and vocational education. Each listing begins with the subject area, gives complete program title, a brief description of the program, the grade level and type of instruction utilized in the program (e.g., drill-and-practice, tutorial, instructional game) plus TRS-80 model compatibility and memory size needed, format availability (cassette, diskette, etc.) and price. Instructor and administrator user classifications include programs specifically designed for noninstructional applications — such as working with class schedules, keeping attendance and test score records — all aimed at reducing the amount of time spent on clerical work by instructors and administrators. Complete ordering information is given at the end of each listing, avoiding the necessity of having to consult a separate publishers' or vendors' list at the end of the directory, a common requirement in other directories. Besides publisher's name and address, all entries have telephone number(s).

A unique and extremely useful feature of this directory is the indexes provided at the end. These include an index by user level and subject and an index by instructional technique and subject. These allow an educator or parent to quickly find programs aimed at a particular grade or difficulty level or using a particular instructional technique in any given subject area. The user levels indexed are pre-school, primary (grades K-3), intermediate (grades 4-6), junior high/middle school (grades 6-9), senior high (grades 9-12), self-study (all ages), instructor, and administrator. The instructional techniques used to classify programs are drill-and-practice, tutorial, instructional game, simulation, problem solving, and inquiry. Each technique is fully defined for the benefit of users who may not be familiar with a particular mode.

While data included on each program are brief, the excellent organization and, in particular, the indexing of this directory, make it extremely useful in identifying appropriate programs which are compatible with the model of TRS-80 which the instructor is using and also fit the requirements of difficulty level and instructional technique. While Radio Shack has not examined or tested the programs listed from other vendors, it does warranty its own program listings and asks publishers and vendors to submit at least one user site reference for the purpose of substantiating validation claims and providing current user testimonials. Two additional aids to selection in the directory are a list of periodicals on computers in education and a list of addresses of associations and organizations involved in instructional computer use.

Vanloves 1983 Apple II/III Software Directory. Vol. 2. Overland Park, Kans.: Advanced Software Technology, 1982. Various paging. $24.95 paper. ISBN 0-941-520-02-1.

Order from: Advanced Software Technology, Inc.
7899 Mastin Dr.
Overland Park, KS 66204
(913) 648-4442

Although each major section has separate numbering, making counting a task, the publisher claims to have over eleven hundred pages containing three thousand program listings for the Apple computer in this directory. The basic arrangement is by broad subject categories many of which are subdivided by more specific topics. Major categories embrace agriculture, Apple III specific programs, business (including accounting, payroll, real estate, stock market, and tax programs), communications, programming aids and utilities, database management, education, engineering, games, graphics, mailing lists, mathematics, medical, music, personal/home use, special interest, time-sharing, and word processing. The subdivisions under education include administration and counseling, computer aided/assisted-instruction, English/grammar, foreign languages, library science, mathematics, music, science, and social studies. Programs are listed alphabetically by title within each subject category.

The main index located in the front of the directory serves as a table of contents and allows the user to find specific application programs. In addition, there is a complete listing at the beginning of each section of all the programs contained within. The lack of continuous paging is not a problem since the letter/number combination paging system used is in general alphabetical and in logical order (e.g., educational programs are on pages lettered E).

Under each program title are found the publisher's name, a description of the program and its special features, and price. Addresses and, in most cases, telephone numbers are given for all publishers whose names are in the vendor list found at the end of the directory. When diskette price is different from that for the cassette or tape version of a program, such prices are quoted separately. Grade levels are not consistently mentioned (a problem for educators using the directory); however, there are over two hundred pages devoted solely to educational software, making the directory a very good resource for Apple compatible program titles.

Other Software Listings

RICE Online Database. Portland, Oreg.: Northwest Regional Educational Laboratory.

Access from: BRS, Inc.
1200 Route 7
Latham, NY 12110

Another source of software listings is that provided by the RICE (Resources in Computer Education) online database designed and developed by the Northwest Regional Educational Laboratory (NWREL) in Portland, Oregon. This database contains information on some two thousand microcomputer courseware items for use in elementary and secondary education. There are five files or categories of information included in RICE: "Software Packages"; "Producers"; "Computer Literacy," containing objectives and test items for computer education curriculum; "Project Register," describing computer application school projects in K-12; and Inventory, or data on hardware installations and their applications in both elementary and secondary schools. NWREL has gathered the software package information, which includes commercial software, in its database through its national network of twenty-six educational institutions. Since NWREL has also developed its own evaluation process, two hundred of the two thousand courseware packages in RICE have been evaluated by staff members at NWREL-affiliated institutions using their "Evaluator's Guide for Microcomputer-Based Instructional Packages."

For each software package included in RICE, the following information is provided: package title, cost, producer, subject area, grade/ability level, ERIC descriptors, medium (cassette, cartridge, disk), required hardware, required software, type of package, instructional purpose, instructional techniques, documentation available, and evaluation information (for those which have been evaluated). Information from the producer's file includes the organization's name; contact person and telephone number; hardware brands, types, and subject areas for which software is produced by that company; age levels; and modes of instruction utilized.

Information about accessing the RICE database is available from BRS (see above for full address). Most cities will have a local telephone number available to access the database so that users will not have to use long distance telephone service. Cost, once the access is established, will be based on a per minute fee for computer time actually used with an anticipated cost for a single search running less than five dollars. Additional information about the RICE database may be obtained by contacting: Judith Edwards Allen, Director of the NWREL Computer Technology Program, Northwest Regional Educational Laboratory, 300 S.W. Sixth Ave., Portland, OR 97204.

1983 Educational Software Preview Guide, edited by Ann Lathrop. Redwood City, Calif.: San Mateo County Office of Education, 1983.

Order from: California TEC Center Software Library
and Clearinghouse
SMERC Library
San Mateo County Office of Education
333 Main Street
Redwood City, CA 94063

The *Preview Guide* is an alphabetical title listing of programs designed to aid educators in locating software for preview. It includes software favorably reviewed by members of the Educational Software Evaluation Consortium representing seventeen organizations involved in computer education throughout North America. The selection of titles on the list was based on critical evaluations conducted on the software by participants at a forum held in Menlo Park, California, in January 1983, supplemented by references to published review sources. While inclusion of a title on the list indicates it has been favorably reviewed, it does not mean that the titles should be bought without examination. The list is divided into two main parts. Part one is an alphabetical listing by title and gives publisher, computer brands for which the program is available, curriculum area(s), subject or topic of the particular program and price. The second part is a listing by curriculum area giving title, publisher, computer brand, grade level, and mode of instruction. A final section includes an alphabetical listing of publishers, providing complete names and addresses for ordering.

"Courseware Directory." In *Courseware in the Classroom*, by Ann Lathrop and Bobby Goodson. Menlo Park, Calif.: Addison-Wesley, 1983.

The "Courseware Directory" is an alphabetical title listing of recommended educational software for the Apple, Atari, PET and TRS-80 computers. Each listing gives besides title, computer brands, subject area, descriptive annotation, documentation, cataloging information (e.g., Dewey classification number and Sears subject heading), publisher, and title(s) — and names and dates of journals publishing positive recommendations of the software. There is a subject index to programs, and an order form is included for an annual spring supplement.

Computer Magazines and Journals

The following computer journals regularly publish computer program listings. While this survey is by no means comprehensive, it does serve as a representative sample of program source journals. The programs offered may be typed in and run by the reader as is, or they may actually exist on preprogrammed disks or cassettes (e.g., *CLOAD, Window*) which come ready to run. Two possible limitations of these programs are the lack of documentation or instructions for use and the fact that they are often written by amateurs who possess varying levels of programming expertise. However, since the high cost of commercial programs is a major constraint for computer users, these inexpensive programs, obtained simply by purchasing a copy or single issue of the journal, should not be overlooked.

Journals on Disk or Cassette

Chromasette, Box 1087, Santa Barbara, Calif. 93102, (805) 963-1066. $50 tape format; $95 diskette format; $6 per tape or $11 per diskette for a single copy of a back issue. Published monthly.

Produced by the same editorial staff as *CLOAD*, (see below) this journal provides actual software programs ready for use to users of the TRS-80 Color Computer. As of July 1983, it is also available on diskette although originally it could only be purchased on cassette tape.

CLOAD, Box 1448, Santa Barbara, Calif. 93102, (805) 962-6271. $50 tape format; $95 diskette format; $6 per tape or $11 per diskette for a single copy of a back issue. Published monthly.

Not a journal really, but a monthly selection of six to eight software programs which may be ordered on tape or diskette for the TRS-80 Model I or III computer. Programs included are games, educational software, utilities; useful applications such as tax recording systems are also included. Accompanying each issue are three to four pages of printed matter which give a paragraph describing each program and directions for use. *CLOAD* also has separately available groups of game programs on either tape or diskette each of which comes with a booklet giving program particulars. Back issues are available from October 1978 on, making this an excellent source of inexpensive software.

Microzine, Scholastic Inc., 902 Sylvan Ave., Englewood Cliffs, N.J. 07632. $149. Published bimonthly.

Another journal on disk, *Microzine* contains four full-length educational programs on each bimonthly issue for a total of twenty-four programs annually. A comprehensive *Student Handbook and Teaching Guide* accompanies every issue. Diskettes are designed for use on Apple II computers with 3.3 DOS for grades 4 through 8. Types of programs included are reusable utility programs such as word processors, electronic filing systems, or data based management; graphics packages; and computer learning activities.

School CourseWare Journal, c/o School and Home CourseWare, Inc., 1341 Bulldog Ln., Suite C-J, Fresno, Calif. 93710. $90; $24.95 for a single copy. Published five times a year.

School CourseWare Journal consists of educational software programs available either on disk or cassette for four different computer brands: Apple, Commodore, TRS-80, and Atari. When either subscriptions or single issues are ordered, both computer brand and format should be designated. A year's subscription consists of five issues, each containing two educational programs providing the subscriber with a total of ten programs per year. Single back issues contain only one program for $19.95 each thus it is considerably cheaper to subscribe on an annual basis as this permits one to purchase the dual program back issues for $24.95.

The publisher promises that all programs provided will include thorough documentation consisting of a teacher's guide, a student's guide, student worksheets, program logic, and complete program listings. Also included will be tutorials on programming quality and style and reader innovations.

Window. *See* entry under Journals on Disk or Cassette in chapter 6.

Journals Which Publish Program Listings

The Alternate Source
Apple Orchard
BYTE
Call—A.P.P.L.E.
Compute!
The Computing Teacher
Creative Computing
Dr. Dobb's Journal
Educational Computer Magazine
80 Microcomputing
80-U.S.
H & E Computronics
inCider
Interface Age
The Journal of Computers in Mathematics and Science Teaching
Microcomputing
Nibble
Personal Computer Age
Personal Computing
The Portable Companion
The Rainbow
Softalk
Softside
SQ: Syntax Quarterly
Syntax
TRS-80 Microcomputer News
Turtle News and LOGO Newsletter

Complete order information for all of the journals listed may be found in chapter 6, along with prices and other subscription information. Refer to the index for page locations.

Books

The best sources for books which contain program listings are your local computer store, your local book store, computer magazine advertisements, catalog listings from both publishers and jobbers carrying computer-related items, and the displays of computer vendors to be found at local, regional, and national conferences. While it would be impractical to list here all the books which carry program listings, the following provide a sampling of the types available:

An Apple for the Teacher: Fundamentals of Instructional Computing, by George Culp and Herbert Nickles. Monterey, Calif.: Brooks/Cole, 1983.

Essentially a text for teachers, this book has program listings illustrating use of BASIC commands and sample programs for the most common modes of computer-assisted instruction including problem solving, drill-and-practice, tutorial, simulation, and testing.

The Computer Tutor: Learning Activities for Homes and Schools, by Gary Orwig and William S. Hodges. Boston: Little, Brown, 1982.

This contains twenty-five programs using linear, branching, and simulation techniques including the well-known Capitals of Nations, Guess the Numbers, Math Tutor, Spelling Quiz, and Stock Market.

Basic Computer Games, by David Ahl. Morristown, N.J.: Creative Computing Press, 1978.

Game Playing with BASIC, by Donald D. Spencer. Rochelle Park, N.J.: Hayden Press, 1977.

More Basic Computer Games, by David Ahl. Morristown, N.J.: Creative Computing Press, 1978.

All three titles above provide listings of computer games.

Problems for Computer Solutions. 2d ed., by Donald Spencer. Rochelle Park, N.J.: Hayden, 1979.

Problems for Computer Solutions Using BASIC, by Henry M. Walker. Boston: Little, Brown, 1980.

The above works challenge the user by setting up problems which must be solved by writing computer programs.

Computer Games for Businesses, Schools, and Homes, by J. Victor Nahigian and William S. Hodges. Boston: Little, Brown, 1979.

Complete programs are provided for a wide variety of highly entertaining games, from traditional to the unusual, with each game written in 8K of memory.

The Mind Appliance: Home Computer Applications, by T. G. Lewis. Rochelle Park, N.J.: Hayden Press, 1978.

Includes useful programs for the home (kitchen, home office, etc.).

SOURCES OF FREE
AND INEXPENSIVE SOFTWARE

The often high prices of commercial computer software will force many users to seek other software sources which are less costly. Five general sources of free and inexpensive computer software have been identified (Price 1982). These include: computing journals, books, clubs and individuals, educational agencies, and software exchanges. Of course, one will always be tempted to use lesser evaluation criteria or standards for programs obtained free or at a fraction of the cost of commercial ones, but at the very least one should ask several pertinent questions about any program. These include: Does it run on my machine? Does it work? And, for educators, Does it serve any significant educational purpose? If these considerations are ignored when obtaining a software product, something even more valuable than money can be wasted—time.

Educational Computer Magazine carries a regular department called Free and Inexpensive Software Review, which provides reviews of software programs that are either in the public domain or are available for less than normal commercial rates. All the software reviewed in this column is judged to be of good quality. Besides the review itself, author and equipment requirements are designated, and source or order information is provided so that users may obtain the programs reviewed.

Computer user groups are springing up all over the country providing a valuable source of information, support, and programming expertise, and even actual programs. The programs obtained from these groups vary greatly in quality and seldom provide the documentation or user support given by the better software publishers, but this is often more than made up for by their reasonable cost (i.e., they are generally free or very inexpensive and many can be obtained merely for the cost of one's own disk or cassette to store a copy of the shared program). User groups are generally composed of members who use a particular brand of computer (e.g., an Apple user group) or who share some geographic affinity (common school district, city, or state).

User groups which are computer specific (i.e., limited to users of a single computer brand) are listed in Part II of the *Classroom Computer News Directory of Educational Computing Resources*. This same directory also lists in a separate section—Part III—those user groups based on a shared geographic location.

Clearinghouses of contributed and public domain (i.e., non-copyrighted) programs have also begun to spring up around the country. None of these provide truly free programs but operate under a variety of "payment" plans. Some sell their disks for a flat, usually nominal, fee. Others require that the user contribute his or her own original programs. Still others charge a membership fee. The following list is far from all-inclusive but provides a start for those wishing to obtain programs through a software exchange. Beginning sources for software exchange programs should always be local user groups.

The Apple Avocation Alliance, 721 Pike St., Cheyenne, Wyo. 82001. $1 per copy.

Programs are available from this library on a broad range of topics, including educational application. A $2.50 mailing list fee brings the user a catalog/newsletter several times a year. Programs may be copied on one's own disk for one dollar per disk or on disks purchased from the exchange at discount prices.

Apple Puget Sound Program Library Exchange, 304 Maine Ave. S, Suite 300 Renton, Wash. 98055. $20 with subscription to *Call—A.P.P.L.E.* plus $25 one-time membership fee.

Operated by the Puget Sound Apple Club, the largest Apple Computer Club in the country, this group also publishes *Call—A.P.P.L.E.* Programs included are both utilities and general interest programs.

Georgia Micro Swap, Department of Mathematics Education, University of Georgia, Athens, Ga. 30602. $15 membership.

Members periodically contribute programs and in return receive programs contributed by other members. One cannot receive programs without contributing some. In some years, contributions are limited to programs for a single brand of computer.

North Dakota Council of Teachers of Mathematics Program Exchange, David McCormack, Makoti, N. Dak. 58756.

Teachers may purchase either the actual programs on tape or simply the source code at minimal cost to cover tapes, postage, etc. If a program is submitted, two free programs may be obtained in exchange with the only charge being postage. Mostly mathematical programs are available but some in classroom management (e.g., student grade record keeping) are also included.

SOFTSWAP, Microcomputer Center, San Mateo County Office of Education and Computer-Using Educators, 333 Main St., Redwood City, Calif. 94063. $10 per disk.

Disks sell for $10 each but users may contribute disks or original programs to receive free disks. The collection includes public domain programs of educational value for a variety of computer brands (Apple, Atari, PET, and TRS-80). Orders must be prepaid. A complete catalog of disks is available for one dollar or the user may refer to the April 1983 issue of *The Computing Teacher* which published the complete catalog. This exchange has a comprehensive listing of available programs on a broad range of topics including mathematics, graphics, games, authoring programs, language arts, social studies, and science.

Two additional organizations which operate a program exchange clearinghouse are the Michigan Association for Computer Users in Learning and the Nebraska Clearinghouse for Microcomputer Software. Both of these groups are described in chapter 7 which also gives the addresses to which one may write for additional information and their program listings. Despite the drawbacks discussed above, these exchange programs are an invaluable source of inexpensive software for computer users and should be fully exploited by anyone wishing to establish a comprehensive software collection.

Programming One's Own Software

Programming or creating one's own software is another solution to the twin problems of poor quality and high cost of commercial software. Such in-house programs have the advantage of immediacy and relevancy, particularly in a school and/or classroom situation. Teachers, administrators, parents, and even students themselves can participate in the programming activity which offers a tremendous learning experience to those who create software.

The authors, however, see two or three rather obvious disadvantages to this practice in an academic setting. In the first place, few teachers or other educators possess the expertise to do a professional, thorough job of programming. Those who have used commercial software are already well aware of how easy it is for even professionals in the business to produce software which contains programming errors and other problems. Another disadvantage, particularly for those who do not possess a computer science background, is the enormous amount of time required to write even a simple program. Teachers are seldom given sufficient release time to write computer programs and, since they generally do not possess the polished skills nor even an awareness of the programming shortcuts available to the professional programmer, they require even more time for writing the programs than would be normal.

There are aids, called authoring systems, which teachers can use to help them in creating their own lessons and Lathrop and Goodson (1983) provide a concise, though brief, description of the types of resources available. A special programming language called PILOT has been developed specifically to help teachers develop their own materials. There are also many other programs available which allow a teacher varying degrees of flexibility in lesson construction ranging from ready-to-use lesson frameworks to more open-ended, less structured authoring systems. Shell Games and The Game Show are two examples of the former while TRS-80 and Apple PILOT are representative of the latter. Lathrop and Goodson caution that learning to use the more advanced authoring systems requires a good deal of time and study but that their potential for helping to create some excellent new educational software is tremendous.

There has been, though, some controversy over the whole question of whether or not teachers should even be involved in writing, at the taxpayers' expense, computer software which if it is later sold, will be in direct competition with that being developed and sold by commercial publishers operating in the free enterprise system. It becomes an ethical and an economic question and possibly even a legal one, which has not been resolved.

OBTAINING SOFTWARE TO
PREVIEW AND OTHER ORDERING TIPS

Microcomputer software, like many other nonprint media formats which represent a sizable monetary investment, can often only be properly evaluated by obtaining a sample of the product itself, called a preview copy, and examining it on a firsthand basis. Until about a year ago, publishers and producers of commercial software programs were extremely reluctant to send preview copies to the potential purchasers of their courseware. As we explained earlier, the reason for this was quite simple: It was an easy matter to copy a software program, return the original version to the publisher indicating it was unsuitable, and end up using the copy without any compensation being provided to the producer. How often this may actually have occurred will probably never be known, but the mere fact that it is possible to perpetrate this sort of software piracy deterred many early producers from extending preview privileges to their customers.

A survey by Hoover and Gould (1982) of software houses which produced Apple compatible programs found that 75 percent did not allow preview although 45 percent permitted purchase with a return option. Either a ten-day or a thirty-day return was the usual policy with almost three-fourths giving a full refund. Ironically, nearly two-thirds of the producers do not copy protect their programs. The survey found that 50 percent of the producers considered illegal copying either a serious or moderate threat to profits, and those least likely to allow preview are the very producers whose programs are *not* copy protected.

Furthermore, almost three-fourths of the producers do *not* provide backup copies. (A backup copy is an extra copy in case the original is damaged, lost, or otherwise unusable.) Those who do provide backup copies for purchase generally charge approximately ten dollars and over 80 percent of the producers are willing to negotiate a special price for school districts desiring multiple copies. Thus, there is a strong case for negotiation on special prices for multiple copies and/or licensing agreements. The making or purchasing of additional copies at a reduced rate should be negotiated and agreed upon in writing at the time of the original purchase to obtain the most beneficial terms or conditions.

Two articles (Glotfelty 1982; Lathrop 1983) indicate how the non-preview practice has been turned around recently and Lathrop's article lists thirteen jobbers or mail-order distributors who sell software allowing full preview privileges and, generally, a thirty-day return option for unsatisfactory courseware. These companies are *

AMERICAN MICRO MEDIA
Box 306
Red Hood, NY 12571
(914) 756-2557   Apple, Atari, PET, TRS-80

---

*Reprinted by permission. Copyright 1983 by Educational Computer, PO Box 535, Cupertino, CA 95015. Sample issue $3.00, 10-issue subscription $25.

CHARLES CLARK CO., INC.
168 Express Drive South
Brentwood, NY 11717
(516) 231-1220   Apple, Atari, PET, TRS-80

EAV (EDUCATIONAL AUDIO VISUAL)
Pleasantville, NY 10570
(800) 431-2196   Apple, PET, TRS-80

EISI (EDUCATIONAL INSTRUCTIONAL SYSTEMS, INC.)
2225 Grant Rd., Suite 3
Los Altos, CA 94022
(415) 969-5212   Apple, Atari, PET, TRS-80

FOLLETT LIBRARY BOOK COMPANY
4506 Northwest Highway
Crystal Lake, IL 60014
(800) 435-6170   Apple, Atari, PET, TRS-80,
                    TRS-80 Color Computer

GAMCO
Box 310-P
Big Spring, TX 79720
(915) 267-6327   Apple, PET, TRS-80

J. L. HAMMETT CO.
Box 545
Braintree, MA 02184
(800) 225-5467   Apple, PET, TRS-80

K-12 MICRO MEDIA
Box 17
Valley Cottage, NY 10989
(201) 391-7555   Apple, Atari, PET, TRS-80

THE MICRO CENTER
Box 6
Pleasantville, NY 10570
(914) 769-6002
(800) 431-2434   Apple, Atari, PET, TRS-80

OPPORTUNITIES FOR LEARNING
8950 Lurline Ave.
Chatsworth, CA 91311
(213) 341-2535   Apple, Atari, PET, TRS-80

SCHOLASTIC
904 Sylvan Avenue
Englewood Cliffs, NJ 07632
(800) 631-1586   Apple, Atari, PET, TRS-80, TI-99/4

SUNBURST
39 Washington Ave.
Pleasantville, NY 10570
(800) 431-1934   Apple, Atari, PET, TRS-80

SVE/SOCIETY FOR VISUAL EDUCATION, INC.
1345 Diversey Parkway
Chicago, IL 60614
(800) 621-1900   Apple, Atari, PET, TRS-80

Since so many publishers and jobbers, who sell software from a number of software companies, are now extending preview privileges, it is incumbent upon purchasers to understand what this service implies. It generally allows a customer to keep the software for a thirty-day trial evaluation period during which the programs may be run for purposes of determining whether or not they suit one's educational objectives and are the best programs available for the money. If, after evaluation against a suitable checklist, they are found to be unsatisfactory, all copies ordered should be sent back within the thirty-day trial period along with a copy of the checklist indicating why they are being rejected. Under no circumstance should copies be made of materials to be returned. In fact, only copies specifically authorized and approved by the publisher through the existence of a written agreement should ever be made. The purchase of a single copy does not permit the making of multiple copies for districtwide, schoolwide, or even classroom use. Unauthorized copies are in direct violation of the U.S. Copyright Act of 1976.

6

AIDS TO SELECTION:
MICROWARE JOURNALS

The rapid changes going on in the computer field make it virtually impossible to keep up with new developments through books alone. Product reviews in magazines and journals have traditionally been one of the most valuable aids to selection of materials in both print and nonprint media formats. These reviews can first identify titles for consideration and then help one to choose among titles on a qualitative basis.

The burgeoning development of microcomputers has been accompanied by a corresponding proliferation of journals. These journals chronicle new developments in the field; announce and review new products, including hardware, peripherals, and software; and provide articles on a broad range of topics from basic education of the new computer user (*Personal Computing*) to advanced programming techniques (*Dr. Dobb's Journal* and *BYTE*). Many journals, as noted in chapter 5, include actual computer program listings which may be typed in and actually run by the computer user.

Computer periodicals may be broadly grouped into two major categories. These include computer-specific journals aimed at owners/users of particular brands of systems (e.g., Apple, Atari) and general interest periodicals written for the enthusiast who might be using any brand of machine. The latter category may be further subdivided by a focus on a specific group such as mathematics teachers or business users, or by a special journal emphasis like software reviews. This chapter provides listings, many with discussions, of those journals felt to be most useful for two major purposes. The first is directly related to the major theme of this book: selection of microcomputer software. Journals which carry reviews of programs are included with, whenever possible, a description of the special features and the nature of the reviews carried. The secondary purpose for consulting the journals listed is simply to keep up with developments in one's field or to find information on a specific brand of hardware. Both of these purposes are significantly related to making software selection decisions; hence, the inclusion here of some journals which, although they do not review software at all, are important to this secondary function.

The best reviews, it is felt, include the following features:

1. reviewer's name, title, and institutional affiliation

2. the complete title or name of the program being reviewed preferably at the beginning of the review and set apart from the text in some manner (e.g., in bold face letters or underlined) so that one can quickly identify the program's name

3. publisher's/producer's name, complete ordering address, and telephone number, as well as program price

4. a clear, concise program description or summary

5. type of program designation (e.g., game, educational, business)

6. computer brand and model compatibility, memory size needed, and any special requirements necessary to run the program (e.g., Apple II Plus, 48K with two disk drives)

7. specific evaluation criteria stated (a set format is helpful)

8. a rating summary using a clearly understandable scale (e.g., letters A through F, or numbers 1 through 5)

9. a final recommendation to purchase or not.

Some common weaknesses in software reviews include omitting many or most of the above items. It is very frustrating to read a review of a truly exciting, highly rated program only to discover that there is incomplete order information and one must then spend an hour or more searching software directories for a complete mailing address. It is particularly helpful in reviews if the format includes a summary rating boxed off from the rest of the review text so that one can tell at a glance whether the reviewer felt the program was worthwhile or not. *Classroom Computer News* includes this summary rating in its "*CCN* Profile" which is set into each software review. These profiles also include the title of the program, price, order information, brand, and other basic data.

Although the quality of reviews varies greatly from journal to journal, in general it is felt that most reviews of microcomputer software contain useful evaluative criticism—reviewers are not hesitant about pointing out major weaknesses or flaws in the programs.

A special feature which many review sources often include at the end of a review is a publisher's response to the written review. Both *Classroom Computer News* and *School Microware Reviews* regularly feature rebuttal comments by the software producer and these are often helpful for an important reason: Microcomputer programs, unlike printed books or films, can be easily and quickly modified in response to weaknesses or problems and, in fact, many software publishers use formative evaluation to improve their products. When one reads, therefore, in the publisher's response to a review that changes have been made which eliminate weaknesses pointed out by the reviewer in an otherwise acceptable program, one could confidently consider that software title for purchase.

The credentials of the reviewers, while not always given, help one evaluate their qualifications for reviewing a particular program. These credentials where they are stated are often quite impressive.

The journals listed and discussed on the following pages are grouped into eleven categories according to the major emphasis or focus of the journal.

These categories are (1) review journals and services, (2) educational computing journals, (3) computer journals, (4) education journals (which include computer articles and/or reviews), (5) computer-specific journals (which are limited to one brand of computer), (6) newsletters from both computer user groups and other groups, (7) publications on microcomputers in libraries, (8) journals on disk or cassette, (9) newsweeklies, (10) computer magazines for children, and (11) computer hardware reviews. A final section lists and discusses indexes to computing journals and other related literature.

Many journals, unfortunately, cannot be neatly categorized and fit into two or more of the groups. The authors' ultimate decision in regard to the appropriate category was based on where it was felt the title would prove most helpful to users of this book and cross references are used wherever deemed necessary. While the majority of the eleven categories above are self-explanatory, two groups may need clarification. Review journals and services includes, besides the typical journal format, those evaluation products published by review services which, while they may not necessarily conform to the standard definition of a journal, are reviews of software published on a regular basis. *Courseware Report Card*, for example, is essentially a set of reports published by a review service three times a year and consists of a series of three-ring loose-leaf sheets of from two to four pages per review.

Journals on a disk or cassette tape are another nonstandard format and an innovation particularly appropriate for computer-related serials. *Window* is one example of this new approach and includes (on an Apple-compatible diskette) articles, programs to be run, and reviews of software which include a sample excerpted from the program being reviewed. The publishers plan to produce similar journals for other computer brands in the future.

All of the journals listed on the following pages include at a minimum the title, publisher's address, telephone number if available, price for one year's subscription, and frequency of publication. Addresses given are for subscription departments, not for the editorial offices which are often located in entirely different cities and, in some cases, even separate states. Often, however, the telephone number of the subscription office was not available, and, therefore, the number given is for the editorial office. Many entries also include a complete annotation with an introductory paragraph giving the nature of the publication, a listing of special features, and a description of the software reviews included in the journal.

In a field which is changing as rapidly as microcomputing, the only way to keep up-to-date with the technology is through periodicals. One may wish to read, besides the quarterly and monthly journals, at least one weekly newspaper such as *Infoworld*, which carries industry news as well as software reviews. Perhaps the only certain thing in this dynamic field is that what is true today will probably appear quite different tomorrow as new products force earlier ones into obsolescence. Keeping up with the periodicals, which fluctuate almost as much as the related technology, will in itself prove to be a challenge.

REVIEW JOURNALS AND SERVICES

Apple Journal of Courseware Review. *See* entry under **Journal of Courseware Review.**

Booklist, American Library Association, 50 E. Huron St., Chicago, Ill. 60611. (312) 944-6780. $40; $2.25 for a single copy. Published twice monthly September through June, monthly July and August.

The purpose of *Booklist*, a long established, standard selection tool, is "to provide a current guide to materials worthy of consideration for purchase by small and medium-sized public libraries, school media centers, and community college libraries." It normally carries book reviews of adult nonfiction and fiction, young adult and children's books, many special thematic sections in each issue (e.g., computer books, picture books for older children), and reviews on nonprint materials including films, filmstrips, video formats, and, recently added, microcomputer software. *Reference and Subscription Book Reviews*, formerly a separate publication, is still an autonomous publication which now comes at the end of the *Booklist* reviews and carries evaluations of both recommended and not recommended books. All works reviewed in *Booklist* itself are recommended and those with an asterisk indicate an item particularly good in its genre. Wide coverage makes *Booklist* an indispensable tool for librarians and media specialists.

Reviews: All reviews regardless of format of the material being reviewed follow a set form. Works are arranged alphabetically by author within the appropriate subject or age categories and each review provides title of the work, date, paging and illustration, publisher, price; if read in galley proofs, month of release; initials of the reviewer; and cataloging information including Dewey number and suggested subject heading. Microcomputer software reviews include machine compatibility, memory and peripheral equipment required, format, and whether a manual is included. There is also an indication of user age level. Reviews run approximately one-third of a column in length.

Courseware Report Card, 150 W. Carob St., Compton, Calif. 90220. (213) 637-2131 or (213) 979-1955. $49.50 elementary grades K-6; $49.50 secondary grades 7-up; or $95 for both levels. Published five times a year.

Basically a service providing evaluations of microcomputer programs for education, *Courseware Report Card* is available in two editions: Elementary for grades K-6 and Secondary for grades 7-12. Each edition appears five times during the school year with a typical issue containing between twenty and twenty-five software reviews from a wide variety of subject areas, formats, and applications including drill-and-practice, tutorials, simulations, games, authoring systems, and management programs. Programs included are for Apple II, Atari 400 and 800, PET/CBM, and TRS-80 computers. To facilitate finding programs for the right brand of computer, a table of contents precedes each issue and, besides an alphabetical listing of each program by title with the producer's name, a chart next to each title indicates the hardware compatibility of the program.

Reviews: All reviews are separate reports on 8½x11-inch three-hole punched sheets, ranging in length from two to four pages. The format is excellent for obtaining both basic information and a rating on each program quickly and efficiently. The first page of each review contains the following information set off in a box in the upper left corner: subject area, grade level, type of program (e.g., tutorial, drill-and-practice), system requirements, price, and order information including publisher and address. In the upper right corner beneath the program title is a brief two to three line description of the program. In the lower right, again boxed, is a capsule summary rating of the program on each of the following six criteria: performance, ease of use, error handling, appropriateness, documentation, and educational value. Ratings range from A to F on the six criteria, and reviews vary from five hundred to two thousand words, many including reproductions or facsimiles of screen displays.

The narrative of each review includes a complete description of the program followed by an evaluation section which covers the six criteria listed above in detail, explaining why each was evaluated as it was. Reviews appear frank and critical and where the reviewers feel there is no educational value they do not appear afraid to rate the program low or to state exactly why.

Mark Falstein, managing editor of *CRC* is the former editor of *The Electronic Classroom*, a newsletter on computer applications in education. Reviews, unless otherwise indicated, are based upon the evaluation of one or more members of the *CRC* editorial staff. Every reviewer is identified as a former classroom teacher, by implication possessing considerable experience in both development and evaluation of curriculum materials. The names and credentials of each reviewer appear in the preliminary sheet which accompanies each issue and also contains a Comments and Complaints section where software publishers may respond to criticisms of their products from earlier issues. Overall, reviews appear high in quality with sound criticism. All school districts and any individual schools which can afford it should subscribe to this excellent service.

Courseware Reviews 1982: Fifty Classroom-Based Evaluations of Micro-computer Programs, SMERC Library Microcomputer Center, San Mateo County Office of Education, 333 Main St., Redwood City, Calif. 94063. (415) 363-5470. $10 for a single copy.

Courseware Reviews is the product of group software evaluations conducted by the California Library Media Consortium for Classroom Evaluation of Microcomputer Courseware. This first set of fifty evaluations of Apple, PET, TRS-80, and Elvie (a *dedicated* educational microcomputer available from Learning Ventures) programs is based on a total of 147 reviews contributed by educators in twelve California counties. At the time of printing, over 200 additional reviews had been received and will be published in future issues. To be included, a program had to have at least two separate reviews, and if the first two reviewers did not agree in their findings, additional reviews were sought until a pattern could be determined. At least one of the reviews included student input and reaction to the program during classroom use.

There is a separate alphabetical list of program titles (although this is the overall arrangement) and reviewers are listed at the beginning though not individually identified for each review. A subject index, a computer brand index, and a publishers' directory complete the work.

An excellent, inexpensive source of software evaluations for those wishing to start a good basic library of reviews, this work and future issues which become available should be seriously considered by educators for purchase.

Reviews: Each review is provided on a standard form which begins with the following information in a box at the top: equipment and language requirements; suggested subject(s), grade level(s) and type of program; publisher and price; contents; appropriate group size(s); and scope of the program. The annotation which follows gives purpose, content, and classroom use of the program and there is a listing of other journals which review the program. Comments are provided for program strengths, weaknesses, and documentation, and for student response. A "Checklist of Evaluation Criteria" completes the form. At the top of this section the total number of reviews is indicated and criteria are grouped under general factors, content, instructions, input, and screen format. The evaluations conclude with an overall opinion which ranges from great program (highly recommend) to not useful (don't recommend purchase). The total number of reviewers checking each choice is indicated.

The Digest of Software Reviews: Education, c/o School and Home Course-Ware, Inc., 1341 Bulldog Ln., Suite C-5, Fresno, Calif. 93710. $38.95 to schools, colleges and educators; $48.95 to others. Published quarterly.

Edited by Ann Lathrop, an educator/librarian active in both evaluation and selection of educational software, this professional quarterly for buyers of microcomputer programs for schools contains profiles of fifty administrative and instructional programs per issue plus digests of two hundred reviews of those programs, gathered from over thirty journals and newsletters which regularly review software. Besides carrying the digests of software reviews, *DSR* provides (1) an easy-to-use cumulative index of reviews published, (2) digests of reviews of important administrative software, and (3) indexing by title, subject, publisher, and microcomputer system.

Providing both an index to reviews and summaries of these reviews, *DSR* should be an invaluable aid in educational software selection.

Reviews: Each program included appears on a single 8½x11-inch, three-ring punched sheet which fits in a special binder provided free to *Digest* subscribers. Entries give title of program, producer's name and address, price, system requirements, contents of package, publisher's suggested grade level, suggested instructional group size, instructional mode, Dewey Decimal classification number, Sears subject heading(s), and ERIC descriptors. Following the publisher's description of each program are digests or excerpts of comments from reviews of the software. Each *Digest* citation gives, besides these excerpts from the reviewers' comments, the journal title, date, reviewer's name, and page to aid easy location of the original review.

Journal of Courseware Review, The Apple Foundation, Apple Computer, Inc., 20525 Marian Ave., Cupertino, Calif. 95014. (408) 996-1010. $5.95 for a single copy. No subscriptions. Available from the Foundation prepaid (no purchase orders accepted) or through local dealers. Published irregularly.

The *Journal of Courseware Review* is published by the Apple Education Foundation's Educational Program Evaluation Centre (EPEC) established by Apple Computer, Inc., to "foster excellence in computer-assisted education." Through its *Journal*, the Foundation aims to establish an impartial source of reviews on quality microcomputer courseware. Apparently the *Journal* was begun with the idea of publication on a regular basis since subscription information in the first issue has been covered with a sticker stating that there are no subscriptions and that copies of current and future issues are available through Apple Computer dealers. To date, only two issues have appeared, both having different numbering systems. Volume I, number 1, appeared in October 1981, and the next issue, called Issue 1, was published in July 1982. Each issue follows the same format and while at least one article in each is devoted to instructional computing concerns (e.g., how to evaluate educational courseware), the remainder of the text is devoted entirely to reviews of educational software programs, which programs have been submitted by their producers. An effort was made to choose some of the better known, more exemplary programs available either from commercial sources or from educational consortia such as the Minnesota Educational Computing Consortium for the initial issues of the *Journal*. The second issue states that the reviews are "intended to identify models of excellence in program design and development." The Foundation, which funds grants for courseware development, plans to announce programs resulting from their grants and to include reviews of these programs in future issues.

Reviews: All reviews are signed by authors whose credentials and institutional affiliations are fully identified. Many are by recognized leaders in the educational computing field although anyone may volunteer to be a reviewer of the programs. There are suggested review criteria available which include instructional design, user level, documentation, support of educational process, user interest, programming quality, importance of subject matter, innovative use of technology, overall recommendation, and suggested improvements.

Besides addressing the above considerations, reviewers identify at least four sample screen displays from the program which are reproduced in the review and give the reader an excellent idea of what the graphics and other program output looks like. Each review also includes the program title, program type, identification, and a brief paragraph describing its operation. At the end of the review, there are two summaries of the basic courseware information: (1) cataloging information, which provides the Dewey decimal number, an ERIC descriptor and Sears subject headings and (2) source information, which restates title, and gives complete order information including publisher's name and address, equipment needed, package components, and price. Reviews average four to five pages, and reviewers appear to be chosen for their special expertise in a particular program area.

The second issue contains a complete index to articles and reviews in both the issues. Reviewers are critical and evaluative in their discussions and, although EPEC has prescreened and preselected programs felt to be exemplary, the authors still do not hesitate to recommend against purchase of some of the software. There are fifteen reviews in each issue, all of educational software. The major limitation of the *Journal* is its exclusion of programs for other computer brands besides Apple. It would be helpful if all manufacturers of computers used extensively in education regularly published similar journals reviewing compatible courseware for their brands.

MACUL Journal. *See* entry under Educational Computing Journals.

Microcomputers in Education, Queue, 5 Chapel Hill Dr., Fairfield, Conn. 06432. (800) 232-2224; in Connecticut, Alaska, Hawaii, and Canada call (203) 335-0908. $33; $4.50 for a single copy. Published monthly.

Published by Queue, Incorporated, which claims to be the oldest distributor (i.e., jobber) of educational software in the world and "the only one with over 2,000 programs from over 100 publishers," this journal includes reviews, analyses of industry developments, articles, and news of interest to computer users in education. Subscribers to *MIE* receive a 10 percent discount and thirty-day return privilege on all software ordered from Queue.

The journal offers a list of new software releases (actually a list of new software available from Queue, arranged by subject), computer company portraits, magazine and book reviews, hardware reviews, and a calendar of shows and meetings.

The frequent typographical errors and small print are somewhat distracting. *MIE* is probably most useful as a finding list of titles for purchase consideration since its major purpose is to help Queue sell software.

Reviews: MIE carries few original reviews but rather excerpts software review comments from *Courseware Report Card*, *The Computing Teacher*, *School Microware Reviews*, *Electronic Learning*, and others, and tells which programs are available from Queue.

MIE contains MicroSIFT reviews from the Northwest Regional Educational Laboratory in the standard "MicroSIFT Courseware Evaluation" format (see page 127). Tables give an evaluation summary and a final comment states whether the three or more reviewers would recommend use of the program. Three MicroSIFT evaluations appeared in a recent issue of *MIE*.

The occasional original reviews by *MIE* writers do not follow a set format but evaluate new programs available from Queue in essay-style reviews running several pages in length. Besides describing program contents, reviews point out major weaknesses and flaws and problems encountered by students who were used for field testing. Since the reviews conclude by saying how to order the software from Queue, one wonders about objectivity.

Micro-Courseware PRO/FILES, EPIE and Consumers Union, Box 839, Water Mill, N.Y. 11976. (516) 283-4922. $125 with monthly updates.

A subscription begins with sixty courseware *PRO/FILES*, updated monthly with additional, current software reviews. There is a companion service available for hardware evaluations (see entry under Computer

Hardware Reviews) called *Microcomputer Hardware PRO/FILES* and various other services which are available from EPIE/CU are described in chapter 7. Selected *Micro-Courseware PRO/FILES* appear in issues of *Computing Teacher*.

Reviews: Reviews begin with title of package; computer brand and system requirements; package components; supplier's name, address and telephone number; curriculum role; copyright date; and author, if applicable. The two to four page product evaluations contain easy-to-scan ratings and in-depth critical reviews of both the instructional and technical qualities of courseware covering major school curriculum areas and grade levels. Included are analyst's summary (including recommendations to the producer); a capsule evaluation rating each program for overall instructional quality, technical quality, cost effectiveness, and ease of implementation; user comments; sample frames showing a typical lesson item; student comments; other reviews of the program with quotes from still other sources; comments on how the teacher and student use the program and on the instructional/educational value of the content including potentially controversial topics; and documentation.

Two-page *PRO/FILES* of smaller packages, while including most of the same information as the regular *PRO/FILES*, do so in condensed form.

MicroSIFT Courseware Reviews, MicroSIFT Project, Northwest Regional Educational Laboratory, 300 S.W. Sixth Ave., Portland, Oreg. 97204. (503) 248-6800. Free.

MicroSIFT reviews are written by the Northwest Regional Educational Laboratory network, called MicroSIFT, and generally disseminated free through two major sources—designated education agencies and journals. A complete list of the agencies providing these courseware evaluation reports appears in chapter 7 at the end of the description of NWREL's activities. Reproduced masters of the reviews are periodically sent to these agencies, who in turn make them available (either free or for a small fee to cover duplication/ distribution costs) to those in their geographic area who form their constituency. There are many journals which publish MicroSIFT reviews including *Microcomputers in Education, School Microware Reviews*, and *Access: Microcomputers in Libraries*, although they do not necessarily include the reviews in each issue.

Both their quality and easy availability make these reviews an excellent source of courseware information. Individual schools, school districts, educational service units and others wishing to establish a library of published reviews should all avail themselves of this service. Consult the agency list in chapter 7 for geographic representatives.

Reviews: MicroSIFT reviews are performed according to a rigorous process which is thoroughly discussed in chapter 7. After an initial identification process called SIFTnet, courseware evaluation is performed by the NWREL MicroSIFT network in a two-step process which employs the use of two standardized forms, one for courseware description and one for the actual courseware evaluation. Copies of these forms appear in chapter 4.

The "MicroSIFT Courseware Description" form is designed to obtain the following preliminary data: title, producer, subject/topics, grade level(s), required hardware and other software, whether software is protected, medium (format), back-up policy, and availability of producer's field test data. Beyond this, the description asks for instructional purposes and techniques, documentation available, objectives and prerequisites (whether stated or implied), and a description of the package's content and structure, including record keeping and reporting functions.

The evaluation form seeks evaluator's name and organization, whether the evaluation is based on observation of student use, and an evaluation of the following on a Likert-type scale: content characteristics, instructional characteristics, and technical characteristics. An overall quality rating is required ranging from a low of 1 to a high of 5 on each of these major characteristics and there is a final recommendation for use or not. Space is also devoted to the evaluator's own comments in regard to potential use in classroom settings; anticipated student time required to meet objectives; strengths and weaknesses. While evaluations of a single title are made by two or more teachers through the MicroSIFT network, MicroSIFT staff members coordinate the summary and final report of these evaluations.

Peelings II, Peelings II, Inc., Box 188, Las Cruces, N. Mex. 88004-0188. (505) 526-8364. $21; $2.50 for a single copy. Published monthly except June, August, and October.

A unique journal devoted exclusively to reviews of Apple microcomputer software and hardware, *Peelings II* is not affiliated with Apple Computer, Inc., and uses a board of what appear to be independent reviewers chosen from business, education, and other professions.

Reviews: The journal has signed reviews by authors whose credentials are identified at the beginning of each issue. Reviews are grouped under broad categories (including business, educational, hardware, simulations, utilities, games, and communications) and range in length from less than one to three or more pages. Standard format is followed which indicates author of program, name and address of producer/publisher, price, language, computer storage capacity needed, whether the program is locked or not, and a general overall rating ranging from AAA to F. Triple A means the software is absolutely astounding, and F means that it is so unacceptable that it should not be marketed. The meaning of the ratings used is given in the back of each issue and should be studied by users. After the rating, format of each review varies, but generally includes a description of the program, comments on documentation, special features (e.g., error-trapping), and ease of use, and ends with a conclusion or evaluation paragraph summarizing the reviewer's analysis.

The number of reviews in each issue varies from sixteen to over twenty. An abundance of game reviews probably reflects the state of the software market. Overall an excellent review source; the rating system used is particularly commendable.

School Microware Reviews, Dresden Associates, Box 246, Dresden, Maine 04342. (207) 737-4466. $45; $1.50 for individual reviews from back issues. Published three times a year: summer, winter and spring.

Unique publication devoted solely to evaluations of precollege educational software for the Apple II, Atari 400 and 800, Commodore PET, and the TRS-80 models I and III. Since these four computers, at least initially, have been the most widely used micros in education, this journal provides excellent coverage for instructional purposes and is one of the best single review sources available. *Reviews* is a companion work to *School Microware Directory*.

School Microware Reviews has four main sections: "Courseware Reviews," which generally contains over forty reviews; "Forum," which contains feedback from those who have used reviewed products, suggestions for improving *SMR*, and reactions from suppliers to reviews in earlier editions; "Index to Reviews in Other Publications"; and "Description of User Software Review Program."

The "Index to Reviews in Other Publications" provided in a recent edition access to over nine hundred reviews of instructional software published over the previous three years by over two dozen different magazines and journals. The index is updated in each edition of *SMR*.

Reviews: A recent issue contained forty-eight reviews from twenty-seven suppliers of software. Included are some reviews from the MicroSIFT Project. Reviews are provided by users/readers on a voluntary basis and follow one of two review formats: (1) the format provided by a form in *SMR* itself, or (2) the courseware description and evaluation forms developed by the MicroSIFT Project.

Those following the *SMR* format begin with the name and type of program, computer compatability (i.e., equipment needed, storage capacity, and language), grade level, supplier, packaging (e.g., eleven programs on protected disk plus backup disk), and price. Evaluation section includes functional description; evaluation including comments; characteristics such as documentation instructions given by program; and student-computer dialog. Evaluators are identified by name, title, and place of work. Suppliers' reactions to reviews are included at the end of many of the evaluations. For a description of the MicroSIFT evaluation format see page 127.

Both review formats include a summary rating or table. Reviews appear to be quite critical and evaluative in nature and often suggest changes necessary before recommending use. *SMR* format has a somewhat confusing system of symbols used to compute a summary rating but since the overall summary is stated on a fractional basis, this is not a major handicap.

The Software Critic, Box 3CH, University Park, N. Mex. 88003. (505) 522-5232. $15; $2.50 for a single copy. Published bimonthly.

Software Critic is devoted to program reviews of software compatible with the TRS-80, although there are occasional hardware and book reviews included. *SC* provides TRS-80 users with a critical guide to software, reviewing approximately ten programs per issue. Types of programs reviewed include database management, spelling checker and grammar, games, geneology, word processing, and utilities programs. Models of the TRS-80 for which programs are reviewed include models I and III and Color Computers. Reviews are individually identified as to author and all reviewers are listed at the beginning of the journal, along with their credentials including computer-related work experience.

Reviews: Reviews begin with an inset giving title of program, price, vendor, address, author if available, and holder of copyright, medium (disk, cassette, etc.), model, program type, and reviewer's name. This is followed by a review summary table which rates the program on the following criteria: usability, program efficiency, documentation, cost/performance, special features, entertainment value, and an overall rating. The scale used ranges from Very Good to Poor.

Reviews, while folksy in style, are frank and evaluative, often comparing one program to another of the same type reviewed in that issue. Reviews point out limitations of the program and weaknesses, and each review concludes with a summary paragraph which generally comments on the cost effectiveness of the program.

Software Review, Meckler Publishing, 520 Riverside Ave., Westport, Conn. 06880. (800) 243-4223 or (203) 226-6967 in Connecticut. $38; $20 for a single copy. Published quarterly: winter, spring, summer and fall.

"Specifically designed to provide the educational and library user with the information required to make intelligent software evaluation and procurement decisions," each issue includes articles on software concepts and evaluations, selection reports on available software products suitable for education and library applications, and reviews of books and other recent publications directly relevant to library users.

Software Review includes a classified bibliography of microcomputer books and articles of interest to educators and librarians, neophyte as well as experienced users. Three categories in the bibliography are devoted to different aspects of software (e.g., educational and library). Articles focus on how to evaluate software (e.g., "Pre-Written Software; Identification, Evaluation and Selection"). The Software: What's Available section lists and describes in one to two page annotations new software under such headings as educational applications, library applications, and systems software. Computer brand needed to run the program is not always included and prices are not given. Names and addresses of producers and distributors are provided. Conferences and Seminars section concludes the issues.

Reviews: Full length reviews are signed by authors whose title and institutional affiliation are given. Typical review runs ten pages and gives price, computer brands, and name and address for purchase. Illustrations are liberally used to illustrate the reviewer's discussion and clarify the program's features. Other items covered include documentation, warranties, weaknesses, and the availability of backup copies. A single review may compare and contrast several similar programs by different producers.

EDUCATIONAL COMPUTING JOURNALS

AEDS Journal, Association for Educational Data Systems, 1201 Sixteenth St., NW, Washington, D.C. 20036. (202) 822-7845. $25 to nonmembers; included as part of $45 dues to AEDS members. Published quarterly.

AEDS, the official publication of the Association for Educational Data Systems, contains articles on the application of computer technology to all areas and levels of education.

Book reviews, historical reviews, bibliographies, and special issues devoted to timely topics (e.g., selection and applications of microcomputers in education) are offered.

Reviews: None on software or hardware.

AEDS Monitor, Association for Educational Data Systems, 1201 Sixteenth St., NW, Washington, D.C. 20036. (202) 822-7845. $22 to nonmembers; included as part of $45 yearly dues to AEDS members. Published bimonthly.

Published by the Association for Educational Data Systems, *AEDS Monitor* carries the organization's news and convention information plus general interest articles on a broad range of educational computer topics, such as student scheduling and tracking with the microcomputer, using the microcomputer to help teach beginning statistics, and using the Apple II in the vocational classroom.

Reviews: None.

Classroom Computer News, Intentional Educations, Inc., 341 Mount Auburn St., Watertown, Mass. 02172. (617) 923-8595. $16; $2.50 for a single copy. Published bimonthly.

Recently added subtitle: *The Magazine for Teachers & Parents. Classroom Computer News* is a general interest journal emphasizing educational programs and uses of microcomputers. Each issue typically carries a special theme, (i.e., simulations, reading programs and games, word processing). Online reports on micro and other computer news items, In Review contains software reviews, Calendar lists computer events, and Treehouse, a feature section written for students, carries software reviews and articles of interest to younger readers.

Reviews: Signed reviews run up to three pages in length and identify the reviewer by title and institutional affiliation. Each review includes sections on features, educational value, design quality, written materials (including documentation, teachers' guide, and worksheets) and ease of use. There is also a *CCN* Profile box set into each review which summarizes the evaluation and gives basic data: title, version of the program tested, author, disk operating system (DOS) required, memory or storage capacity required, whether disk drive(s) are required and how many, price, publisher/producer with address, and a five point evaluation summary which gives ratings for the following criteria on a scale of 1 to 5: educational value, design quality, written materials, ease of use, captivation, and fun. A special feature of the reviews is the Publisher's Response, included at the end of the review and providing the producer with the opportunity to respond to criticisms and weaknesses identified in the reviews. Besides the regular reviews, there are mini-reviews called Reader's Reports contributed by readers which, though generally shorter and lacking the structured format and profiles found in the longer reviews, are evaluative and informative. These are also signed by individuals whose credentials are at least credible if not downright impressive.

The Computing Teacher, Education 135, University of Oregon, Eugene, Oreg. 97403. (503) 686-4414. $16.50; $3 for a single copy. Published nine times a year.

Published by the International Council of Computers in Education, this journal features articles for those interested in the instructional use of computers including teaching about computers, teacher education, and the impact of computers on curriculum.

Beginning with the January 1983 issue, *CT* includes *MICROgram*, the newsletter of the newly created consortium formed by the merger of the EPIE Institute and the Consumers Union which are jointly providing evaluations of microcomputer hardware and courseware. There are also book reviews and one recent issue had two special departments: Computer Literacy Film Reviews and Computers in the Media Center.

Reviews: Software Reviews section has its own separate editor and generally only carries one review which is signed, with author identified by title and organization. Reviews run from one to two and a half pages in length and provide at the beginning: name of program, publisher and address, price, computer model, memory and peripherals needed, and reviewer. Essay-type reviews describe the program, discuss the major features and documentation, and point out weaknesses with a final purchase recommendation being made.

CT also occasionally includes "MicroSIFT Courseware Evaluations" reviews in its Software Reviews section and regularly publishes at least one full length EPIE/CU *Micro-Courseware PRO/FILE* and evaluation review along with the *MICROgram* mentioned above.

Educational Computer Magazine, Edcomp, Inc., Box 535, Cupertino, Calif. 95015. (408) 252-3224. $15; $3 for a single copy. Published bimonthly.

This journal has as its subtitle *Educating Tomorrow's Computer Users.* It is an excellent source for a broad range of educational computing articles, reviews, and special columns. Some sample article topics include microcomputer art, an innovative class registration system, Apple PILOT, games as teaching tools, and teacher education curriculum.

Regular columns include Viewpoint, Bittersweet, Administrative Perspectives, The Micro in the Media Center, People and Their Computers, and Preschools + Computers = ABC. There are also Book Reviews, Courseware Reviews, and SECTOR Courseware Reviews. A recently added feature is a column reviewing free and inexpensive software. There are also conference reports, computer news announcements and dates of upcoming computer conferences.

Reviews: The regular Courseware Reviews include, for each, the title of the program, producer's name and address, and name of the reviewer. Boxed-in data provides background information such as target group, equipment requirements, materials included in the package, and price. Reviews themselves provide a general description of the program, student response when available, special program characteristics, and comments on documentation and directions. Most reviews provide a final recommendation as to purchase advisability, and range in length from one-third of a page to over two pages. This column reviews from two to four software programs per issue.

Besides the regular courseware review section, recent issues of the journal have published SECTOR Project reviews of software. This project is funded by a grant from the Utah State Office of Education and the reviews follow a set format including program name, publisher, subject, grade level, price, overview, content and instructional design, record keeping/management capabilities, ease of use, validation, and conclusions. The November-December 1982 issue of the journal describes the SECTOR evaluation process and provides a copy of the evaluation forms used. The final review section, that of free and inexpensive software, is described in chapter 5.

Electronic Education, Electronic Communications, Inc., Suite 220, 1311 Executive Center Dr., Tallahassee, Fla. 32301. (904) 878-4178. $18; $3 for a single copy. Published nine times a year: monthly September through June, with March/April issue combined.

General interest computer journal which nonetheless emphasizes instructional computing for kindergarten through college level, *EE* features industry news and updates of interest to the beginning computer user. Recent sample articles include suggestions on how to tell if the college of your choice is computer literate, and discussions of electronic newspapers and the merits of arcade video games.

Journal features include Looking Ahead, a calendar of national and regional computer conferences and workshops; Around the Circuit, featuring news of the microcomputer industry, and summaries of statistical reports, new product announcements, etc.; Hardware and Software Reviews; and Book Reviews.

Reviews: Software reviews are not included in every issue. Reviews are essay-style, run several pages in length, and are written by outside reviewers identified by name, title, and institutional affiliation.

Electronic Learning, Scholastic, Inc., 902 Sylvan Ave., Englewood Cliffs, N.J. 07632. (212) 944-7700. $19; $3.50 for a single copy. Published eight times a year: monthly during school year.

Published by Scholastic, Incorporated, this journal features articles of interest to those just getting started in the educational use of computers. Some features added recently include: Technology-Using Educator of the Year (a focus on an individual), School of the Month (how particular school districts implement computer education), and a series on computer literacy.

Features include news on developments in the computer world and educational software publishing, book reviews, new products, books, and software listings. Also, *EL*'s Software Reviews on File, a regular section containing listings of software reviews from past issues grouped by grade level (Elementary-Junior High, Secondary, and Professional—for classroom management). Each profile contains, besides the basic ordering information, comments excerpted from the review and a reference to the complete review source (month and year) in *Electronic Learning*. The profiles may be clipped and put on index cards for future reference.

Reviews: The review section is devoted entirely to educational software. According to the journal, each program or package is reviewed by a team which consists of a content area specialist, classroom teacher(s) or school administrator(s), and target age students. The reviewer comments on the software cover content accuracy, quality of information presentation, accessibility to users, specific strengths and weaknesses, instructional usefulness, potential applications, and overall educational value. The printed review is a synthesis of all these reviewers' comments. Besides title of the program, each review includes the necessary hardware, the subject area, grade level, source (producer/publisher and address), and the cost of the software. Names, titles, and instructional affiliations are given for reviewers. A recent issue contained five critical, evaluative reviews.

Journal of Computer-Based Instruction, Gordon Hayes, Executive Secretary, ADCIS International Headquarters, Computer Center, Western Washington University, Bellingham, Wash. 98225. $18 to nonmembers; free to members of the Association for the Development of Computer-Based Instructional Systems; $6.50 for a single copy. Published quarterly.

Purposes of the ADCIS organization include promoting the use of computer-assisted instruction (CAI), and specifying requirements and priorities for hardware and software development. Issues focus on special aspects (e.g., aviation use of CAI).

Reviews: None.

The Journal of Computers in Mathematics and Science Teaching, Box 4455, Austin, Tex. 78764. (512) 258-9738. $15; $5 for a single copy. Published quarterly.

Membership to the Association for Computers in Mathematics and Science Teaching includes a subscription to *JCMST*, their official journal. This is an excellent, semischolarly publication with articles on a broad range of computer topics beyond the narrow scope that its title suggests. Some recent articles included an introduction to LOGO, short biographies of prominent women in the history of the development of computers, and a bibliography on computers in elementary education.

Special features include The ComputerBook Center, which is a service of the Association and consists of a listing or catalog of over three hundred best selling computer books which may be ordered for from 10 to 30 percent discounts; Software Resources, which includes listings of software available at reasonable prices for particular applications (e.g., administrative grade management programs for under one hundred dollars); New Products listings including software, peripherals, and instructional materials; and a calendar of computer events.

The LOGO and Educational Computing Journal, Al Weiner, Editor, Suite 219, 1320 Stony Brook Rd., Stony Brook, N.Y. 11790. $20. Published five times a year.

This is a new periodical for classroom teachers, software developers, and parents and children with home computers. The journal reports on research, instructional software, and CAI methods.

MACUL Journal, Michigan Association for Computer Users in Learning, Lary R. Smith, Wayne Intermediate School District, Box 807, Wayne, Mich. 48184. (313) 326-9300. $5 which includes membership to MACUL and a bimonthly newsletter *Checkpoint*; $5 for a single copy. Published two to three times a year.

The *MACUL Journal* is primarily a state computer club publication but periodically has devoted entire issues to software evaluation. Two volumes publishing only reviews of computer programs are the spring 1980 and winter 1981 issues which may be ordered for five dollars each and between the two of them contain reviews of 257 software titles. The second issue (winter 1981) contains in the appendixes the following indexes which greatly simplify finding reviews on particular programs: (1) an alphabetical list of titles reviewed from both volumes, which also gives subject area and machine compatibility of the program, (2) a subject index, and (3) an index by computer brand. A final section lists sources or publishers of the software reviewed with mailing addresses and telephone number where available.

Reviews: Arrangement of the reviews is alphabetical by title. Reviews include the brand compatability plus memory requirements, subject, grade level, author if known, producer, cost, program description, evaluation and criteria rated on a five-point scale, special requirements, and the date of the review and initials of the reviewer (although all the reviews examined in the second volume were written by James Winebrener of the Livonia Michigan Public Schools). The five items rated on the five-point scale were program polish, use of machine capability, written documentation, ease of use, and educational value. Reviews were one page or less in length, reduced in print size, and formatted two to a page in the journal. Many of the more popular educational software programs are found in these reviews such as those available from the Minnesota Educational Computer Consortium (MECC) as well as public domain programs obtainable from MACUL itself. Types of programs reviewed, besides instructional ones, include teacher authoring systems, programming aids, management programs, readability indexes, and introductory computer lessons. The two volumes combined form a good initial library of software reviews although the use of a single reviewer is perhaps a disadvantage.

Microcomputers in Education. *See* entry under Review Journals and Services.

Pipeline, CONDUIT, The University of Iowa, Box 388, Iowa City, Iowa 52244. (319) 353-5789. $10. Published twice a year.

This is the major journal of CONDUIT, a nonprofit organization whose major purpose is to promote the use of instructional computing at the college level. Besides containing thematic articles of general interest, each issue contains two separate catalog listings: Catalog of Standard FORTRAN and BASIC Packages, and Catalog of Microcomputer-Based Packages. These software programs are all available for purchase from CONDUIT and have been reviewed and tested by them. The microcomputers for which programs are available include: Apple II, Radio Shack TRS-80, Commodore PET 2000 and 4000 Series, Atari 800, and Monroe EC 8800. While programs are generally college level, some could be used with accelerated high school students.

Reviews: The New Packages section contains descriptive reviews by outside reviewers of approximately ten new programs available through CONDUIT. They tend to focus on the special features but many include colorful sample screen outputs from the programs. Each review gives price and machine requirements plus catalog order number.

T.H.E. Journal, Information Synergy, Inc., Box 992, Acton, Mass. 01720. $15; $2.50 for a single copy. Published eight times a year: January through May, September through November.

T[echnological] H[orizons in] E[ducation] *Journal* regularly features articles on the use of computers in education. It also includes a calendar of computer conferences; lists of new publications catalogs of computer software and equipment, educational materials, and magazines; conference proceedings listing; and sources of free software. Books section lists and annotates computer books, buyer's guides, dictionaries and directories.

The Software and Courseware section briefly describes new software available. Most descriptions run one or two paragraphs and lack prices and addresses needed to order and, often, grade or age level of intended user for educational programs. Further information may be obtained by means of an inquiry card. Additional software programs are included in New Products section where they are sometimes hard to distinquish from the equipment and other peripherals listed.

Reviews: No critical reviews.

COMPUTER JOURNALS

BYTE, Box 590, Martinsville, N.J. 08836. (603) 924-9281. $19; $2.95 for a single copy. Published monthly.

BYTE is a general magazine subtitled *The Small Systems Journal* featuring articles somewhat technical in nature but still of popular interest: a recent issue contained articles on games and electronic music synthesizers.

Features of interest are book reviews, listings of software and books, Event Queue (computer conferences, seminars, workshops) and Bytelines (news of interest in the computer world). Also included are the Product Description column and System Notes. Cumulative index in December issue aids in finding particular articles or software reviews. Reviews listed are arranged under broad subject categories and by computer brand.

Reviews: Most reviews are not of educational software but do include utilities programs, business games, graphics, mathematics, word processing and statistics. Signed reviews give addresses, but not title/occupation of the reviewers. Each review gives program name, computer needed, type of program, distributor, documentation, price, and intended audience. Reviews average four to six pages and a recent issue carried three software and one hardware review. Reviews may be a bit technical for the novice computer user.

Compute!, Box 914, Farmingdale, N.Y. 11737. (800) 334-0868. $20; $2.50 for a single copy. Published monthly.

Compute! considers itself the leading magazine of home, educational, and recreational computing. Emphasis is on personal computers and popular usage. Articles, regular columns, and complete BASIC and machine language listings of games, utilities, and other applications are included. While principal editorial coverage is for the Atari, Apple, Commodore PET, CP/M and VIC 20, this is expanding to include TI 99/4A, Sinclair ZX-81, and the Radio Shack Color Computer. Contents are divided into Features, Education and Recreation, Reviews, Columns and Departments, and the journal articles.

New Products lists both software and equipment. Guide to Articles and Programs serves as the table of contents and indicates the computer brands to which the articles or reviews refer. Included are language programs, book reviews, games, peripherals, and regular software reviews.

Reviews: Evaluations are signed and tend to be descriptive; some are as long as three pages. Title, prices, and ordering information are given. Some reviewers have their titles and institutional affiliations given while others do not.

Computers & Electronics, Box 2774, Boulder, Colo. 80321. (212) 725-3500. $15.97; $1.25 for a single copy. Published monthly.

Formerly *Popular Electronics, C & E* now has as its major focus the microcomputer field and, in particular, the home computer. Recent representative articles address microcomputer joystick interfacing methods and communications networks, and provide an equipment hookup guide for using videocassette recorders with cable TV.

Special features include Programmer's Notebook, with tips to aid programmers; Software and Hardware Reviews; Solid-State Developments, which discusses new peripherals available; Operation Assist, a column to aid readers in obtaining information on outdated or rare equipment; Computer Hotline, a column where *C & E* staff answer readers' questions about computers; and New Products listings. Another regular feature is the construction articles for the do-it-yourself electronics builder.

Reviews: A recent issue reviewed three software programs, all of computer video games. Reviews were unsigned and ran about one column in length. Each gave the title of the program; the producer, but not the address or price; and generally, but not always, the format available. All programs were for the Atari computer and the reviewer was frank about not recommending purchase in the brief essay-style reviews. Although reviews vary, items discussed included a summary of the program, documentation and/or directions for use, graphics, music, vendor support, availability of backup copies, and skill levels needed to play.

Creative Computing, Box 5214, Boulder, Colo. 80321. (800) 631-8112, in New
Jersey call (201) 540-0445. $24.97; $2.95 for a single copy. Published
monthly.

Creative Computing considers itself a computer education publication
and regularly carries articles on designing and evaluating educational
software, teaching concepts and terminology in computer education, text
editing applications for literature, and computer simulations in the classroom
plus many additional features of general interest (e.g., word processing). All
brands are included.

The journal also has sections on legal processing, reviews, games, and
organizations, as well as interviews with experts in the field, a software legal
forum, and book reviews. Equipment profiles evaluate new products on the
market. Many useful programs are included for a variety of microcomputers.

Reviews: Both comparative and single program in-depth reviews are
included for popular, business, and educational software. Reviews are signed,
many being submitted by reader contributors whose names and addresses are
included. Although each reviewer follows his/her own format, there is a
standard Software Profile included within a shaded box for each program
which gives program name, type (e.g., game, graphics, art, teaching), system
needed (i.e., brand and storage or memory size need to run the program, such
as 16K Apple II), format which program is available in, summary of program,
price and manufacturer/producer's name, address, and telephone number for
ordering. Single reviews typically run two to three pages and describe the
program, point out shortcomings and problems encountered, and discuss
documentation and user support available (i.e., telephone assistance and
program updates). Usually each program review also has a reproduction of a
sample frame to provide an example of the program's graphic displays.
Comparative reviews like those for arcade games run half a page in length. No
index to reviews is provided and many of the programs reviewed are not listed
by name in the table of contents, although such listing is a common practice in
many other journals.

Desktop Computing, 1001001, Inc., Box 917, Farmingdale, N.Y. 11737. $25;
$2.95 for a single copy. Published monthly.

Subtitled *The Plain Language Computer Magazine for the Businessman*,
DC focuses on the needs and concerns of small businesses using
microcomputers. Sample topics include word processing, use of computers by
farmers, how to choose a microcomputer system, and even small town
government uses of computers. Special features include Book Reviews, New
Products listings, News Briefs, and Calendar of computer-related events.

Dr. Dobb's Journal, People's Computer Company, Box E, 1263 El Camino
Real, Menlo Park, Calif. 94025. (415) 323-3111. $25; $2.50 for a single
copy. Published monthly.

Formerly called *Dr. Dobb's Journal of Computer Calisthenics and
Orthodontia, Dr. Dobb's Journal: For Users of Small Computer Systems*
features articles, book reviews and software reviews of general interest to

computer users. Also included are actual software programs. This journal is somewhat technical for the beginner as it is aimed at the "serious computing professional or enthusiast."

Reviews: Brief, announcement-type descriptions of new software are combined in a single review. In addition, there is a section called Software Review which focuses on a single program in rather technical terms.

Interface Age, 16704 Marquardt Ave., Cerritos, Calif. 90701. (213) 926-9540. $21; $2.50 for a single copy. Published monthly.

Primarily for business users, *Interface Age* nonetheless devotes about one issue a year to educational applications. Individual articles on educational topics or software are included throughout the year. An index in the December issue covers both software and hardware reviews.

Reviews: Though limited to business programs, some reviews (of word processing programs, for example) are of potential use in educational settings. Signed reviews of three to five pages offer thorough description and remarks on equipment compatability, but do not provide ordering information like producer's address and the price of the software.

Micro, Box 6502, 10 Northern Blvd., Amherst, N.H. 03031. (800) 345-8112. $24; $2.50 for a single copy. Published monthly.

Devoted to "expanding computer knowledge," *Micro* includes articles on language, enhancements, and basic aids; and educational updates on a broad range of computers (Apple, Atari, PET, VIC, etc.). Regular columns discuss developments for particular brands: Micro: From Here to Atari, PET Vet, CoCo Bits, and Apple Slices. Micro Software Catalog lists new software programs with very good descriptions and complete order information including price, addresses, and telephone numbers. Micro Hardware Catalog does the same thing for computers and peripherals.

Reviews: Brief one-fourth to one-half page reviews on software for many brands of microcomputers are signed by reviewers who are not, however, identified by title or institutional affiliation. Review format is clear and simple to follow. Each review begins with product name, equipment requirements, price, and manufacturer's name and address. These are followed by a brief description of the program, its good points, it disadvantages or weaknesses, documentation, and skill level required to use the program. A recent issue had six reviews, two of which were for educational programs.

Microcomputing, Box 997, Farmingdale, N.Y. 11737. (603) 924-9471. $25; $2.95 for a single copy. Published monthly.

Microcomputing, formerly called *Kilobaud*, publishes general interest articles. Topics include applications, education, languages, programming techniques, software and reviews. The same publisher (Wayne Green, Inc.) produces *inCider* magazine, *BYTE*, and *Microcomputing Industry*. This journal does not appear quite as technical as *BYTE*.

Special features include programs, computer club notes, calendar of computer events, micro quiz, and new products and software listings. An annual index to articles and software reviews appears in the December issue.

The Micro Software Digest section is a collection of "capsulized" software reviews taken from other computer journals. Digests or excerpts are presented in an index-card format so they may be clipped and pasted on 3x5 cards. Listings are arranged by and begin with the computer brand followed by title, system requirements, manufacturer, price, and excerpts from and source of the review. Also included are reviews for Apple, Commodore, IBM, Atari, Heath, and other computer brands.

Reviews: Signed reviews identify location of authors but not occupation. Reviews average about one page in length and do not follow a set format. Producer/publisher, address, and price are given at the end of reviews. Some also give the computer brand compatability, system needed, etc., but in others one must search the review text for this data. Reviews may include system needed, documentation comments, description of the program, what the program does, and generally a positive recommendation to purchase although drawbacks are discussed. A recent issue contained seven reviews of programs, including graphics, word processing, and a spelling checker. Educational programs are reviewed periodically as well.

Personal Computing, Box 2942, Boulder, Colo. 80322. (201) 843-0550. $18; $2.50 for a single copy. Published monthly.

Published by Hayden which produces a number of other computer periodicals, books, and software, this journal has as its main audience the personal home computer owner. It contains general interest articles (e.g., "Computing Your Family Tree," "Making a Calculator Out of a Computer") plus articles under Education, Business and Professional/Managerial categories for a wide range of computers (TRS-80, PET, IBM, Apple II, etc.).

The journal offers Book Reviews, Hardware of the Month, Hardware Index (a listing of new products), Software of the Month (products considered to be most useful and exciting in this month's crop), and Software Index (a listing of new products arranged under broad subject categories including educational software), are all special features.

Reviews: Software of the Month reviews a fairly small number of programs in short descriptive essays which tend to sound more like product promotions than reviews. The format obscures the basic information about each since the title of the program, computer compatability, and price (if it is even included) have to be dredged out of the narrative. The editors do admit that they are simply commending these programs "for your closer examination" and provide company name, address, and telephone number for further information from the producer. Reviews are unsigned. In a recent issue there were three reviews; only one pertained to educational software, referring to the PLATO educational software now being rewritten for the Apple II Plus, TI 99/4A and Atari 800 computers.

Popular Computing, Box 307, Martinsville, N.J. 08836. $15; $2.50 for a single copy. Published monthly.

Published by the same company as *BYTE* magazine, this journal carries general interest articles on various computer brands for business, education, and home computer users and is a good journal for the beginner as it is not too technical. Typical topics are a user's guide to electronic mail, and banking and shopping by mail. Articles of special interest to educators appear in a regular section called Educational Computing. A recent article was entitled "Which Computer Should a School Buy?" Ask Popular is a column that answers readers' questions about small computers. Book reviews and new products and software lists appear monthly. Software programs are grouped by application and include a Home/Education category.

Reviews: There are two separate sections of reviews. Hardware Reviews evaluates and compares computers and equipment. A recent review compared four low-cost daisywheel printers. Software Reviews is a new section grouping formerly scattered reviews into one easy-to-read section. Each month a lead review which covers a particular program in depth is followed by several shorter software reviews. Reviews frequently compare two or more programs of a similar type. Accompanying charts called "At a Glance" contrast comparable programs and give name, type, manufacturer (including address), price, format, computer compatability, documentation, and intended audience. Reviewers have personally used the programs and describe not only the documentation but also the problems and weaknesses of each. Regular reviews run two to four pages and are both descriptive and evaluative with reviewers not hesitating to recommend against purchasing a particular program. Five software reviews appeared in a recent issue.

Small Business Computers Magazine, Box 789-M, Morristown, N.J. 07960. $19.97. Published bimonthly.

This is similar in scope and coverage to *Desktop Computing* aimed at small business users of microcomputers.

SoftSide, SoftSide Publications, Inc., 100 Pine St., Holmes, Pa. 19043. (800) 345-8112. $30; $3 for a single copy. Published monthly.

This is a general interest journal which emphasizes home and recreational computer uses. There are separate sections for articles and features on four major computer brands and models: the Atari and the Apple computers, the IBM PC and the TRS-80.

Within each of the four sections listed above are actual programs for users, reviews of compatible software, and relevant articles. A typical issue contains three to five programs ready to be keyed in and used on one's own computer. Or, readers may, by means of a special subscription, at a slightly higher rate, receive each month's programs delivered on cassette or disk in addition to the regular magazine issue.

Reviews: The majority of software reviewed consists of recreational games. Reviews give name of reviewer, program name, name and address of producer, system requirements (i.e., brand and storage capacity required) and price. Reviews vary from one to one and a half pages in length.

EDUCATION JOURNALS

Arithmetic Teacher, 1906 Association Dr., Reston, Va. 22091. $30 dues to the National Council of Teachers of Mathematics includes subscription. Published monthly September through May.

An official journal of the National Council of Teachers of Mathematics (which also publishes *Mathematics Teacher*), this periodical is "a forum for the exchange of ideas and a source of techniques for teaching mathematics in grades kindergarten through eight."

The Reviewing and Viewing section contains (1) reviews of New Books for Pupils, (2) Etcetera, reviews of books for teachers including computer books, and (3) Software, reviews of microcomputer software programs.

Reviews: Signed reviews of mathematics software programs give, besides title, computer brand and model, memory needed, language, price, producer and complete address.

Reviews run approximately one-third of a page, and besides generally describing the program, point out major strengths and weaknesses. Reviewers are identified by geographic location and sometimes place of work but the addition of job title would help in judging reviewers' qualifications. One sample issue has three software reviews.

Curriculum Review, Curriculum Advisory Service, 517 S. Jefferson St., Chicago, Ill. 60607. (312) 939-3010. $35. Published five times a year: February, May, August, October, December.

Curriculum Review publishes evaluations of textbooks, supplementary materials, and computer software in all K-12 curriculum areas. It also carries articles reporting on trends in curriculum development and innovations in materials selection and curriculum design.

Contents are arranged under the following categories: Articles (of more general interest), Feature (which focuses on some particular topic such as global education or the creative process), Computer Center (which features software reviews), Language Arts/Reading, Mathematics, Science, Social Studies, and Departments. The Computer Center provides, besides a feature article, a series of software reviews, often also including computer book reviews. In addition, numerous courseware reviews are found in the respective subject sections preceded by a "C" indicating they are computer programs. Another special feature is the cluster review which groups several evaluations of materials on a single theme or subtopic in the larger categories listed above. These appear in the Computer Center section and in most of the others.

Reviews: Reviews, whether in the Computer Center section or under specific subjects, follow the same standard format. Included are title, producer's name, copyright date, machine requirements (brand, model, memory, etc.), format, price, language, approximate running time, subject area, and grade level. The actual evaluation is essay style and deals with content focus, educational purpose, method of operation, technical features, and final recommendations and summary evaluation. Reviews are signed by authors, who are fully identified, and run from one-half to one and one-half pages in length. The evaluation form used by *CR* reviewers appears in chapter 4 of this book.

Educational Technology, Educational Technology Publications, Inc., 140 Sylvan Ave., Englewood Cliffs, N.J. 07632. (201) 871-4007. $49; $6 for a single copy. Published monthly.

Subtitled *Magazine for Managers of Change in Education*, this journal is aimed at educational leaders at all levels, including school administrators, instructional designers and developers, educational researchers, media technologists and others interested in the improvement of instruction and learning. Special issues in the past have included "The Computer and Education," "Computer Aided Test Construction," "Microcomputers in Education," and "Computers in the Schools." Although the journal encompasses all media and instructional design, in recent issues it has emphasized the computer in education.

Computer News contains a monthly column of news and commentary; Educational Technology Product Reviews, which includes a section called Computer Media regularly containing microcomputer software reviews by independent reviewers; New Services and New Products, a monthly annotated listing that contains, among others, two sections: Computer Courseware and Software and Computer Hardware.

Reviews: The publication contains excellent evaluative reviews written by educators who are sent a one-page set of "Guidelines for Educational Technology Product Reviews" to use as a basis for their work. Reviewers try out the product under consideration with members of the intended audience and many of the evaluators include comments on user response and performance with the software. Each review includes name of the program, type of program, price, name and address of publisher/producer, name and title and complete address of reviewer. Beyond this basic information, reviews vary as to format but generally include a description of the content and purposes of the program, a list of equipment with which the program is compatible, a discussion of problems encountered in using the program, and a final summary or conclusion. Reviews vary from a half to one and a half pages in length. Many conclude with a very frank summary evaluation.

Two unique features help update these reviews since software producers frequently revise their programs before the review can be published. Update paragraphs describe recent modifications, which generally improve the product, and a response by publisher section allows the software producers to respond to the criticisms of the reviewers and provide additional information. Response by authors provides the same data from the author(s) themselves. Software evaluators are identified and range from professional evaluation consultants to graduate students. The number of reviews per issue varies. No index to reviews is provided.

The Mathematics Teacher, 1906 Association Dr., Reston, Va. 22091. $30 dues to the National Council of Teachers of Mathematics includes subscription. Published monthly September through May.

This is the official journal of the National Council of Teachers of Mathematics, devoted to the improvement of mathematics instruction in junior high through college level, and includes articles on the use of microcomputers and computer-assisted instruction in math education.

Reviews: The courseware section includes under New Products, signed reviews of software specifically designed for teaching mathematics concepts. Each review gives the name, computer system compatability (i.e., brand and storage capacity of computer needed to run the program), package components, price, and name and address of producer/distributor. Thoughtful, critical reviews average half a page in length and identify the author by name and institutional affiliation. An index to courseware reviews appears in the December issue and lists programs reviewed for the previous year under the following headings: algebra, applications, arithmetic, calculus, computer science, games and puzzles, geometry, statistics, tests, trigonometry, and word processing. Besides the program name, the index gives the machine capacity needed to run the program, as well as, of course, the date and page number of the review.

COMPUTER-SPECIFIC JOURNALS

Apple

Apple Education News, 20525 Mariani Ave., Cupertino, Calif. 95014. Free. Published three times a year.

Apple Education News is a company newsletter designed to disseminate information from the Apple Computer Company to educational users of Apple computers. It is particularly useful for its announcements of new Apple compatible software and software company developments, but it also includes brief articles on special new uses of the Apple, (e.g., for an elementary school library catalog). Software descriptions appear to be based on publisher's promotional materials and are not evaluative.
Reviews: None.

Apple Orchard, International Apple Core, Inc., 908 George St., Santa Clara, Calif. 95050. (408) 727-7652. $19.50; $3.25 for a single copy. Published nine times a year.

Apple Orchard is published by the International Apple Core, a worldwide federation of Apple Computer User Groups, and is devoted exclusively to concerns of Apple users. Articles are on a broad variety of topics in non-technical language. The Forbidden Fruit column highlights and lists new products for the Apple including hardware and software, and includes a special section on educational programs. Listings include a very good program description and complete order information.
Reviews: Reviews are signed and include somewhere in the text the name of the program, the publisher, but unfortunately not always the price or complete order address. Reviews run one to one and a half pages in length and include both description and evaluative, critical comments dealing with difficulty level, documentation, and special features. Reviews often combine two similar programs in a single review for comparative purposes. A recent issue reviewed six programs in four different reviews. Most were entertainment or business programs.

Apple: The Personal Computer Magazine and Catalog, Apple Computer, Inc., 10260 Bandley Dr., Cupertino, Calif. 95014. $2.50 for a single copy. Published semiannually.

Call-A.P.P.L.E., Apple Puget Sound Program Library Exchange, 304 Maine Ave. S, Suite 300, Renton, Wash. 98055. Included free as part of the annual Exchange membership dues of $20 per year (first time members must pay an additional $25 one time "Apple-cation" fee); $2.50 for a single copy. Published monthly.

This journal is published by the Apple Puget Sound Program Library Exchange. Some recent articles included fare for both the beginning user ("Beginner's Guide") and the more advanced user ("Password Protection").

The *Call-A.P.P.L.E.* Hot Line is available during specified hours and provides technical and programming assistance to users. Product Review Column reviews peripherals; Technique describes useful programming techniques; and Tomorrow's Apples Today provides new Apple product announcements. A list of Apple consultants is also included.

Reviews: No regular software reviews.

inCider, Box 911, Farmingdale, N.Y. 11737. (603) 924-9471. $25; $2.95 for a single copy. Published monthly.

A new magazine by an independent publisher designed to promote use of the Apple microcomputer, *inCider* includes articles, programs to run, and reviews of hardware and software. It is similar to magazines promoting use of the TRS-80.

Special features include Applesoft Adviser, book reviews, descriptive listings in New Software and New Products sections.

Reviews: The magazine offers half to full page reviews of software programs predominately games (five out of six in one issue). The reviews are signed, and both describe the programs and offer criticism and evaluation. Most reviews give software producer/distributor's name and address and price but do not indicate the storage space necessary to run the programs.

Microzine. *See* entry under Journals on Disk or Cassette.

Nibble, Box 325, Lincoln, Mass. 01773. (617) 259-9710. $19.95; $2.50 for a single copy. Published eight times a year.

Nibble is subtitled *The Reference Manual for Apple Computing* and includes actual programs for the home, small business, and entertainment plus articles for both the beginner and more advanced programmer on graphics, games, systems programming, hardware construction, projects, and product news. New software is announced in Nibble Software Column.

Reviews: The On the Scene column briefly reviews new software and peripherals in a one-paragraph format mainly descriptive in nature.

Peelings II. *See* entry under Review Journals and Services.

Softalk, Box 60, North Hollywood, Calif. 91603. (213) 980-5074. $24; $3 for a single copy. Published monthly.

Softalk is directed at the Apple computer owner or user, and those purchasing an Apple may receive a complimentary trial subscription to the journal. Articles for home, business, and education users of the microcomputer are included as well as new product developments and announcements.

Special features and columns include Marketalk News (industry news and new product announcements on books, programs, etc., available); Marketalk Reviews of software programs; Graphically Speaking (a column on creating computer graphics); Beginners' Corner (a tutorial on BASIC programming); and Bestsellers, which includes lists of the current and previous month's top selling software in the following program categories: Apple III, arcade, business, hobby, home, home education, and word processors. There are separate lists of the top selling adventure, fantasy, and strategy games; and there is a final list summarizing the top thirty programs in sales for all categories. Fastalk lists Apple compatible software programs available under such categories as adventure, business, communications, fantasy, graphics, home, and home education.

Reviews: There were two separate review sections in a sample issue. The Schoolhouse Apple, which is a regular column but does not always carry evaluations, reviewed only educational software with a total of eight instructional programs being discussed. Reviews were contributed by four different authors not individually identified. The other regular review section, Marketalk Reviews, contained fourteen reviews of all types of programs ranging from games to Pascal programming to the reading of tarot cards. Both review sections follow the same basic format with reviews running from one-fourth to one-half a page in length. Reviews concentrate on description and begin by naming the program and producer. Complete order information follows the review along with telephone number and price. Basic information such as grade level and overall evaluation given the program is hard to extract from reviews; however, such useful components as documentation and teacher's manuals are discussed.

Window. *See* entry under Journals on Disk or Cassette.

Atari

A.N.A.L.O.G. 400/800, Analog Magazine Corp., Box 23, Worcester, Mass. 01603. $12. Published bimonthly.

Antic: The Atari Resource, Antic Publishing, 600 Eighteenth St., San Francisco, Calif. 94107. (415) 864-0886. $15; $2.50 for a single copy. Published bimonthly.

Commodore

PET: Cursor, Box 550, Goleta, Calif. 90317. $20. Published bimonthly. Available on disk or cassette.

Commodore: The Microcomputer Magazine, Commodore Business Machines, Inc., Box 651, Holmes, Pa. 19043. $15. Published bimonthly.

Commodore Vic 20, Commodore Computer, 681 Moore Rd., King of Prussia, Pa. 19406.

Commodore Power/Play, Commodore Business Machines, Inc., Box 651, Holmes, Pa. 19043. $10. Published quarterly.

IBM

PC, Software Communications, Inc., 1528 Irving St., San Francisco, Calif. 94122. $27. Published monthly.

Subtitled *The Independent Guide to IBM Personal Computers*, this journal features articles pertaining to business, communications, education, law, and programming applications.

Reviews: Reviews of software and hardware are included.

Personal Computer Age, Box 70725, Pasadena, Calif. 91107. $24; $2.50 for a single copy. Published monthly.

Reviews: Software reviews are included.

Softalk for the IBM Personal Computer, 11021 Magnolia Blvd., Box 60, North Hollywood, Calif. 91603. Free to owners of the IBM PC; $24 for others; $2 for a single copy. Published monthly.

North Star

North Star Notes, North Star Compute, 14440 Catalina St., San Leandro, Calif. 94577. Free. Published quarterly.

Osborne

OS/TECH, Box 517, Clearwater, Fla. 33517. (813) 446-7239. $9; $1.50 for a single copy. Published bimonthly.

Source of public domain programs available for Osborne.
Reviews: OS/TECH includes software reviews.

The Portable Companion, 26538 Danti Ct., Box 18, Hayward, Calif. 94545. (415) 887-8080. $25; $2.95 for a single copy. Published monthly.

Limited to the Osborne I.
Reviews: The journal includes software reviews.

Radio Shack TRS-80

80 Microcomputing, Box 981, Farmingdale, N.Y. 11737. $25; $2.95 for a single copy. Published monthly.

Aimed specifically at the TRS-80 user, a typical issue contains articles for the home, education, and business user on a wide variety of topics including specific business applications, games, graphics, hardware, utility programs, tutorials, and new product listings. It also includes a calendar of computer events and reviews of books, hardware, and software programs.

This journal contains actual program listings and indicates which are available on tape. A special issue on education contained over ten articles of interest to educators, including "An '80 in the Apple," "Grade Book," "Computer Etch-a-Sketch," and "To Comma or Not to Comma."

Reviews: Though signed, reviews do not identify the authors by title or institution. A recent issue contained nine software reviews which averaged less than one page in length. Reviews included name of program, name of publisher and place but not address, model of TRS-80 needed, price, and format of program (disk or cassette).

The majority of reviews appear to be of games or utility programs. Book reviews mixed with software reviews are somewhat confusing.

80-U.S., 3838 S. Warner St., Tacoma, Wash. 98409. (206) 475-2219. $16; $3 for a single copy. Published monthly.

Subtitled: *The TRS-80 Users Journal,* this is an independently published magazine devoted almost exclusively to Radio Shack TRS-80 model microcomputers including the new Color Computer. It includes general interest articles primarily for the home computer user on a broad range of topics from recipes for generating pi on a computer to microcomputers in church.

Includes actual program listings for the TRS-80 New Product listings.

Reviews: The reviews section combines reviews of computer courses, books, hardware and peripherals, and software all in one confusing section where a review often must be re-read several times before one discerns whether it is for a new program or a printer. Software reviews are signed but do not identify the author by title or institutional affiliation. Title and complete order information are included (price, name and address of publisher, and often author) but reviews vary in quality and follow no particular format. One issue examined reviewed three software programs all of which were games.

H & E Computronics, 50 N. Pascack Rd., Spring Valley, N.Y. 10977. $24; $3 for a single copy. Published monthly.

The purpose of this journal is to "provide and exchange information related to the care, use and applications of TRS-80 computer systems," although it is not sponsored by or in any way officially connected with Radio Shack which markets the TRS-80 microcomputer.

Special features include lists of software exchange programs and articles on educational programs. Descriptive announcements of new software are included in regular features such as Bits and Pieces (which recently listed The Instructors' System Which Permits Teachers to Keep Student Records and Create and Print Exams) and The Crystal Ball (which recently described COMPUTER SAT, a new package consisting of textbook, floppy disks, and a user's manual designed to help high school students prepare for the Scholastic Achievement Test). Descriptions are approximately five to six paragraphs long, and generally include price and publisher's name and address for ordering.

Reviews: None.

The Rainbow, Falsoft, Inc., Box 209, Prospect, Ky. 40059. (502) 228-4492. $22; $2.95 for a single copy. Published monthly.

The Rainbow is devoted to articles and features of interest to users of TRS-80 Color Computer, a specific model marketed by the Radio Shack company. While it contains articles and programming news and tips which may be of general interest, most articles only apply to this one model of computer. Articles are included about business and home applications, and about educational topics such as grammar programs and the advantages of using the Color Computer in your school.

The journal includes regular columns such as Education Notes, Bits and Bytes of Basic, Using Graphics, and Product Reviews. The latter includes reviews of books, hardware, software, and peripherals or additional equipment. Actual programs which may be typed in and run on the Color Computer are included in articles.

Reviews: All items reviewed, hardware and software, are listed in the table of contents. The disadvantage of this index is that, although it is conveniently arranged alphabetically by product name, it does not identify what the product is. Thus, if one wishes to find all the software reviews, one has to look up each product reviewed.

Reviews typically run less than one page and are either by *Rainbow* staff or by others who are named. Each reviewer follows his own format and there is no rating system used. Reviewers are very frank in their criticisms of program weaknesses or flaws and provide good descriptions which address actual use situations. All appear not only to have used the programs thoroughly but some also used them with appropriate target users such as school children. Prices and order information are included but not always the memory and equipment or language requirements, and all programs are Radio

Shack Color Computer compatible. Software reviewed includes games, instructional programs, and utility or management programs. One issue examined had over twenty-five software reviews, including three of educational programs, and over half a dozen games.

Software Critic. *See* entry under Reviews Journals and Services.

TRS-80 Microcomputer News, Box 2910, Fort Worth, Tex. 76113-2910. (817) 390-3835. Free six-month subscription available to purchasers of new TRS-80 microcomputer systems with addresses in the United States, Puerto Rico, and Canada; others $12; $1.50 for a single copy. Published monthly.

Exclusively addressed to users of TRS-80 computer systems, each issue publishes programs written and submitted by readers plus information about new hardware and software. Programs may be used and/or reproduced without obtaining publisher's permission if used for personal, noncommerical use.
Programs are produced "as is," and, although some effort to ensure that programs do work is made, Radio Shack assumes no liability for accuracy or results obtained. Names and addresses of program authors are provided.
The Education section contains descriptions of new educational software (e.g., "Chemistry Simulations for Secondary Students"). An annual cumulative subject index appears in the December issue.
Reviews: This journal offers no critical reviews; articles on software packages are noncritical descriptive only, designed mainly to promote product sales.

two/sixteen Magazine, Box 1216, Lancaster, Pa. 17604. (717) 397-3364. $30; $5.95 for a single copy. Published bimonthly.

This is a fairly new journal for business, professional, and scientific users of the TRS-80 Model II and 16 computers.
Reviews: Reviews are primarily of business and management software. Two programs reviewed in a typical issue examined word processing tools— Proofreader and Grammatik. Reviews are signed by identified reviewers who have used the programs, run as long as five pages, and are quite entertaining. Order information and prices, including telephone numbers are provided.

Texas Instruments

99'er Home Computer Magazine, Box 5537, Eugene, Oreg. 97405. (503) 485-8796. $25; $3.50 for a single copy. Published monthly.

Reviews: This magazine includes software reviews.

TI Source & LOGO News, Microcomputers Corporation, 34 Maple Ave., Armonk, N.Y. 10504. (914) 273-6480. Free. Published monthly.

Essentially an advertising vehicle to announce software available for the Texas Instruments TI 99/4A microcomputer, this describes new courseware and has an order form. However, the newsletter states: "We in no way intend these descriptions to be an endorsement of specific products." Products included have been rated for "ease of use, clarity of instruction, appropriateness of material for the intended population, availability of documentation and depth of support material provided." Reviewers are both educators and programmers who have had an opportunity to test the courseware. Most of the items are either described briefly or simply listed. Also included is a listing of TI hardware and peripherals.

Timex/Sinclair

SYNC Magazine, 39 E. Hanover Ave., Morris Plains, N.J. 07950. (800) 631-8112, in New Jersey call (201) 540-0445. $16; $2.95 for a single copy. Published bimonthly.

Reviews: Software reviews are included.

SYNTAX, The Harvard Group, RD 2, Box 457, Harvard, Mass. 01451. (617) 456-3661. $29; $4 for a single copy. Published monthly.

Reviews: Software reviews are included.

SQ: Syntax Quarterly, The Harvard Group, RD 2, Box 457, Harvard, Mass. 01451. (617) 456-3661. $15; $4.95 for a single copy. Published quarterly.

Reviews: Both hardware and software reviews are included.

NEWSLETTERS FROM USER GROUPS AND OTHER GROUPS

Computer Update, Boston Computer Society, Inc., 3 Center Plaza, Boston, Mass. 02108. (617) 367-8080. $20; $2 for a single copy. Published bimonthly.

This is the official newsletter of the Boston Computer Society, the largest computer user group in the United States (see chapter 7 for a description of BCS).

ComputerTown™ News Bulletin, Box E, Menlo Park, Calif. 94025. (415) 323-3111. $25 membership fee. Published bimonthly.

This is the official newsletter of the ComputerTown organization, an international, nonprofit educational corporation (see description in chapter 7) dedicated to the promotion of universal computer literacy. Through its newsletter, ComputerTown provides consulting and support services to some two hundred ComputerTown sites worldwide. Groups and leaders, as well as those under the age of sixteen, have a different dues structure. The *ComputerTown News Bulletin* provides organization news, microcomputer news, discounts on selected computer journal subscriptions, a listing of computer courses available in Menlo Park, funding tips, a complete listing of members, a bulletin board of computer conferences, and software reviews.

Reviews: Reviews of educational software are included. They provide name, distributor/producer, address, system requirements, summary of the program, audience level, and price. Description of the program includes discussion of the documentation and purposes of the software.

CUE Newsletter, Computer-Using Educators, c/o Don McKell, Box 18547, San Jose, Calif. 95158. Free to CUE members. Published six times a year.

The *CUE Newsletter* is published by Computer-Using Educators, a non-profit California corporation founded by teachers in 1978 to promote and improve computer use in schools and colleges. CUE is affiliated with the International Council for Computers in Education which publishes the *Computing Teacher*. General interest articles for educators keep one up-to-date on new developments, publications, review sources, books, etc.

The Soft Swap Notes column updates readers on the activities of SOFT-SWAP, an educational software library and exchange program sponsored by CUE. While actual programs are not included in the newsletter, complete order information and order blanks are included for obtaining the SOFTSWAP programs.

Reviews: None.

Etc.: Educational Technology & Communication, Far West Laboratory, 1855 Folsom St., San Francisco, Calif. 94103. (415) 565-3000. $36. Published eleven times a year.

Etc. is the newsletter of the Far West Laboratory for Educational Research and Development (see description in chapter 7). It is designed to keep educators abreast of developments in technology and their applications in education, and to serve as a forum for the discussion of issues and problems confronting the schools. Included are general technology news developments, hardware and software data, and information about programs and projects, new publications, research studies, and computer events.

Hands On!, Technical Education Research Centers, 8 Eliot St., Cambridge, Mass. 02138. $10 contribution. Published quarterly.

This quarterly newsletter of TERC (see description in chapter 7) contains articles on a broad range of educational microcomputer topics including languages, software evaluation, graphics, word processing, and computing events. It also includes announcements of TERC activities such as workshops and computer classes. The journal contains software reviews, book reviews, a listing of TERC publications which are for sale, and an idea exchange.

Reviews: The reviews are not thorough evaluations of individual titles but rather articles which provide an overview or state-of-the-art survey of software in broad subject categories. A recent one focused on the sciences and discussed programs and producers of chemistry, physics, astronomy, biology, earth sciences and geology, and general science software. That issue included a bibliography of the programs mentioned in the article including addresses; prices were not included.

The Jeffries Report, Ron Jeffries, Editor, Box 6838, Santa Barbara, Calif. 93111. (805) 967-7167. $30; $3 for a single copy. Published monthly.

Subtitled *A Personal View of Computing*, this newsletter contains industry news on microcomputers, software, and new publications including books, magazines, and other newsletters.

MACUL Journal. *See* entry under Educational Computing Journals.

MEAN BRIEF, Microcomputer Education Applications Network, 256 N. Washington St., Falls Church, Va. 22046. (703) 536-2310. $10. Published quarterly.

MEAN BRIEF is the newsletter of the Microcomputer Education Applications Network, a national communications network designed to facilitate the exchange of information among developers of educational software in remedial and special education areas. Its focus is administrative. Membership is included in the subscription fee. The newsletter provides technology news from Washington and the Department of Education, survey results, new software releases, hardware developments and other features including a subscriber information exchange, all for a variety of computer brands.
Reviews: None.

MICROgram, EPIE and Consumers Union, Box 839, Water Mill, N.Y. 11976. (516) 283-4922. $48; free with subscription to *The Computing Teacher*. Published monthly.

MICROgram is the newsletter of the Consortium for Quality in Educational Computing Products which is sponsored by the Educational Products Information Exchange (EPIE) and Consumers Union who publish *Micro-Courseware* and *Hardware PRO/FILES*. This newsletter allows consumers of microcomputer products to voice their concerns and recommendations to those companies which produce these commodities and is automatically sent to all individuals or organizations which subscribe to the *PRO/FILES* service. *MICROgram* provides consumers with industry news, purchasing tips, and educational computing developments.
Reviews: None.

Turtle News and LOGO Newsletter. *See* entry under Computer Magazines for Children.

Users: The MECC Instructional Computing Newsletter, 2520 N. Broadway Dr., St. Paul, Minn. 55113. (612) 376-1117. Sent upon request. Published monthly.

This is the newsletter for members of the Minnesota Educational Computer Consortium and others using MECC materials who wish to keep apprised of new products available through the consortium. Materials available include software, books, and teaching manuals. These materials support the use of three computing alternatives: the MECC Timeshare System (available to cooperating schools in Minnesota), the Apple II computer, and the Atari computer.

Reviews: Software reviews are limited to MECC programs and are written by MECC evaluators with each review giving the following basic data: title, producer (including name, address, and telephone number), support materials and program components, and price and equipment needed including memory size. This is followed by a general product description and a statement of the MECC classroom review situation if there was an actual field test performed. The MECC evaluators' critique discusses educational content or value, ease of use, level of student interest, how well the program uses microcomputer capabilities, and support materials. Reviews end with an evaluation summary. A recent issue contained two reviews.

PUBLICATIONS ON
MICROCOMPUTERS IN LIBRARIES

Access: Microcomputers in Libraries, DAC Publications, Box 764, Oakridge, Oreg. 97463. $11; $3 for a single copy. Published quarterly.

Special interest journal geared to the needs of smaller libraries (public, school, small college) or those who can use the microcomputer for library instruction or data based management applications. The journal offers general articles on software, automation, special projects, etc. Book reviews are included and new products listed.

Reviews: Two-page descriptive and evaluative comprehensive reviews are included. Reviewers have used the programs discussed and experienced the problems and processes firsthand. Documentation is evaluated, and specific purchasing recommendations are given according to the user's experience, need, and ability. Price, complete order information (name, address), and type of program are listed. Signed reviews identify the reviewer by title and institutional affiliation. *Access* also publishes MicroSIFT reviews.

CMC News, 515 Oak St. N, Cannon Falls, Minn. 55009. $3; $1 for a single copy. Published three times a year: spring, fall, winter.

Subtitled *Computers and the Media Center*, this newsletter is published and edited by Jim Deacon in Minnesota and contains news, views, ads, bibliographies of articles and books, and software reviews. It is a good means of keeping up with use of microcomputers in small libraries, particularly the school media center. Its critiques of magazine articles help keep one up-to-date on the rapid developments in the field.

Reviews: CMC News includes reviews written by subscribers about programs they have actually used, as well as some reprinted from other sources including Minnesota Educational Computer Consortium. While there are no set guidelines or format followed for the reviews, they are both informative and evaluative, and typically run about one page in length. There are sometimes two reviews of the same software program. Reviewers are identified by name and generally title and position. The lack of standard format often makes it difficult to find basic program information (i.e., brand, memory needed, source) on titles reviewed. The number of reviews per issue varies from none to four.

Small Computers in Libraries, Graduate Library School, College of Education, University of Arizona, 1515 E. First St., Tucson, Ariz. 85721. (602) 626-3566. $20; $1.75 for a single copy. Published monthly.

Prepared by the Graduate Library School at the University of Arizona, this newsletter primarily carries news notes on publications and products and reader contributed articles on how libraries throughout the country are using microcomputers in their operations. It claims to be the only monthly publication devoted to the library use of microcomputers.

Reviews: A recent issue contained one review, a page and a half long on a data based management software program appropriate for library use. The review included a thorough description of the program and the documentation, discussed drawbacks or weaknesses, explained computer system necessary to run the program, and offered price and complete order information including telephone number.

Software Reviews. *See* entry under Review Journals and Services.

JOURNALS ON DISK OR CASSETTE

Chromasette. *See* entry under Journals on Disk or Cassette in chapter 5.

CLOAD. *See* entry under Journals on Disk or Cassette in chapter 5.

Microzine. *See* entry under Journals on Disk or Cassette in chapter 5.

School CourseWare Journal. *See* entry under Journals on Disk or Cassette in chapter 5.

Window, 469 Pleasant St., Watertown, Mass. 02172. (617) 923-9147. $95; $24.95 for a current issue. Published five times a year.

Window is a "learning magazine on a disk" available either for the Apple II or Apple II Plus computer with one disk drive, at least 48K of memory and DOS 3.3. Instead of a traditional magazine issue, subscribers receive a disk on which there are actual microcomputer programs.

Each issue includes a feature program (e.g., a recent one was a program for learning BASIC), a feature article (e.g., a computer detective mystery), educational games, and interactive reviews of software programs available from such major publishers as McGraw-Hill. There are computer utilities tools (such as database systems), music composition programs, turtle graphics, and economic analysis programs provided on a regular basis as well as previews of new software releases and regular columns on Visicalc, LOGO, and other current computer topics.

Reviews: Interactive reviews are provided of some of the best educational software from major publishers. Reviews actually allow the user to experience the program by including a portion of it on the disk and allowing the subscriber to evaluate it her/himself before considering purchase. Although this is somewhat comparable to previewing a publisher's demonstration disk, which only includes a portion of a total lesson or set of lessons, it is still better than buying programs without ever having seen the software demonstrated.

NEWSWEEKLIES

Computerworld, C W Communications, Inc., Box 880, Framingham, Mass. 01701. $44; $1.50 for a single copy. Published weekly.

Subtitled *The Newsweekly for the Computer Community*, *Computerworld* does not limit its news coverage to microcomputers but includes the entire spectrum from main frame to home computers in its pages. Articles are grouped under general news, software and services, communications, systems and peripherals, office automation, and the computer industry. While *InfoWorld*, which limits itself to microcomputers and has software reviews might be a first choice for micro users, *Computerworld* keeps one abreast of developments in the entire computer industry and carries an impressive listing of job position announcements and other computer-related classifieds.

InfoWorld, Box 880, Framingham, Mass. 01701. (800) 343-6474, in Massachusetts call (617) 879-0700. $25; $1.25 for a single copy. Published weekly except in January.

The newsweekly specifically for microcomputer users, this newspaper comes out every week except for a single combined issue published the first two weeks of January by Popular Computing, Inc. *InfoWorld* may be the only way for anyone to keep up with the rapidly developing microcomputer field these days as it covers industry news for a broad variety of computer brands and software publishers. Some sample topics featured in recent articles include compatibility of the new Apple IIe with the old Apple II Plus software, the new smaller disk size, and the availability of new online personnel job recruiting services. Besides the news articles, there are regular columns and features each week, including New Technologies, Education, Business, Getting Started, Industry Report, Software News, Graphics, and software, hardware, and book reviews.

Reviews: Reviews are signed (although reviewers are not identified by title, etc.) and follow a standard format addressing features, performance, documentation, ease of use, and error handling. Besides the critical essay which runs approximately one page (newspaper size), there is an inset box called the *InfoWorld* Software Report Card which gives a capsule rating of the last four evaluation criteria listed above on a four point rating scale which includes poor, fair, good, and excellent. Beneath this are given system requirements (computer brand, model, memory, etc.), price and publisher's name, address, and telephone number. At the end of each review, there is a capsule summary of the evaluation with a final recommendation for purchase. Reviewers point out weaknesses and problems encountered in using the programs.

One typical issue has two software reviews, both for noneducational programs. The December 6, 1982, issue contains a Software Review Recap, which is an alphabetical listing of all software reviewed in the past year. Other review aids are charts comparing similar types of programs (e.g., a word processing program comparison chart appeared in the January 13, 1983, issue).

COMPUTER MAGAZINES FOR CHILDREN

DIGIT, Box 29996, San Francisco, Calif. 94129. (415) 931-1885. $18.95. Published bimonthly.

Subtitled *The Video/Computing Connection for Young People,* this is a new magazine written especially for children and designed to assist young people in taking full advantage of the electronics revolution.

Microzine. *See* entry under Journals on Disk or Cassette in chapter 5.

Student Computer News, Box 87H, Kickapoo, Ill. 61528. $14. Published monthly.

This is a newsletter featuring software and hardware listings, programming tips, and a question and answer column.

Turtle News and LOGO Newsletter, Young People's LOGO Association, Inc., 1208 Hillsdale Dr., Richardson, Tex. 75081. (214) 783-7548. Free to members. Published monthly.

This newspaper format newsletter contains *Turtle News* (the major portion) and within its pages a section called the *LOGO Newsletter.* It is sent to members of the Young Peoples' LOGO Association. Written specifically for children, *Turtle News* contains articles, programs for six computer brands, news about computer camps, columns, stories, contest announcements, and information on the association's software exchange program.

COMPUTER HARDWARE REVIEWS

Computer Equipment Review, Meckler Publishing, Box 405, Saugatuck Station, Westport, Conn. 06880. $85-$150 depending on the size of one's library materials budget. Published semiannually.

Formerly *Library Computer Equipment Review.*

Computer Shopper, Patch Publishing Company, Box F, Titusville, Fla. 32780. $10. Published monthly.

Microcomputer Hardware PRO/FILES, EPIE and Consumers Union, Box
839, Water Mill, N.Y. 11976. (516) 283-4922. $125 with monthly updates.

Essentially a hardware review service, *Microcomputer Hardware PRO/
FILES* begins with a basic set of twenty-five microcomputer equipment and
peripheral reviews sent in a plastic filebox which are updated with additional
product reports on a monthly basis. Computer brands reviewed include Apple,
Atari, Commodore, IBM, Osborne, Radio Shack, and Texas Instruments.
There are also reviews for printers and other microcomputer peripherals. The
MICROgram newsletter comes free to all *PRO/FILE* subscribers.

Reviews: All hardware evaluations are based on laboratory tests
performed by Consumers Union with feedback included from actual user
experience. Information for each hardware *PRO/FILE* includes photographs
of the unit and its character display, laboratory test findings in regard to the
keyboard's susceptibility to damage, character legibility on screen and printer
copy, ease of operation, disk drive performance specifications, type and
quality of cables and connectors, and shock hazard; summative evaluation of
unique capabilities and limitations; pricing; manufacturer's information;
"brain power" data on memory size, expansion capability, microprocessor
model, and resident language and operation manuals.

A sample *PRO/FILE* may be ordered from EPIE/CU. The format of
these reviews is excellent.

INDEXES

ACM Guide to Computing Literature, Association for Computing Machinery,
Box 64145, Baltimore, Md. 21264. (301) 528-4261. $50 to nonmembers;
$25 to members.

This guide includes educational listings although it is primarily an index to
computer science literature. The 1980 guide lists over fifty thousand books,
papers and reports with nearly eighteen thousand authors included. There are
six separate indexes: titles, authors, keywords, topics, sources, and reviewers.
All the items reviewed and abstracted in ACM's *Computing Reviews* are listed.
The 1981-82 edition will be out early in 1984.

Color Computer Index, American Library and Information Service, 3705
Mary Ellen, NE, Albuquerque, N. Mex. 87111.

This index contains citations and brief annotations of articles, programs,
reviews, and news releases solely about the color computer. Items are listed by
title, author, and subject from a variety of magazines.

The Index, W. H. Wallace, Missouri Indexing, Inc., Box 301, St. Ann, Mo.
63074. (314) 997-6470. $15 per volume.

Aimed at the home personal computer user, *The Index* provides in two
volumes a guide to articles in eighty journals and newsletters from early 1975
through the spring of 1983. Volume 1 indexes forty-four magazines from 1975
to the summer of 1981. Volume 2 picks up additional titles from 1975 and
updates the earlier titles from fall of 1981 to early 1983. Indexing is by

keyword from the titles, and entries are grouped by computer system brands. Program listings are indicated and reviews of both hardware and software are included.

Micro Publications in Review, Vogeler Publishing, Inc., Box 489, Arlington Heights, Ill. 60006. (312) 255-6385.

This index reprints the tables of contents from approximately seventy journals, magazines, and newsletters aimed at users of the small computer. Besides the contents, there is a subject index of twenty-six broad subject categories subdivided into more specific topics and a listing of publishers' addresses.

Microcomputer Index, Microcomputer Information Services, 2464 El Camino Real, #247, Santa Clara, Calif. 95051. (408) 984-1097. $38. Published quarterly.

This is a subject index covering over 1,250 abstracted articles in forty microcomputer journals including five titles which focus particularly on educational computing. *MI* is now available online through Dialog Information Retrieval Services as file #233 and as Comp 3 on Knowledge Index (another database) as well as in print form and carries abstracts of articles, indexes, reviews, and program listings. It goes through each journal indexed month by month and article by article, including book reviews as well as reviews of microcomputer software, thus providing quite comprehensive coverage of the microcomputer literature available.

RICE. *See* entry under Other Software Listings in chapter 5.

School Microware Reviews. *See* entry under Review Journals and Services.

7

AIDS TO SELECTION: MICROCOMPUTER CONSORTIA, USER GROUPS, AND REGIONAL EDUCATIONAL ORGANIZATIONS

Since software evaluation has become a major concern of educators and other microcomputer users throughout the country, a number of consortia, regional educational organizations, and even user groups either have been established specifically to develop and/or evaluate microcomputer software or have taken this on as a project of their organization. Although it would be impractical to discuss here all of the organizations involved in such computer-related activities, a representative cross section of some of the larger or better-known groups will be described along with the nature of their activities. More importantly, the reader will be told about the actual software programs and the reviews which these groups provide. The journals and newsletters of these groups are described in previous chapters and can be most easily accessed through the index of this book.

An additional source is the annual *Classroom Computer News Directory of Educational Computing Resources*, Part III: Local and Regional Resources, which, as the discussion in chapter 5 explains, lists by geographical location throughout the United States and Canada the following types of organizations: resource centers, ongoing projects, user groups, educators' organizations, and computer learning centers that can provide local help in selection and evaluation of software.

Some of the major organizations included in this chapter had been in operation and actively involved in other types of research and development activities prior to their involvement with microcomputers. The following descriptions of these organizations include information culled from published sources (in most cases provided by the organizations themselves) and a questionnaire which was sent to each group. A brief history of each organization is provided along with a discussion of the scope and nature of its computer-related activities.

Association for Educational Communications and Technology, 1126 Sixteenth St., NW, Washington, D.C. 20036. (202) 466-4780.

The Association for Educational Communications and Technology (AECT) was founded in 1923 and considers itself the only national professional association dedicated to the improvement of instruction through media and technology. Microcomputers are only one segment of the interests of AECT's fourteen thousand members who work as audiovisual, media, and library specialists; educational administrators; researchers; teachers and professors; media service directors; and communications specialists; and specialize in numerous other instructional technology fields. AECT's general purposes include advancing the interests of communications technology, promoting the integral role of instructional technology in the educational process, and monitoring government policies that affect instructional technology. AECT has forty-eight statewide and thirteen national affiliates.

AECT's computer-related activities include publications, workshop presentations at its national and regional conventions, and, most recently, a two-year federally funded program called Project BEST, which has established an electronic mail service via computer for state education agencies and initiated development of video satellite teleconference programs for microcomputer inservice training for educators. AECT's official journal *Instructional Innovator* regularly offers articles on microcomputers. Additionally, the organization publishes numerous books, both on the use of microcomputers in education and on computer literacy, and produces a range of audiovisual instructional aids. One can obtain AECT's list of publications and productions, or membership information, by writing to the above address.

Association for Educational Data Systems, 1201 Sixteenth St., NW, Washington, D.C. 20036. (202) 822-7845.

The Association for Educational Data Systems (AEDS) is an international professional organization founded in 1962 to promote the advancement of educational technology. AEDS has three divisions (Instructional, Computer Science, and Administrative), and twenty-four chapters.

Its major purposes include providing a forum for the exchange of ideas regarding the impact of educational technology, promoting greater understanding of technology at all levels of education, promoting recognition of the professional role of the educational data processor, and assuming an active leadership role by keeping educators and computing specialists informed of technological developments.

Membership is open to all persons interested in the use of computers in education and includes educators and technical experts from the United States and Canada and other foreign countries. These members represent public and private schools, higher education, state or provincial departments of education, the federal government, and professional and technical groups.

AEDS's activities include publications, workshops, an annual convention, and a computer programming contest. The *AEDS Journal*, the *AEDS Monitor*, and the *AEDS Newsletter* are all sent as benefits of membership and provide readers with association news plus articles on the state of the art in educational computing and selection and evaluation of microcomputer software. The programming contest is open to students in grades 7-12. Additional information may be obtained about AEDS membership by writing to the above address.

The Boston Computer Society, Three Center Plaza, Boston, Mass. 02108. (617) 367-8080.

The Boston Computer Society (BCS), the largest nonprofit personal computer association in the United States, is actually a consortium of user groups representing owners of the computer systems in common use today including Apple, Atari, TRS-80, IBM, North Star, OSI, PET, Robotics, and Sinclair and information utilities such as The Source. BCS additionally serves as a computer resource center and provides monthly meetings as well as seminars on a broad range of topics for home, educational, and business users. Through its Educational Resource Exchange it provides information on funding, teacher training, equipment selection, availability of software, and a host of other issues of interest to educators. Special events sponsored by the BCS have included two national computer shows and a forum on the future of personal computers.

A BCS discount program available in New England entitles members to special discounts at most computer retail outlets. Publications include its bimonthly *Boston Computer Update* and *The First New England Microcomputer Resources Handbook*. To order these publications or obtain additional membership information, contact the Society.

California TEC Center Software Library and Clearinghouse, SMERC Library and Microcomputer Center, San Mateo County Office of Education, 333 Main St., Redwood City, Calif. 94063. (415) 363-5470.

The California Teacher Education and Computers (TEC) Center provides for the division of California into fifteen service regions. Each region containing a local TEC Center provides its teachers with inservice training in science, mathematics, computer literacy, and other subject areas.

The Microcomputer Center in the SMERC Library of the San Mateo County Office of Education has been designated as the statewide Software Library and Clearinghouse with its major purpose being the provision of support services to these TEC Centers. In providing this support, the Clearinghouse has four major responsibilities: the training of software evaluators who can then train teachers in software evaluation, the developing of a subject area/grade level matrix of favorably reviewed software, the rotating of new software collections at each TEC Center for preview/evaluation purposes, and the collecting and disseminating of critical evaluations of instructional software throughout California.

The Clearinghouse also supports the efforts of the California Library Media Consortium for Classroom Evaluation of Microcomputer Courseware in its efforts to collect teacher evaluations of software currently being used in the classroom. The Consortium was organized in 1981 and consists of fifty-four librarians and media specialists from twenty-three California counties. Their reviews are based on classroom use of the software by at least two teachers or librarians. Among the members of the Consortium are representatives from all fifteen TEC Centers. The first fifty reviews of the Consortium have been published and are available as *Courseware Reviews 1982: Fifty Classroom Based Evaluations of Microcomputer Programs*.

Further activities of the Clearinghouse itself include the compiling of an index of over sixteen hundred software reviews from local and national sources, including the Consortium's teacher reviews. It also publishes the California reviews for distribution to the TEC Centers and maintains a computerized catalog of its extensive K-12 software library which may be searched by title, subject, grade level, availability, instructional mode, or publisher. The Clearinghouse's software evaluations are available through occasional publications.

The TEC Centers are the local communication and dissemination outlets for the Clearinghouse which in turn provides them with a number of additional services including a monthly newsletter of reviews, resources, and information. The Clearinghouse supports the SOFTSWAP Program (a software exchange program described in chapter 5) in its efforts to collect, edit, and disseminate public domain software and to translate programs into additional computer systems. It also serves as liaison between the TEC Centers and software publishers concerning the need for software development in neglected areas and the matter of software copyright issues.

The California Clearinghouse is funded by the state and the Computer-Using Educators (see information about CUE in this chapter).

Other computer-related benefits provided by the SMERC Library and Microcomputer Center include access to a wide range of microcomputer equipment available for use in the Center, blank diskettes for sale, access to a library of commercial software programs which may be previewed and evaluated in the Center, an *Advisory List* of favorably reviewed software, and a number of additional direct services such as workshops.

For more information about the activities of the California TEC Center or to order *Courseware Reviews*, write to SMERC Library and Microcomputer Center at the above address.

Center for Children and Technology, Bank Street College, 610 W. One Hundred and Twelfth St., New York, N.Y. 10025. (212) 663-7200.

The Bank Street College of Education Center for Children and Technology was founded in 1979 as a research and development laboratory to investigate the impact of the new electronic technologies on children's lives and their ways of thinking, learning, and relating to one another. The original work has broadened to include teaching and outreach as well as some software development. Funding has been provided by both federal grants and private foundations including the Spencer Foundation, the Xerox Foundation, the Richard Lounsbery Foundation, the Ford Foundation, the International Paper Company Foundation, and the U.S. Department of Education.

Research projects conducted have included a study of the social and cognitive implications of programming on children learning this skill, a study of the effect of using a word processing program on children's writing and editing, software and curriculum development in science and mathematics for elementary education students, pilot research on use of computers with deaf students, and the design of models of staff development for schools wishing to implement microcomputer education. As part of their writing project, staff members developed the popular Bank Street Writer, a word processing program designed especially for students and available commercially for purchase.

The Center for Children and Technology regularly offers microcomputer courses at the professional and graduate level through the College, and it makes its research findings available through a long list of publications. To obtain this list or other information about the Bank Street Technology Center, write to the Bank Street College.

ComputerTown™, Box E, Menlo Park, Calif. 94025. (415) 323-3111.

ComputerTown is an international organization dedicated to the advancement of universal computer literacy. It pursues this goal through offering basic computer books, introductory classes, and membership. Publications include a series of guidebooks on short topics and full-length books published in conjunction with Reston Publishing Company. Introductory and intermediate computer classes are available in the San Francisco Bay area.

ComputerTown has over 250 affiliates worldwide offering computer literacy activities and services to members of their communities. Originally begun as a research project with some temporary funding from the National Science Foundation, the model organization ComputerTown, USA! has been a prototype for later ComputerTown affiliates.

Members receive both discounts on certain computer magazine subscriptions and search and referral service from the ComputerTown staff on computer-related inquiries including course design.

The *ComputerTown News Bulletin*, is the bimonthly newsletter of the organization.

Those wishing additional information should write to Fritzi Lareau at the above address.

Computer-Using Educators, Box 18547, San Jose, Calif. 95158.

Computer-Using Educators (CUE) is a nonprofit organization committed to the promotion and improvement of computer use in schools and colleges. It has approximately five thousand members from both the United States and foreign countries. CUE helps fund the Microcomputer Center of the SMERC Library at the San Mateo County Office of Education. It also publishes a bimonthly newsletter, sponsors several major computer conferences every year, and runs the educational software library and exchange program called SOFTSWAP described in chapter 5.

CONDUIT, Box 388, Iowa City, Iowa 52244. (319) 353-5789.

Five regional computer centers (at Oregon State, North Carolina Educational Computing Service, Dartmouth College, the University of Iowa and the University of Texas at Austin) joined together in 1971 to form CONDUIT. Their mutual concern was the lack of sharing of computer-based instructional ideas and their initial support was provided by a grant from the National Science Foundation (NSF) which permitted a three-year experimental study to be conducted. This experiment sought to identify ways of eliminating barriers to the more widespread use of computer materials. Using the results of their experiment, CONDUIT proposed a system for collecting, evaluating, and distributing instructional materials for use in higher education; and in 1975

CONDUIT received additional support from the NSF to develop a prototype system. In 1977, the EXXON Educational Foundation became a contributor.

Today CONDUIT exists as a nonprofit organization devoted to promoting the use of instructional computing primarily at the college level, though many of its materials have been used for secondary school students. Based at the University of Iowa and supported partially by revenue from its services and sale of instructional materials, CONDUIT has two major thrusts for its activities: providing instructors with ideas, curriculum materials and information about instructional computing; and assisting instructors and development teams to produce computer-based learning materials. Thus, CONDUIT is a research and development laboratory that both distributes courseware and assists authors in creating this software. Authors are generally college or university faculty whose materials have been produced as a result of teaching and use with their own students.

CONDUIT also provides a peer review system for software under development involving educators in the appropriate content area of the software who use the materials in their classroom. These reviewers report their findings on the "CONDUIT Review Rating Form" and from these reviews CONDUIT can determine if the material is substantively sound. Evaluators suggestions are incorporated into the final software package design. CONDUIT staff also evaluate programs for accuracy and prepare them for use and installation on a variety of computers.

The CONDUIT library of software currently contains over 160 packages in biology, chemistry, economics, education, English, geography, languages, management science, mathematics, music, physics, sociology, political science, psychology, and statistics. Many units have been written specifically for use on such computers as the Apple II, the PET 2000 and 4000 series, the TRS-80 models I and III, and the Atari 800. Along with the software, each package contains a student's manual, an instructor's guide, and notes describing how to install materials on the computer.

In conjunction with research and development activities, CONDUIT publishes the biannual magazine *PIPELINE*. CONDUIT also publishes two reports on CONDUIT standards: the CONDUIT *Author's Guide* describing how to design, develop, and package instructional software materials and the *CONDUIT BASIC Guide* describing how to write or transform programs into various BASIC dialects. CONDUIT's recent research activities have included studying the educational value and effectiveness of such features of microcomputers as graphics, color, audio, and animation through an NSF grant; and a project, financed by the Fund for the Improvement of Postsecondary Education, to identify, review and distribute thirty-five software units for several different brands of microcomputers.

Membership in CONDUIT is open to institutions and entitles the member to receive all publications produced by the organization, demonstration copies of selected packages, and substantial discounts on purchased packages. In addition, one may ask to be placed on a specific discipline mailing list which enables one to receive announcements of new programs in that particular area plus related disciplines. CONDUIT's software packages are listed in two catalogs which are published separately: (1) standard BASIC and FORTRAN packages and (2) microcomputer packages. The catalogs are free and may be ordered by writing CONDUIT.

EPIE Institute, Box 839, Water Mill, N.Y. 11976. (516) 283-4922.

The Educational Products Information Exchange (EPIE) was chartered by the Regents of the State University of New York in 1967. Thus, it is probably one of the oldest groups involved in the evaluation of both microcomputer software and hardware although this activity is a recent addition to the numerous services which are provided to educators. EPIE grew out of the need expressed by U.S. Commissioner of Education Harold Howe II for an educational "consumer's union." Through Commissioner Howe's support and a planning grant from the U.S. Office of Education, EPIE materialized and continues its efforts and ongoing research through additional funding from the Ford Foundation, the Lilly Endowment, the Carnegie Corporation, the Sloan Foundation, the Clarke Foundation, and the National Institute of Education. It does not accept funds from any companies which produce or market educational products and considers itself "the country's only full-time consumer advocacy group dedicated to improving the quality of learning in all educational environments."

Its broad scope of activities includes comprehensive services for curriculum selection, professional development workshops, educational consulting, and the production of a number of consumer publications including the well-known *EPIEgram*, and the *EPIE Reports* series which appears quarterly for both equipment and materials.

EPIE has been conducting research and evaluations on both instructional materials and equipment, including everything from textbooks to video equipment, for over a decade. Most recently, microcomputer software and hardware have been included. These latest activities have developed from the combined efforts of the EPIE Institute and the Consumers Union (CU) and have resulted in a new service which provides its subscribers with detailed reports on computers, monitors, printers, and software, as well as a monthly consumer newsletter geared to schools. Their evaluations of computer products are available as regularly updated expandable files called *Microcomputer Hardware PRO/FILES*, providing detailed reviews of tested products.

The hardware evaluations reported on in this service are based on laboratory tests performed by Consumers Union. Besides the lab testing, however, feedback from users is considered.

Courseware evaluations are conducted by teams of trained experts operating throughout the country in various school districts and universities in a similar manner to that employed by EPIE for the evaluation of other educational materials.

Besides providing these evaluation services, CU and EPIE cosponsor a Consortium for Quality in Educational Computing Products which has been established to aid educators in obtaining leverage with computer product manufacturers. Membership in this consortium includes all schools subscribing to the *PRO/FILE* service, who additionally receive *MICROgram*, the consortium's official newsletter.

MICROgram is also available through *The Computing Teacher*, the monthly publication of the International Council for Computers in Education. Not only do *Computing Teacher* subscribers obtain a discount rate when they order a special Elementary School Package containing *Micro Courseware PRO/FILES* for grades K-8, but sample EPIE/CU reviews also regularly appear in each issue of *The Computing Teacher*. Subscriptions as well as additional information about the extensive array of EPIE services available may be obtained by writing to the EPIE Institute.

ERIC Clearinghouse on Information Resources, School of Education, Syracuse University, Syracuse, N.Y. 13210. (315) 423-3640.

The ERIC Clearinghouse on Information Resources is one of the sixteen major regional subject-specialized document clearinghouses operated as part of the Educational Resources Information Center (ERIC). ERIC is a federal information system established in 1966 and currently sponsored by the National Institute of Education within the U.S. Department of Education to provide users with ready access to primarily English-language literature dealing with education. ERIC offerings include databases, abstract journals, microfiche, computer searches, online access, document reproductions, analyses, and syntheses.

The Information Resources Clearinghouse is located at Syracuse University and is the major ERIC source for computer-related materials. The Clearinghouse publishes *ERIC Fact Sheet* reviews on relevant topics (e.g., computer literacy), bibliographies of computer publications, and *ERIC/IR Update*, a semiannual bulletin containing computer and other media news plus brief reviews of new books, as well as ERIC documents and other recent publications. The Clearinghouse will also conduct literature searches of their database on microcomputer topics. Currently, there are six InfoSearch annotated bibliographies available on selected microcomputer topics from the ERIC database including an overview of microcomputers, computer literacy, hardware, software, elementary/secondary education, and specific applications of microcomputers. All are available for five dollars each from ERIC.

Far West Laboratory for Educational Research and Development, 1855 Folsom St., San Francisco, Calif. 94103. (415) 565-3221.

The Far West Laboratory for Research and Development was founded in 1966 with the basic objective of utilizing research grants and other funds for the qualitative improvement of education. By 1981, it had spent over eighty million dollars producing 750 technical reports (600 of which became ERIC documents), 300 school improvement products (manuals, guides, films, handbooks, directories, curriculum units, etc.), 300 professional articles or books, and face-to-face services to over 35,000 professional educators. Funding has come from many sources including federal grants (from both the Office of Education and the National Institute of Education), state funds, private foundations, and users' fees.

A sample of Far West's activities gives an indication of the diversity of its endeavors: interactive research and development projects, Native American student career educational materials, toy lending library, materials and technical assistance to aid schools in desegregation projects, an international center of educational methodology, a major computer-based information acquisition and dissemination system for women's concerns in education, and a Teacher's Center Exchange which provides a self-help network for staff development throughout the nation. The Far West Laboratory also played a significant role in promoting the U.S. Department of Education's National Diffusion Network (NDN), which was established in 1978 to publicize exemplary educational programs developed through federal funding. State facilitators disseminate the information and aid local school districts in adapting these programs to their needs. Services provided by Far West to these facilitators include a newsletter, an annual catalog of developer/demonstrator projects called *Educational Programs That Work*, and a training program for both developer/demonstrators and state facilitators.

Most recently, the Far West Laboratory has begun writing and developing educational software programs geared to the needs of school administrators. When completed, these packages will be available for sale. Currently, Far West performs evaluations on commercial software. These reviews are available to educators as a quarterly feature of Far West's newsletter *Etc.: Educational Technology and Communication* which also carries computer-related news and is published eleven times a year. Other computer services provided by Far West include demonstrations of both hardware and software at the Technology Learning Center and microcomputer workshops.

The International Council of Computers in Education, Education 135, University of Oregon, Eugene, Oreg. 97403. (503) 686-4414.

The International Council of Computers in Education (ICCE) is a professional computing association founded in 1979 as an outgrowth of the Northwest Council for Computers in Education to publish *The Computing Teacher* and to further the interests of the classroom teacher involved in instructional computing. Today ICCE has twenty-seven organizational members whose names and addresses appear at the end of this discussion and a total membership of twenty-thousand people including those belonging through its affiliates. Individual members of ICCE number close to eight thousand and include all persons who subscribe to *The Computing Teacher*. Professional organizations which are working to enhance the instructional use of computers at the precollege level can become organization members at no charge. ICCE helps the formation of groups working to facilitate instructional uses of computers by providing a free announcement in its journal of the proposed group's organizational meeting, a list of the journal's subscribers in the proposed group's region, a sample constitution, advice via telephone, free sample copies of *The Computing Teacher* to attendees at an organizational meeting, and a one-time reduced subscription rate to *Computing Teacher* for people who join the new organization. Organization members must be nonprofit, educationally oriented, have well-defined membership criteria, encourage their members to belong to ICCE, and be approved by ICCE's Board of Directors. Such member organizations receive free advertising for their conferences and activities, discounts on publications, and other benefits.

ICCE also publishes numerous computer books and manuals including *Introduction to Computers in Education for Elementary and Middle School Teachers, An Introduction to Computing: Content for a High School Course*, and the *Evaluator's Guide for Microcomputer—Based Instructional Packages* developed by the MicroSIFT project of the Northwest Regional Educational Laboratory.

For a complete listing of ICCE publications or further information on the organization, write to Dick Ricketts, Managing Editor of *The Computing Teacher* at ICCE.

ICCE ORGANIZATION MEMBERS

Alaska Association for Computers in Education (AACE), Anchorage, AL 99502

Alberta Association for Educational Data Systems, 2500 University Dr. NW, Calgary, Alberta T2N 1N4

Association for the Development of Computer-Based Instructional Systems (ADCIS), Bellingham, WA 98225

Computer Education Society of Ireland, Mt. Anville Secondary School, Goatstown, Dublin 14, Ireland

Computers, Learners, Users Educators Association (CLUES), Wayne, NJ 07470

Computer-Using Educators (California), San Jose, CA 95133

Computer-Using Educators of British Columbia (CUEBC), 509 Alder Street, Campbell River, British Columbia, Canada V9W 2N9

DIDACOM, Avenbeeck 98, 2182 RZ Hillegom, The Netherlands

Educational Computing Consortium of Ohio, Cleveland, OH 44124

Educational Computing Organization of Ontario (ECOO), 252 Bloor Street West, Toronto, Ontario M5S 1X6 Canada. *(This organization has absorbed the Ontario Society for Microcomputers in Education.)*

Educators Interest Group of the San Diego Computer Society, San Diego, CA 92138

Illinois Association for Educational Data Systems (ILAEDS), De Kalb, IL 60115

Indiana Computer Educators, Ft. Wayne, IN 46802

Manitoba Association for Educational Data Systems (MAN AEDS), Neepawa Area Collegiate, Box 430, Neepawa, Manitoba R0J 1H0 Canada

Michigan Association for Computer Users in Learning (MACUL), Wayne, MI 48184

Minnesota Association for Educational Data Systems, St. Paul, MN 55113

New Hampshire Association for Computer Education Statewide (NHACES), Durham, NH 03824

Northwest Council for Computer Education (Oregon and Washington), La Grande, OR 97850

Oklahoma Educational Computer Users Program (OECUP), Norman, OK 73019

Pennsylvania Learning Resources Association (PLRA), Lancaster, PA 17601

Saskatchewan Association for Computers in Education, 2200 Rusholme Road, Saskatoon, Saskatchewan S7L 4A4

The Science Teachers' Association of Ontario, 306 Beulea Dr., Nepean, Ontario K2G 4A8

Society of Data Educators (SDE), Memphis, TN 38117

Texas Computer Education Association, Dallas, TX 75230

The Utah Council for Computers in Education, Mapleton, UT 84663

West Australian Computer Educators, 12 Lilac Place, Dianella, 6062, Western Australia

Wyoming Educational Computing Council, Cheyenne, WY 82001

Michigan Association for Computer Users in Learning, Wayne Intermediate
School District, Box 807, Wayne, Mich. 48184. (313) 326-9300.

The Michigan Association for Computer Users in Learning (MACUL)
was founded in 1975 by twelve people interested in the instructional uses of
computers from micros to mainframe systems. Today MACUL, which is
representative of a successful state level computer organization, boasts a
membership of twenty-eight hundred from throughout the United States and
Canada and from several foreign countries. It is an affiliate organization
member of the International Conference of Computer Education, discussed in
this chapter, and publishes a magazine called the *MACUL Journal.*

Specific objectives of MACUL are to encourage the dissemination of
information on computer uses in learning; to assist in planning for computer
uses in learning; to prepare specifications for computer courseware including
software, hardware, and related peripherals; to promote and catalog research
on computer uses in learning; to provide for cost-reducing group purchases;
and to coordinate the development of courseware.

MACUL members are drawn from all levels and types of education, both
public and private. Each year MACUL sponsors a statewide conference and
maintains a software exchange which permits anyone attending the conference
to copy contributed programs free of charge. Mail order cost for these
diskettes is ten dollars each with programs available for the Apple II Plus, the
PET 4040, the TRS-80 Model I and the Atari 800.

The *MACUL Journal* contains both original software reviews and
reprints of *MicroSIFT* reviews. In addition, two special issues are devoted
entirely to software evaluations. To order program diskettes or to subscribe to
the *MACUL Journal* and thus join the organization contact Lary R. Smith,
Communications Secretary of MACUL, at the above address.

Microcomputer Education Applications Network, 256 N. Washington St.,
Falls Church, Va. 22046. (703) 536-2310.

The Microcomputer Education Applications Network (MEAN) is a
national communications network which provides the following services: (1)
microcomputer workshops for state and local educational administrators
geared to providing orientation and familiarization with microcomputers in
both general and specific areas of application, (2) a quarterly newsletter, the
MEAN BRIEF, which alerts readers to applications of microcomputers in
both educational instruction and administration, and (3) assistance to state
and local education agencies in the development of microcomputer software
for administrative applications.

MEAN has also developed software packages in the areas of special
education administration, fiscal management, and remedial programs in
reading and mathematics. MEAN is designed to bring together people desiring
to learn more about microcomputer applications being developed in the local
educational setting. It provides members with a network for selling proven
programs to other MEAN members, provides help in packaging programs,
and ensures that royalties are paid for sales achieved through the MEAN
network.

A subscription to the *MEAN BRIEF* is all that is required for
membership.

Microcomputer Evaluation and Resource Center, Indiana Department of Public Instruction, Division of Federal Resources and School Improvement, 3833 N. Meridian St., Indianapolis, Ind. 46204. (317) 927-0296.

The Microcomputer Evaluation and Resource Center (MERC) located in Indianapolis, Indiana, provides teachers, administrators, and other educators with an opportunity to preview and evaluate commercially available microcomputer hardware and courseware. It is representative of the state level clearinghouses and resource centers which have been set up throughout the country to aid educators in the selection of computer equipment and software.

Computer brands which have been made available on a loan basis from the vendors include Apple II Plus, Commodore PET, Atari 800, and the TRS-80 Model III. Each system also has a collection of compatible software available for preview and evaluation. Evaluations may be conducted by educators or Education Department personnel with evaluations being kept on file for review by visiting educators. Those desiring more information about the MERC evaluation and resource center or wishing an appointment to visit should contact the center at the above address.

Minnesota Educational Computing Consortium, 2520 Broadway Dr., St. Paul, Minn. 55113. (612) 638-0600.

The Minnesota Educational Computing Consortium (MECC) was created by the Minnesota State government in 1973 for the express purpose of providing coordination and direct services to students, teachers, and administrators in support of their educational computing efforts throughout the state. Members within the state include the public school systems of Minnesota, the University of Minnesota, the state university system, the state community college system, and the state Department of Education. In addition, approximately one hundred educational computing service organizations in some forty states and ten foreign countries have institutional memberships with MECC.

MECC has produced a well-known and widely used set of instructional courseware for microcomputers which is available for purchase. Besides developing software, MECC's activities include the delivery of training sessions, informational workshop presentations, and site visitations by MECC staff members to educators within the state.

MECC offers three types of services within the state: (1) a time-share system encompassing the whole state, including higher education institutions, which links together about 90 percent of Minnesota's schools, (2) a broker service for the PLATO system, and (3) support services for software and training programs. The latter includes translating the time-share software into Apple compatible courseware resulting in one of the first libraries of "downloaded" programs in the country.

MECC is currently organized to include three divisions which provide the services described:

1. Instructional Services

This division provides and coordinates instructional computing activities throughout the state of Minnesota including operating the statewide time-share computer network with two thousand terminals and four thousand microcomputers. User Services provides statewide services through ten coordinators while the Technical Services staff maintains the time-share computer system. The Communications Network reduces long distance telephone line costs permitting access to the computers in Minneapolis/St. Paul. Instructional Systems Development produces computing courseware products for the Apple II and ATARI 400 computers. The Documentation Center sells courseware and other support materials. Program libraries are maintained for time-share and microcomputer programs at the elementary, secondary, and college levels.

2. Management Information Services

Comprehensive and flexible software has been developed and is supported to assist in school district management, data processing, and reporting in the areas of personnel, finance, and student and instructional management. Planning and technical assistance is offered to regional service centers with support provided to microcomputer-based administrative applications. State computing equipment contracts permit the purchase of compatible equipment at discount rates.

3. Special Projects

Along with providing assistance in securing funds, research projects related to computer use in education are conducted and have been supported through National Science Foundation and National Institute of Education grants. Development activities have focused on finding new applications for the computer in education. Evaluation studies are conducted to measure the effectiveness of computer-based systems.

The majority of MECC's support comes from state funding, although it has received a few grants from the NSF and NIE described above. It is considered by many to be a national model for a state level educational computing consortium.

MECC publishes a newsletter called *DATA LINE* and also evaluates commercial software using the MicroSIFT evaluation form. The evaluations are available to educators by means of MECC's bimonthly publication called *Users*. MECC sponsors an annual conference which in 1982 drew twelve hundred participants from all over the United States and many foreign countries. Further information about MECC or details on how to obtain its software may be obtained by writing to the above address.

Nebraska Clearinghouse for Microcomputer Software, Teachers College, University of Nebraska-Lincoln, Lincoln, Nebr. 68588-0472. (402) 472-3158.

The Nebraska Clearinghouse for Microcomputer Software is a service activity begun at Teachers College, University of Nebraska-Lincoln, to provide schools with information and access to low-cost educational software. It is an outgrowth of the Committee for Utilization of Technology in Education (CUTE), a statewide organization which attempts to coordinate educational computing activities of public schools, educational service units, and the State Department of Education.

The Clearinghouse has a twofold purpose: (1) to evaluate software programs developed by educators throughout the state and region and to make the evaluation summaries available to program authors for future improvement of their programs and (2) to provide a vehicle for making "acceptable" programs available to potential users. Twice each academic year (in September and February) a call for programs to be evaluated is sent to selected schools, agencies, and individuals throughout the state. Evaluations are conducted on a trimester cycle (beginning in January, May, and August). Graduate-level students in educational computing courses serve as evaluators.

Program disks of evaluated software are available for ten dollars each and are listed in a catalog which may be obtained by writing to Dr. Ward Sybouts at the above address.

Northwest Regional Educational Laboratory, 300 S.W. Sixth Ave., Portland, Oreg. 97204. (503) 248-6800.

A major activity of the Northwest Regional Educational Laboratory (NWREL) located in Portland, Oregon, has been the establishment of a clearinghouse for microcomputer software and teacher information. Supported through a contract with the National Institute of Education and under the direction of Dr. Judith Edwards and Donald Holznagel, this clearinghouse called MicroSIFT (Microcomputer Software and Information for Teachers) is a central project of NWREL's Computer Technology Program. MicroSIFT has been developing methods and materials for the use of computers in education for over a decade, concerning itself with both instructional and administrative applications although the initial focus of evaluation efforts was on instructional programs due to the high demand for and proliferation of such packages.

Key objectives of the MicroSIFT clearinghouse are to develop and implement (1) a model for the dissemination of microcomputer software, information, and materials for grades K-12; (2) a suitable evaluation model for computer-based instructional packages; (3) a user support and technical assistance program in the Northwest region which provides aid to local and state education agencies in the choosing and implementing of microcomputer applications in education; and (4) a feedforward model for guiding and directing the development of new computer-assisted instruction (CAI) materials.

To conduct this clearinghouse activity, NWREL established a network of existing computer centers serving a large number of schools. Thus, MicroSIFT utilizes established educational institutions and consortia as a major mechanism for its collection, evaluation, and dissemination activities. This ensures the use of experienced personnel whose centers have a need to evaluate their own software but individually could not support a large-scale, continuous evaluation project. Currently there are over two dozen geographically representative members of the network, called SIFTnet, including school districts and regional service centers. SIFTnet is crucial to the success of the project because it provides both reviewers and test sites needed for software evaluation. The centers also provide a variety of local resources, hardware configurations, and brands, besides the expertise of their inhouse evaluators.

MicroSIFT evaluations are performed using three major components: the SIFTnet network of educational institutions described above, a set of forms developed by MicroSIFT, and the *Evaluator's Guide*. The *Guide*, revised in late 1982, is a book designed to be used by teachers and others evaluating courseware for MicroSIFT. Besides generally describing the use of the description and evaluation forms, it provides complete guidelines and interpretations of all items on the evaluation form.

The forms used by MicroSIFT were originally patterned after those used by the CONDUIT Project (described on pp. 164-65) for evaluating CAI programs used in postsecondary institutions; the forms were later modfied by SIFTnet members. Copies of both the description and the evaluation forms appear in chapter 4.

Ordinarily the evaluation process is performed in three stages:

1. "Sifting" to obtain suitable programs (done by MicroSIFT staff).

2. Filling out the description form (done by the producer and MicroSIFT staff).

3. Conducting a "Peer Review" evaluation (performed by two appropriate subject/grade level teachers at a chosen SIFTnet site) followed by an evaluation by a SIFTnet expert, who then writes up a summary review of the three evaluations.

Completion of the MicroSIFT evaluation process normally takes three months.

MicroSIFT's courseware evaluations are currently available through an online database, many state and local education agencies, and a number of professional magazines and journals. The database which disseminates MicroSIFT evaluations is RICE (Resources in Computer Education), an information base designed to provide a state of the art review of computers in the schools. RICE, designed by NWREL staff and supported by the National Institute of Education, is currently available through the computer of the Bibliographic Retrieval Services, Inc. (BRS) in Latham, New York. Since the RICE database is described in detail in chapter 5 under Other Software Listings, along with the address to write for more information, the reader is referred there for additional details.

A list of the state agencies receiving reproduction masters of all MicroSIFT evaluation reports appears at the end of this section. Educators may contact them directly to obtain these evaluations. Professional journals now publishing the evaluations include *The Computing Teacher*, *ACCESS*, *School Microware Reviews*, and a growing list of other professional magazines which request them for reproduction. See chapter 8 for information on ordering the MicroSIFT *Evaluator's Guide*.

NWREL's Technology Center for Demonstration and Training conducts microcomputer workshops on a regular basis and the *Developers Advisory*, a quarterly memorandum, publicizes information about software needs which have been identified from contacts with teachers, SIFTnet members, and other school agencies. The organization also publishes a newsletter and maintains an active mailing list. To obtain further information about their activities or workshops, write the Northwest Regional Educational Laboratory.

DISSEMINATION LIST FOR
MicroSIFT COURSEWARE REVIEWS

WESTERN STATES

ALASKA

Mr. Ed Obie
Department of Planning
Alaska Department of Education
Pouch F
Juneau, AK 99811

ARIZONA

Dr. Beverly Wheeler
Director of Information
Dissemination
Department of Education
State of Arizona
1535 West Jefferson
Phoenix, AZ 85007

CALIFORNIA

Ms. Ann Lathrop
SMERC Library/Microcomputer
Center
333 Main Street
Redwood City, CA 94063

COLORADO

Mr. Gene Collins
Jefferson County Schools
13300 W. Ellsworth Avenue
Golden, CO 90401

HAWAII

Ms. Kathleen D. Steffen
Hawaii Educational Dissemination
Diffusion System
Office of Instructional Services
Curriculum Materials and Services
Development Section
233 Vineyard Street
Honolulu, HI 96813

IDAHO

Mr. Charles A. Brown
Coordinator, Management
Information
Department of Education
State of Idaho
Len B. Jordan Office Building
Boise, ID 83720

Mr. George Tucker
Basic Skills
Idaho State Department of
Education
LBJ Office Building
Boise, ID 83720

MONTANA

Dr. William Connett
Planning and Evaluation
Office of Public Instruction
State of Montana
Helena, MT 59601

Mr. Dan Dolan
Math Specialist
Office of Public Instruction
State of Montana
Helena, MT 59601

NEW MEXICO

Mr. Bill Trujillo
Math Specialist
Department of Education
Santa Fe, NM 87503

Mrs. Dolores Dietz
FOCUS
New Mexico State Department
of Education
Santa Fe, NM 87503

OKLAHOMA

Mr. Jack Craddock, Administrator
Communications Section
State Department of Education
State of Oklahoma
2500 North Lincoln Boulevard
Oklahoma City, OK 73105

OREGON

Mr. Jim Tompkins
Multnomah County ESD
P. O. Box 16657
Portland, OR 97216

Jerry Larer
North Clackamas School District
14211 S. E. Johnson Road
Milwaukie, OR 97222

Ben Jones
OTIS
1200 Highway 99N
Eugene, OR 97402

George Katagiri
Oregon Department of Education
700 Pringle Parkway S.E.
Salem, OR 97310

TEXAS

Ms. Nancy Baker Jones
S.W. Educational Development
Laboratory
Regional Exchange Project
211 East 7th Street
Austin, TX 78701

Ms. Marj Wightman
Project CITE
Texas Education Agency
201 E. 11th Street
Austin, TX 78701

Ms. Marilyn Fricks
Region IV ESC
P. O. Box 863
Houston, TX 77001

TEXAS (cont'd)

Mr. Tommy Wade
Region IV ESC
P. O. Box 1300
Richardson, TX 75080

UTAH

Dr. Kenneth P. Lindsay
Project Director
Utah State Board of Education
Division of Research and
Development
250 E. Fifth Street
Salt Lake City, UT 84111

WASHINGTON

Ms. Sue Collins, Coordinator
KNOW-NET Project
Division of Instructional and
Professional Services
Superintendent of Public
Instruction
7510 Armstrong Street S.W.
Tumwater, WA 98504

Ms. Kristi Harwood
Director, Educational Services
ESD #1
P. O. Box 5436
Spokane, WA 99206

Ms. Catherine Hardison and
Ms. Bridget Lambert
Co-Directors, Curriculum Services
ESD #105
33 S. Second Avenue
Yakima, WA 98902

Mr. John Pope
Administrative Assistant
Instructional Services
ESD #112
1313 N.E. 134th Street
Vancouver, WA 98665

WASHINGTON (cont'd)

Mr. C. E. Redfield
Administrative Assistant
Curriculum and Instructional
Materials
ESD #113
601 McPhee Road S.W.
Olympia, WA 98502

Mr. Richard L. Colombini
Assistant Superintendent
ESD #144
Box 155, Federal Building
Port Townsend, WA 98368

Dr. James J. Kiefert
Assistant Superintendent
Curriculum and Instruction
ESD #121
1410 S. 200th Street
Seattle, WA 98148

Mr. Marv Purvis and
Ms. Louise Gustafson
ESD #123
124 S. Fourth
Pasco, WA 99301

Mr. Harold Kafer, Consultant
Curriculum and Instruction
ESD #171
Box 1847
Wenatchee, WA 98801

Mrs. Margret Jackson
Coordinator
Curriculum and Instruction
ESD #189
330 Pacific Place
Mt. Vernon, WA 98273

EASTERN STATES

ARKANSAS

Ms. Dianne Williams
Information Center
Arkansas Department of
Education
Education Building 103A
Capitol Mall
Little Rock, AR 72201

CONNECTICUT

Ms. Elizabeth M. Glass
Consultant Computer Technology
Department of Education
State of Connecticut
165 Capitol Avenue
Hartford, CT 06115

Mr. Peter C. Young
Area Cooperative Education
Services
800 Dixwell Avenue
New Haven, CT 06511

CONNECTICUT (cont'd)

Dr. John Allison, Jr.
Capitol Regional Education
Council
212 King Philip Drive
West Hartford, CT 06117

Dr. Peter T. Willner
Cooperative Educational Services
11 Allen Road
P. O. Box 2087
Norwalk, CT 06852

Mr. George Bondera
Cooperative Special Services
Center
Carl Allgrove School
East Granby, CT 06026

Francis D. Robinson
Long-Range Educational
Assistance for Regional Needs
P. O. Box 220
East Lyme, CT 06333

CONNECTICUT (cont'd)

Ms. Kathryn Smith
ACES Computer Services
800 Dixwell Avenue
New Haven, CT 06511

Ms. Jean Muccini
Cooperative Educational Services
P. O. Box 2087
Norwalk, CT 06852

DELAWARE

Mr. Wilmer E. Wise
State Director
Planning, Research and
Evaluation Division
Department of Public Instruction
State of Delaware
P. O. Box 1402
Dover, DE 19901

FLORIDA

Dr. Ralph G. Vedros, Director
Public School Resource Center
Division of Public Schools
Department of Education
Knott Building
Tallahassee, FL 32301

Ms. Pristen Bird
Educational Technology Section
Florida Department of Education
109 Knott Building
Tallahassee, FL 32301

GEORGIA

Mr. John A. Barker
Principal Operations Analyst
Operational Systems Support
State Department of Education
16th Floor, Twin Towers East
Atlanta, GA 30334

Mrs. Joan Moore
Research Specialist
Education Information Center
18th Floor, Twin Towers East
State Department of Education
Atlanta, GA 30334

ILLINOIS

Ms. Sandra Cunningham
IER
793 N. Main Street
Glenn Ellyn, IL 60137

INDIANA

Mr. Dave McGaw
West Lafayette High School
West Lafayette, IN 47906

IOWA

Mr. Doug Archer
Green Valley AEA 14
Green Valley Road
Creston, IA 50801

KENTUCKY

Ms. Lydia Wells Sledge, Director
Unit for Educational Improvement
Kentucky Department of
Education
1808 Capital Plaza Tower
Frankfort, KY 40601

LOUISIANA

Mrs. Sue Wilson
Assistant Director for
Dissemination
State Department of Education
P. O. Box 44064
Baton Rouge, LA 70804

MAINE

Mr. Richard K. Riley
Educational Microcomputer
Consultant
Maine Department of Education
and Cultural Services
State House Station #23
Augusta, ME 04333

MARYLAND

Ms. Beverly Sangston
Montgomery County Public
Schools
850 Hungerford Drive
Rockville, MD 20850

MASSACHUSETTS

Mr. Tim Barclay
Technical Education Research
Center
8 Eliot Street
Cambridge, MA 02138

MICHIGAN

Mr. Tom Hartsig
Macomb ISD
44001 Garfield
Mt. Clemens, MI 48043

Mr. Tom Schmeltzer
Oakland ISD
2100 Lake Road
Pontiac, MI 48054

Mr. Lary Smith
Wayne ISD
33500 Van Born Road
Wayne, MI 48184

MINNESOTA

Ms. Sue Talley
TIES
1925 W. County Road B-2
Roseville, MN 55113

Mr. Kent Kehrberg
MECC
2522 Broadway Drive
Lauderdale, MN 55113

MISSISSIPPI

Mr. John Barlow
Supervisor
Educational Media Services
State Department of Education
Suite 301, Sillers Building
Jackson, MS 39205

Mr. Thomas A. Saterfiel
PREPS
P. O. Box 5365
Mississippi State, MS 39762

NEW JERSEY

Mr. Daniel W. Kunz
Division of Research, Planning
and Evaluation
Department of Education
State of New Jersey
225 West State Street
CN 500
Trenton, NJ 08625

NEW YORK

Mr. Robert M. Trombly
Coordinator
EPSIS
Room 330
New York State Education
Department
Albany, NY 12234

Center for Learning Technologies
125 EB
New York State Education
Department
Albany, NY 12234

NORTH CAROLINA

Ms. Vergie Cox
Materials Review and Evaluation
Center
Division of Educational Media
Department of Public Instruction
Raleigh, NC 27611

Ms. Ann Fowler
Education Information Specialist
State Department of Public
Instruction
Raleigh, NC 27611

PENNSYLVANIA

Ms. Shirley D. Douglas
Division of Intermediate Unit
Services
Department of Education
Box 911
Harrisburg, PA 17108

PENNSYLVANIA (cont'd)

Mr. Leroy Tuscher
Educational Technology Program
Lehigh University
524 Brodhead Avenue
Bethlehem, PA 19019

Ms. Barbara Doersom
PDE Resource Center
Pennsylvania Department of
Education
P. O. Box 911, 11th Floor
Harrisburg, PA 17108

Mr. Gary Neights
School Improvement Division
Pennsylvania Department of
Education
Harrisburg, PA 17102

Ms. Lois Perkins
RISE
725 Caley Road
King of Prussia, PA 19400

SOUTH CAROLINA

Mr. William B. Hynds, Unit
Coordinator and Mathematics
Consultant
Curriculum Development Section
South Carolina Department of
Education
Rutledge Building—Room 803
1429 Senate Street
Columbia, SC 29201

TENNESSEE

Ms. Betty Latture,
Educational Specialist
Research and Development
Tennessee Department of
Education
Room 128,
Cordell Hull Building
Nashville, TN 37219

VERMONT

Ms. Mary Terry, Director
State Capacity Building Project
Division of Federal Assistance
Vermont Department of Education
120 State Street
Montpelier, VT 05602

VIRGINIA

Dr. Kenneth Magill
Director of Instructional Media
and Technology
Virginia Department of Education
P. O. Box 6Q
Richmond, VA 23216

WASHINGTON, D.C.

Ms. Heather Harney
Capital Children's Museum
800 Third Street, N.E.
Washington, D.C. 20002

Ms. Mildred Cooper
Assistant Superintendent
District of Columbia Public
Schools
Division of Quality Assurance
415 12th Street, N.W.
Washington, D.C. 20004

WEST VIRGINIA

Ms. Ernestine Capehart
Coordinator, Mathematics
West Virginia Department of
Education
Capitol Complex
Building 6, Room B-330
Charleston, WV 25305

Ms. Sevilla Finley
Information Specialist
Resource and Referral Center
Appalachia Educational
Laboratory
P. O. Box 1348
Charleston, WV 25325

OTHER

Dr. Dennis Bybee
Office of Dependents Schools
2461 Eisenhower Avenue
Alexandria, VA 22331

Technical Education Research Centers, 8 Eliot St., Cambridge, Mass. 02138.

Technical Education Research Centers (TERC) is a nonprofit educational research and development corporation committed to improvement of education through encouraging the appropriate use of microcomputers in the classroom and the laboratory. TERC is supported by various funding sources including federal and private foundation grants, state funds, user fees, and tuition.

The organization publishes the quarterly newsletter *Hands On!*, which deals with issues and innovations related to microcomputers in education. TERC also has a number of works for sale such as the *Microcomputers in Education Resource Handbook*. Other TERC activities include trainer preparation workshops, special interest and computer language workshops (e.g., microcomputers in science instruction, LOGO, BASIC, and graphics), and a hardware/software hotline for consultations. In addition, TERC staff develop and evaluate software. Evaluations appear in the newsletter as do announcements of TERC software available for purchase. Two examples of programs for sale are a graphing/modeling program and a package designed to help users interface a computer with the laboratory. The latter includes ten sample experiments on such topics as kinematics, insolation, and calibration. For a complete listing of TERC materials or to obtain more information on its activities write to the above address.

8

ANNOTATED BIBLIOGRAPHY

Anderson, Cheryl A. **Microcomputers in Education.** Bethesda, Md.: ERIC Document Reproduction Service, ED 198 812, 1980.

Discusses identifying instructional and management needs.

Anderson, Eric. "Software Selection Considerations." **ACCESS: Microcomputers in Libraries** 2 (July 1982): 10-11, 17, 23.

Suggests criteria for selection of both software and hardware.

Ankers, Joan. "Classrooms Make Friends with Computers." **Instructor** 89 (Febrary 1980): 52-58.

Barden, William. "How to Buy Software." **Popular Computing** 2 (January 1983): 54-57.

Offers tips for making intelligent choices in the purchase of software. Concludes with a software evaluation checklist.

Barrette, Pierre P. "Selecting Digital Electronic Knowledge: A Process Model." **School Library Media Quarterly** 10 (Summer 1982): 320-36.

Proposes policies and procedures for selecting microcomputer software. Identifies five types of reinforcers. Explains MICROSIM projection model designed to determine the number of microcomputers needed given various access times.

Beechhold, Henry F. "Real-World Software in the Classroom." **Curriculum Review** 22 (May 1983): 141-44.

Beiser, Karl. "Microcomputer Periodicals for Libraries." **American Libraries** 14 (January 1983): 43-48.

Bitter, Gary G., Ruth A. Camuse, Marilyn S. Ford, Roger L. Goodberlet, Janine M. Muto, and Nancy R. Watson. **Microcomputers in Education.** Tempe, Ariz.: Office of Field Services, College of Education, Arizona State University, 1982.

Botterell, Art. "Which Micro for Me? A Guide to the Prospective User." **Educational Computer Magazine** 2 (January-February 1982): 30-31, 50-51.

Braun, Lud. "The Cost of Good Software." **Electronic Learning** 1 (November-December 1981): 36.

Bukoski, W. J. **A Survey of Computing Activities in Secondary Schools.** Washington, D.C.: ERIC Document Reproduction Service, ED 160 043, 1975.

Coburn, Peter, Peter Kelman, Nancy Roberts, Thomas Snyder, Daniel Watt, and Cheryl Weinger. **Practical Guide to Computers in Education.** Reading, Mass.: Addison-Wesley, 1982.

Two chapters deal specifically with selection—one with choosing hardware systems and the other with educational software. Appendix material includes charts comparing various computer systems, an annotated bibliography, and a resources section listing user groups and computer clubs, software directories, clearinghouses, computer associations, periodicals, and funding sources. A glossary of terms.

Cohen, Vicki Blum. "Criteria for the Evaluation of Microcomputer Courseware." **Educational Technology** 23 (January 1983): 9-14.

Seventeen attributes considered in software design identified and described in detail by a review team from the Microcomputer Resource Center at Columbia University's Teachers College. These suggested criteria provide a potential checklist for the selection and evaluation of microcomputer software.

Cohen, Vicki Blum. **Evaluating Instructional Software for the Micro-computer.** Bethesda, Md.: ERIC Document Reproduction Service, ED 216 704, 1982.

Provides a copy of an evaluation form designed as the result of a joint research project conducted by the Educational Products Information Exchange (EPIE) Institute and the Microcomputer Resource Center at Columbia University. Besides a complete description of the form development and evaluation processes used, there is a flow chart outlining the process and a thorough discussion of the evaluation criteria.

Computer Guide 1983. Cambridge, Mass.: CESS, 1983.

A buyer's guide to both hardware and software systems containing machine descriptions for over 250 computer systems and listing more than 2,000 applications programs. Hardware products from 150 manufacturers are represented.
Discusses computer languages providing the name, machine requirements, and documentation of over five hundred dialects for more than fifty languages. List vendors by location and product. Vendor data includes first shipping date, shipping rate, number installed to date, prices and purchasing

terms, and warranties offered. Complete names, addresses, and telephone numbers provided for manufacturers, dealers, and computer stores throughout the United States.

"Computer Use: The Beginning of a Revolution." **Education USA** 24 (4 January 1982): 143.

Conkling, Richard D. "The Nuts and Bolts of Selecting a Computer Assisted Instructional Program." **T.H.E. Journal** 10 (April 1983): 101-4.

Reports on 1980 Flager County (Florida) School System study of computer-assisted instruction. Six-page bibliography on the development and design of CAI materials.

Crandall, N. D. **CAI: Its Role in the Education of Ethnic Minorities.** Whittier, Calif.: ESAA Project, Los Nietos Elementary School District, 1975.

Crawford, Stuart. **A Standard's Guide for the Authoring of Instructional Software. Reference Manual Volume III.** Bethesda, Md.: ERIC Document Reproduction Service, ED 211 062, 1981.

Detailed, step-by-step instructions for authoring CAI materials plus advice on planning, coding, documenting, and evaluating courseware. An evaluation form for analysis of software under development is provided.

"Curriculum Review's Guidelines for Evaluating Computer Courseware." **Curriculum Review** 21 (May 1982): 149-51.

Curriculum Review has developed its own evaluation form and invites readers to use the form for their own classroom evaluations of software.

Dearborn, Donald E. "A Process for Selecting Computer Software." **NASSP Bulletin** 66 (September 1982): 27-30.

Describes the microcomputer software evaluation procedure used in the public schools of Alexandria, Virginia.

Deitel, Harvey M. **Introduction to Computer Programming with the BASIC Language.** Englewood Cliffs, N.J.: Prentice-Hall, 1977.

Deken, Joseph. **The Electronic Cottage.** New York: William Morrow, 1982.

Delf, Robert M. "Primer for Purchasing Software." **American School and University** 53 (July 1981): 44-45.

Discusses how to obtain the best administrative software for the money.

Delf, Robert M. "Primer for Purchasing Computer Programs: Part 2." **American School and University** 54 (September 1981): 30-31.

Offers bid solicitation tips and program evaluation techniques to aid in purchasing software.

Delf, Robert M. "Primer for Purchasing Computer Programs: Part 3." **American School and University** 54 (October 1981): 36.

Deals with hardware requirements, program considerations, and evaluation techniques.

Dennis, J. Richard. **Evaluating Materials for Teaching with a Computer.** The Illinois Series on Educational Application of Computers, no. 5E. Bethesda, Md.: ERIC Document Reproduction Service, ED 183 185, 1979.

Suggests an evaluation process for commercially prepared courseware.

Dlabay, Les R. "The Educator's Guide to Computer Periodicals." **Curriculum Review** 21 (May 1982): 144-46.

Doerr, Christine. **Microcomputers and the 3 R's: A Guide for Teachers.** Rochelle Park, N.J.: Hayden, 1979.

Program listings and discussions of BASIC commands. A syllabus outlining a seven-week computer literacy course. Discussions of which computer to buy, contrasting features of the various machines, and concluding with a comparative system chart.

Douglas, Shirley, and Gary Neights. **Instructional Software Selection: A Guide to Instructional Microcomputer Software.** Microcomputers in Education Series. Bethesda, Md.: ERIC Document Reproduction Service, ED 205 201, 1981.

A hardware/software interface analysis sheet. A software evaluation form. Appendixes listing computer resources such as user groups and clubs, other organizations, and bibliographies. A six-page glossary of micro-computer terms.

Dyer, Susan R. and Richard C. Forcier. "How to Pick a Computer Software." **Instructional Innovator** 27 (September 1982): 38-40.

Edwards, Judith B., Antoinette S. Ellis, Duane E. Richardson, Donald Holznagel, and Daniel Klassen. **Computer Applications in Instruction: A Teacher's Guide to Selection and Use.** Hanover, N.H.: Time Share, 1978.

A useful sourcebook for those who need to look up such specific information as differences between translators and programming languages or the different languages and their uses. Section on instructional uses of the computer provides a model illustrating five basic categories of computer use in education (e.g., computer as laboratory). Each category is further subdivided into the appropriate modes which would be used for teaching purposes in that category and results in a comprehensive model. Section on selecting computer-based instructional units outlines a theoretical but nonetheless workable selection process and provides both selection criteria and forms. Provides readings on a broad variety of subject areas. Lists sources of computer-based instructional materials.

Eldredge, Bruce, and Kenneth Delp. "But What's a Software? How to Evaluate Educational Computer Programs." **Media and Methods** 17 (February 1981): 4.

Discusses criteria for evaluating microcomputer software.

"Evaluating Software: Be Hard on Software." **Education USA** 24 (January 1982): 146.

Evaluator's Guide for Microcomputer-Based Instructional Packages. Eugene, Oreg.: International Council for Computers in Education, 1983.

"For Your Information: Computers in Schools." **Education Times** 3 (27 September 1982): 8.

Frederick, Franz J. **Guide to Microcomputers.** Washington, D.C.: Association for Educational Communications and Technology, 1980.

Gerhold, George. "An Overview of Educational Software." **Micro** 57 (February 1983): 86-88.

Deals with educational systems software, specialized languages, and systems designed especially for educational applications. Discusses LOGO and PILOT.

Glotfelty, Ruth. "Stalking Microcomputer Software." **School Library Journal** 28 (March 1982): 91-94.

Provides a case study of the introduction of microcomputers into the Pontiac Township Illinois High School media center and the problems encountered in establishing a collection of programs. Briefly describes each program previewed and why the decision was made either to purchase or not.

Golas, Katharine C. "The Formative Evaluation of Computer-Assisted Instruction." **Educational Technology** 23 (January 1983): 26-28.

Describes special considerations in the evaluation of CAI, outlines a recommended approach for evaluating these materials, and offers suggestions to CAI evaluators for process simplification.

Golden, Frederic. "Here Come the Microkids." **Time** 119 (3 May 1982): 50-56.

Good, Phillip. "Choosing the Right Business Software." **Popular Computing** 1 (April 1982): 33-38.

Three charts, including a list of software guides, guides to business software, and guidelines for selecting word processing software make this an excellent introductory article for anyone considering data based management, business-type applications of computer software.

Gordon, Anitra, and Karl Zinn. "Microcomputer Software Considerations." **School Library Journal** 28 (August 1982): 25-27.

Grady, M. Tim, and Jane E. Gawronski, eds. **Computers in Curriculum and Instruction.** Alexandria, Va.: Association for Supervision and Curriculum Development, 1983.

A book of readings providing both an introduction to instructional computing and a closer look at such specialized topics as computer literacy, computer consortiums (MECC), state-level associations (Texas Computer Education Association), applications in specific subject areas and predictions on the future of computing. An entire section is devoted to choosing computers. Six criteria for software and a software evaluation form are provided.

Guide for Selecting a Computer-Based Instructional System. Austin, Tex.: Texas Education Agency, n.d.

A set of guidelines for selecting computer-assisted instruction systems. Appendixes include criteria for selection of courseware and hardware, a selected list of sources for courseware reviews, implementation questions, a review list of the implementation steps, and a glossary of computer terms. Copies are available for one dollar from the Texas Education Agency, 201 E. Eleventh St., Austin, TX 78701.

Hakansson, Joyce. "How to Evaluate Educational Courseware." **The Journal of Courseware Review** 1 (1981): 3-5.

Proposes a set of basic questions to ask when considering purchase of a program.

Heck, William P., Jerry Johnson, and Robert J. Kansky. **Guidelines for Evaluating Computerized Instructional Materials.** Reston, Va.: National Council of Teachers of Mathematics, 1981.

An excellent, brief introduction to instructional computing. Provides for a variety of different user levels, ranging from those with no computer experience to persons with a broad range of programming skills. Tips on obtaining software, resources for finding programs (directories, books, consortia, research labs), evaluation guidelines, and an outline of steps involved in the software review process. An evaluation checklist appears at the end of the guide and is reproduced in chapter 4 of this book. Copies of this handbook may be obtained by writing National Council of Teachers of Mathematics, 1906 Association Dr., Reston, VA 22091.

Hirschbuhl, J. J. **Blueprint for the Future of Computer Based Instruction.** Akron, Ohio: Akron University, 1977.

Hoover, Todd, and Sandra Gould. "The Pirating of Computer Programs: A Survey of Software Producers." **Educational Technology** 22 (October 1982): 23-26.

Survey of a random selection of sixty-eight software houses marketing Apple compatible programs.

"How to Be a Software Whiz." **The Executive Educator** 4 (March 1982): 29-31.

Describes the MicroSIFT materials for evaluating educational software programs.

Jay, Timothy B. "The Cognitive Approach to Computer Courseware Design and Evaluation." **Educational Technology** 23 (January 1983): 22-26.

Discusses how cognitive research can be translated into computer courseware guidelines.

Joiner, Lee Marvin, Sidney R. Miller, and Burton J. Silverstein. "Potential and Limits of Computers in Schools." **Educational Leadership** 37 (March 1980): 498-501.

Joint Committee on Programmed Instruction and Teaching Machines, Division of Audiovisual Instructional Services, National Education Association. **Recommendations for Reporting the Effectiveness of Programmed Instruction Materials.** Washington: NEA, 1966.

Kansky, Bob, William Heck, and Jerry Johnson. "Getting Hard-Nosed about Software: Guidelines for Evaluating Computerized Instructional Materials." **Mathematics Teacher** 74 (November 1981): 600-604.

Sources of software are discussed as well as preliminary selection considerations. A step-by-step process for securing courseware, testing it, and evaluating it is described. Two sample sets of evaluation criteria are provided.

Kearsley, G. P. **The Cost of CAI: A Matter of Assumptions.** Bethesda, Md.: ERIC Document Reproduction Service, ED 153 600, March 1977.

Kehrberg, Kent T. "Microcomputer Software Development: New Strategies for a New Technology." **AEDS Journal** 13 (Fall 1979): 103-10.

Suggestions for developing microcomputer materials.

Kelly, Mahlon G. "Buying Software." **Popular Computing** 1 (April 1982): 27-30.

Some guidelines to facilitate the search for software.

Kingman, James C. "Designing Good Educational Software." **Creative Computing** 7 (October 1981): 72-80.

Eight characteristics of good educational software. A guideline for frame size. Classification of motivational feedback.

Klassen, Daniel. "Introduction to Computers in the Curriculum." In **Computer Applications in Instruction: A Teacher's Guide to Selection and Use,** by Judith B. Edwards et al., 109-11. Hanover, N.H.: Time Share, 1978.

Kleiman, Glenn, Mary M. Humphrey, and Trudy Van Buskirk. "Evaluating Educational Software." **Creative Computing** 7 (October 1981): 84-90.

Questions to ask.

Knapper, Christopher Kay. **Evaluating Instructional Technology.** London: Croom Helm, 1980.

Komoski, P. Kenneth. "The Educational Revolution Is Not 'In the Chips.' " **Education Week** 21 (April 1982): 20-24.

Lathrop, Ann. The Micro in the Media Center. **Educational Computer Magazine** 3 (January-February 1983): 34-37.

"Classroom Test Your Courseware before You Buy It," a discussion of software previewing procedures and a listing of thirteen mail-order distributors who offer liberal approval and return policies. A complete list of these distributors appears in chapter 5 of this book. Lathrop also provides an annotated bibliography of journals which either regularly or periodically review educational software.

Lathrop, Ann. "The Terrible Ten in Educational Programming: My Top Ten Reasons for Automatically Rejecting a Program." **Educational Computer Magazine** 2 (September-October 1982): 34.

Lathrop, Ann, and Bobby Goodson. **Courseware in the Classroom: Selecting, Organizing, and Using Educational Software.** Menlo Park, Calif.: Addison-Wesley, 1983.

A brief introduction to educational computing, advice on the selection of software, and suggestions for its effective organization and utilization. Considers classroom applications and appropriate curriculum objectives. Identifies types of software such as tutorials, simulations, etc., considers reinforcement and remediation, problem solving, program development aids, and tools for classroom management. Discusses courseware evaluation, including criteria, forms, and a description of the evaluation process; the courseware library, including how to organize and process the software collection and suggestions for a policies and procedures manual. Provides a list of recommended K-12 computer programs. Appendixes and indexes provide the copyright regulations pertaining to software, a bibliography of evaluation and authoring guidelines, sources of courseware reviews and directories, and a subject index to software listed in the book. An annual supplement will update the listings of educational courseware.

Lathrop, Ann, and Bobby Goodson. "How to Start a Software Exchange." **Recreational Computing** 10 (September-October 1981): 24-26.

Discusses the cooperative efforts and services provided at the Microcomputer Center in the Library of the San Mateo Educational Resources Center (SMERC). Also describes the steps followed in the evaluation and preparation of contributed programs for the software exchange, SOFTSWAP. (For more information on SOFTSWAP see Sources of Free and Inexpensive Software in chapter 5. For more information on SMERC see California TEC Center in chapter 7.)

Levin, Dan. "These Experts Can Wake You from the Software Nightmare." **The Executive Educator** 4 (March 1982): 26, 28.

School executives and computer users offer advice, based on experience, about microcomputer software.

Loertscher, David V. "Analyzing Microcomputer Software." **School Library Journal** 29 (November 1982): 28-32.

Provides sample notebook pages illustrating types of programs which teachers can create themselves and discusses both positive features and pitfalls. A number of commercial "skeleton" programs are reviewed and discussed in terms of how they might be used in creating lessons.

Marler, Jerilyn, ed. **MicroSIFT News. October 1980 and October 1981.** Bethesda, Md.: ERIC Document Reproduction Service, ED 216 671, 1981.

Combining the first two issues of the MicroSIFT newsletter, this document provides an overview of the MicroSIFT Clearinghouse and its computer-related activities. The first issue describes the MicroSIFT Project, the network formed to implement it, courseware evaluation procedures, hardware available at the Clearinghouse, and other activities. There is also information regarding the workshops and seminars offered, a list of computer publications, and regional news from MicroSIFT participants. The second issue contains a bibliography on selecting microcomputer hardware, a list of the criteria which MicroSIFT evaluators use, several sample evaluations which have been done, and a list of microcomputer software catalogs and directories.

Maryland State Department of Education. **Criteria for Evaluating and Selecting Microcomputer Courseware.** Baltimore, Md.: Maryland State Department of Education, Division of Library Development Services, 1982.

Guidelines developed by the Maryland Department of Education to serve as an aid to local school systems in evaluating and selecting educational computer software. Provide definitions of computer terms, a discussion of hardware considerations, suggested evaluation criteria, sources of courseware reviews including databases, copyright information, and a useful bibliography. Could serve as a model for other states. Order copies from Maryland State Department of Education, Division of Library Development and Services, 200 W. Baltimore St., Baltimore, MD 21201-2595.

Mathews, Walter M., and Linda Wyrick Winkle. "Microliteracy, School Administrators and Survival." **Compact** 15 (Fall 1981): 22-23, 37.

Matthews, John I. "Problems in Selecting a Microcomputer for Educational Applications." **AEDS Journal** 13 (Fall 1979): 69-79.

Outlines the characteristics of both a minimum and an ideal classroom computer system and provides a set of questions to be asked regarding software.

Michelsen, James. **A Survey of Selected Computer-Related Periodicals.** Lansing, Mich.: ERIC Document Reproduction Service, ED 208 946, 1981.

MicroSIFT. **Evaluator's Guide for Microcomputer-Based Instructional Packages.** Eugene, Oreg.: International Council for Computers in Education, 1983.

Contains the MicroSIFT evaluation documents, copies of which appear in chapter 4 of this book. *The Evaluator's Guide* provides complete descriptions and discussion of all items found on these forms. Other information includes a description of the process which MicroSIFT uses in evaluations and definitions. Sample reviews are included. The document may be ordered from ICCE for $2.50 by writing: ICCE, 135 Education, University of Oregon, Eugene, OR 97403. It is also available through the ERIC Database, ED 206 330.

Miller, Inabeth. "The Micros Are Coming." **Media and Methods** 16 (April 1980): 32-34, 72, 74.

Milner, Stuart D. "How to Make the Right Decisions about Microcomputers." **Instructional Innovator** 25 (September 1980): 12-19.

Minnesota Association for Supervision and Curriculum Development, Minnesota Association of School Administrators, and Minnesota Department of Education. **A Compilation of Considerations Regarding the Use of a Computer to Help Teach the School Curriculum.** St. Paul, Minn.: Minnesota Department of Education, n.d.

Provides sources of computing information in Minnesota. Covers curriculum considerations, software and hardware selection criteria, software development considerations, and in-service training of teachers. Bibliography. Could provide model for states seeking to develop resource manuals. Can be ordered from Gilbert Valdez, Supervisor Curriculum Development, 684 Capitol Square Bldg., 550 Cedar St., St. Paul, MN 55105.

Mitchell, P. David. "Can Computer Simulation Improve the Effectiveness of College Teaching?" **Educational Technology** 13 (December 1973): 14-19.

Morgan, C., and W. M. Richardson. "The Computer as a Classroom Tool." **Educational Technology** 12 (October 1976): 71-72.

National Center for Education Statistics. **Student Use of Computers in Schools, Fall 1980: A Survey of Public School Districts.** FRSS Report no. 12. Washington, D.C.: U.S. Department of Education, 1982.

1983 Classroom Computer News Directory of Educational Computing Resources. Watertown, Mass.: Intentional Educations, 1982.

North Dakota Department of Public Instruction. **Microcomputer Guide.** Bismarck, N. Dak.: North Dakota Department of Public Instruction, 1979.

Designed as a resource for teaching use of computers and computing in introductory and advanced mathematics courses in the North Dakota public schools. Included are an introduction to the use of computers and goals for computer education, a source in North Dakota for pre-written programs, tips on choosing a microcomputer system, an outline for a computer programming course to teach BASIC, topics for computer application in the science and mathematics classroom, chemistry and physics problems, a bibliography of resources (textbooks and periodicals), and a glossary of terms. The Appendix contains a list of computer careers, and a discussion with samples of flow charting. May be obtained by writing Dr. Joe Crawford, Superintendent, North Dakota Department of Public Instruction, Bismarck, ND 58505.

Olds, Henry F. "Evaluating Written Guides to Software." **Classroom Computer News** 3 (November-December 1982): 54.

Deals with the evaluation of documentation.

O'Neal, Sharleen, Dan Kauffman, and David Larry Smith. "Cost Effectiveness of Computerized Instruction." **International Journal of Instructional Media** 9 (1981-82): 159-65.

Perry, Nancy N. "Mini or Maxi: Which Computer Is Right for You? **Audiovisual Instruction** 24 (February 1979): 16-18.

A useful introduction to these types of systems. A chart compares features of maxicomputers and minicomputers in regard to instructional computer applications.

Peters, Harold J., and Molly H. Hepler. "Reflections on Ten Years of Experience." **AEDS Monitor,** 20 (April-May-June 1982): 12-15.

Pogrow, Stanley. "Microcomputerizing Your Paperwork, Part II: Scheduling and Attendance Packages." **Electronic Learning** 2 (October 1982): 20-27.

The second in a series of three articles discussing ways that school administrators can use microcomputers and offering a buyer's guide to available software. Offers some sound principles for evaluating administrative software. Provides a chart comparing features of sixteen administrative packages.

Pogrow, Stanley. "On Technological Relevance and the Survival of U.S. Public Schools." **Phi Delta Kappan** 63 (May 1982): 610-11.

Price, Robert. Free and Inexpensive Software Review. **Educational Computer Magazine** 3 (January-February 1983): 54-55.

"Programs for the Apple" is the first in a series of review articles in an *EC* department called Free and Inexpensive Software Review which aims to locate and evaluate programs which are either in the public domain or available for less than normal commercial rates. All programs included are judged to be of good quality and while the first three programs reviewed are for the Apple computer, subsequent issues will carry other computer brands. Reviews are for such popular programs as Oregon Trail and include the program source as well as the other pertinent data.

Price, Robert V. "Selecting Free and Inexpensive Computer Software." **Educational Computer Magazine** 2 (May-June 1982): 24-26.

Provides an excellent discussion and overview of free and inexpensive computer software, including sources, selection criteria, special cautions, and an appraisal checklist. The list of sources appears in chapter 5 of this book.

"Quality Software: How to Know When You've Found It." **Electronic Learning** 1 (November-December 1981): 33-36.

Riordon, Tim. "How to Select Software You Can Trust." **Classroom Computer News** 3 (September-October 1982): 56-60.

Discusses attributes of "user friendly" software. Evaluates program titles from half a dozen educational software publishers by means of a chart.

Roblyer, M. D. "The Case For and Against Teacher-developed Microcomputer Courseware." **Educational Technology** 23 (January 1983): 14-17.

Ronan, F. D. **Achievement of Middle Ability Mathematics Students Using Computer Assisted Instruction.** Bethesda, Md.: ERIC Document Reproduction Service, ED 171 433, 1973.

Rowe, Neil C. "Some Rules for Good Simulations." **Educational Computer Magazine** 1 (November-December 1981): 37-40.

A list of evaluation criteria for simulations.

Safdie, Robert, Keith Peterson, and Bill Murray. "Educational Software—A New Challenge for Publishing Companies." **Educational Computer Magazine** 2 (September-October 1982): 38-40.

Offers suggestions to publishing companies entering the field of computer software production for the college market.

School Microware Reviews. Evaluations of Educational Software for Apple, PET, TRS-80, with Index to Evaluations in Other Publications. Bethesda, Md.: ERIC Document Reproduction Service, ED 213 389, 1981.

This is the initial issue containing fifty program evaluations produced by *School Microware Reviews* (see full annotation in chapter 6 under Review Journals and Services). This edition limits reviews to programs for the Apple II, Commodore PET, and Radio Shack TRS-80 Model I.

Schramm, W. **Big Media, Little Media.** Washington, D.C.: Academy for Educational Development, 1974.

Scriven, Michael. "The Methodology of Evaluation." In **Curriculum Evaluation,** edited by Robert E. Stake. American Educational Research Association Monograph Series on Evaluation, no. 1. Chicago: Rand McNally, 1967.

"The Software Line-Up: What Reviewers Look for When Evaluating Software." **Electronic Learning** 2 (October 1982): 45-48.

Concludes with a two-page, three-part evaluation form which is a synthesis of many such forms currently available.

"Software Will Make or Break the Computer Revolution." **Education USA** 25 (13 September 1982): 17, 24.

Spitler, C. Douglas, and Virginia E. Corgan. "Rules for Authoring Computer-Assisted Instruction Programs." **Educational Technology** 8 (November 1979): 13-20.

Steffin, Sherwin A. "A Suggested Model for Establishing the Validity of Computer-Assisted Instructional Materials." **Educational Technology** 23 (January 1983): 20-22.

Discusses the difficulties involved in establishing appropriate evaluation models for computer-assisted instructional materials. Describes the process used for selecting software test sites for Edu-Ware Services, Inc., for which Steffin is director of Research and Development, and the methods and procedures which are followed at these sites in order to measure the instructional validity and utility of courseware being developed and ultimately offered to the general consumer by this company.

Steinberg, Esther R. "Reviewing the Instructional Effectiveness of Computer Courseware." **Educational Technology** 23 (January 1983): 17-19.

Comprehensive courseware reviews consider the administrative, the implementation, and the instructional effectiveness of software. "Administrative" includes memory requirements, cost, and system reliability, while implementation evaluation considers such matters as report-generating capability and the amount of teacher time needed to help students do the lessons.

"Study Shows Schools Take to Computers." **Educational and Industrial Television** 14 (September 1982): 6.

Taylor, Alexander L. "How Programmers Get Rich." **Time** 120 (13 December 1982): 56.

Thomas, David B., and Donald H. McClain. "Selecting Microcomputers for the Classroom." **AEDS Journal** 13 (Fall 1979): 55-68.

A five-phase model is proposed to systematize the selection of a microcomputer to meet both present and future instructional needs. The authors have developed an Instructional Requirements Matrix which indicates the necessary computer characteristics to support each of eleven instructional activities. Other tables include computer capabilities by size, microcomputer requirements by instructional type, and a chart comparing the features of twelve computer models.

U.S. Congress. Office of Technology Assessment. **Information Technology and Its Impact on American Education.** Washington: U.S. Government Printing Office, 1982.

Vinsonhaler, John F., and R. A. Bass. "A Summary of Ten Major Studies of CAI Drill and Practice." **Educational Technology** 12 (July 1972): 29-32.

Wager, Walter. "Issues in the Evaluation of Instructional Computing Programs." **Educational Computer Magazine** 1 (September-December 1981): 20-22.

Examines basic assumptions underlying authoring guides and evaluation instruments and discusses some of their strengths and weaknesses.

Wager, Walter. "The Software Evaluation Dilemma." **AEDS Monitor** 20 (April-May-June 1982): 5-6.

Watson, Nancy A., ed. **Microcomputers in Education: Getting Started.** Bethesda, Md.: ERIC Document Reproduction Service, ED 205 216, 1981.

This paper presents the proceedings and write-ups from the fifty-five presentations given for "Microcomputers in Education: Getting Started," the Ninth Annual Math/Science Conference held at Arizona State University in January 1981. Besides presenting on a broad variety of general computer topics, speakers discussed computer-assisted instruction in the areas of business education, gifted studies, mathematics, music, basic programming, science, and special education. Provides a good introductory overview of computer books, journals, and films, and a listing of microcomputer manufacturers and software vendors.

Watt, Dan. "Which Computer Should a School Buy?" **Popular Computing** 2 (December 1982): 140-44.

Outlines a school purchasing scheme based on three budget scenarios— $500 to spend, $2,500, and $15,000. Charts illustrate the computer brands and models available for under $500 and under $2,500 per machine.

Webster, Tony. **Microcomputer Buyer's Guide.** Los Angeles: Computer Reference Guide, 1981.

A detailed guide to purchasing microcomputers. One chapter is devoted to microcomputers in education. The microcomputer models of over sixty computer companies are described in detail.

Williams, Dennis A., Patricia King, Donna Foote, Pamela Abramson, and Mary Lord. "The Classroom Computers." **Newsweek** 97 (9 March 1981): 88, 91.

Williams, Warren S., and Jules Shrage. "Microcomputers and Education: An Overview of Popular Hardware and Software." **Educational Technology** 23 (February 1983): 7-12.

An excellent overview of both hardware and software available for micro-computer brands popular in education. Charts compare features of models marketed by Commodore, Radio Shack, Apple, Atari, Texas Instruments, and IBM. Tables show characteristics of the different storage media. Tables show the scope of software available for the different microcomputer brands and break down available software by source and type.

Williams, Warren S., Robert Smith, and Wayne Esch. "Using New Computer Software Products to Manage and Report Educational Data." **Educational Technology** 21 (February 1981): 46-51.

Demonstrates the application of two software packages to typical education problems. Provides a set of guidelines for evaluating and selecting educational software. Fourteen guidelines are offered as aids in the selection of administrative software.

Wold, Allen L., and C. Bruce Hunter. "Computerspeak: A Brief Glossary for the New User." **Curriculum Review** 22 (February 1983): 35-37.

Provides definitions of forty commonly used computer terms and suggests titles for those seeking more extensive glossaries (Sippl's *Microcomputer Dictionary*, the *International Microcomputer Dictionary*, and Spencer's *Computer Dictionary for Everyone*).

Woolls, Blanche E., and David V. Loertscher. "Some Sure-Fire Microcomputer Programs." **School Library Journal** 28 (August 1982): 22-24.

A set of selection criteria for software is suggested. A list of software programs judged satisfactory for instructional purposes is provided. The programs, recommended for first purchase, all cost one hundred dollars or less and cover a variety of subjects.

Worthen, Blaine R., and James R. Sanders. **Educational Evaluation: Theory and Practice.** Worthington, Ohio: C. A. Jones, 1973.

INDEX